Where is Love?

Creation, the Cross, and the Cosmic Christ

Hugh P.C. Broadbent

**Grosvenor House
Publishing Limited**

Scripture quotations taken from the HOLY BIBLE,
NEW INTERNATIONAL VERSION.
Copyright © 1973, 1978, 1984 by International Bible Society.
Used by permission.

This book is published by
Grosvenor House Publishing Ltd
Link House
140 The Broadway, Tolworth, Surrey, KT6 7HT.
www.grosvenorhousepublishing.co.uk

A CIP record for this book
is available from the British Library

ISBN 978-1-83975-208-7

The painting on the front cover, 'Alpha and Omega', depicts the process of cosmic redemption, from the creation of the universe through to the final completion of God's purposes. The Alpha rises above the primaeval waters of chaos described in the first Genesis creation story. The wind of the Spirit, God's active presence in the world, fills the sail on the bow of a boat, a symbol of the Church, as everything moves towards the final Omega, and the heavenly river and trees of life described at the end of the book of Revelation. At the centre of the picture lies the cross and the hint of a Chi Rho sign, the first two letters in the Greek word for Christ.

"For Bernard, Ivor and Digby"

*"God is love. Whoever lives in love lives in
God, and God in him."
(1 John 4:16b)*

CONTENTS

PREFACE

I have learnt that I am dying – hopefully not in the next week or so, or even perhaps within the next few months; but in November 2019 I was diagnosed with advanced pancreatic cancer and from that moment onwards doctors have been advising me to think of my life expectancy in terms of months rather than years, and to recognise that all treatment offered will only be palliative in intent.

My time is clearly limited and I have been forced to prioritise. Who are the people I need to see? What are the things I really want to do? This book has been one of my priorities, and it has been a race against time to finish it. Ideas central to my life and ministry, which I have been reflecting upon over many years, and which I was hoping to work on during a long retirement, have had to be thrown together with a certain degree of haste. If the published product appears somewhat rough at the edges, please forgive me.

As a Christian I have always had an overriding desire to promote the message of God's love in Jesus, and to do so in such a way that it will speak inclusively not only *to* every single human being (the marginalised in particular), but *for* every living creature and the whole created order. This book shows how I have come to see God's love undergirding our values and the dignity of all living creatures in a modern scientific age, and confronting the problem of a suffering world, 'red in tooth and claw', supremely in the mystery of the cross.

Not everyone will find it an easy read. The range of topics covered is broad and varied, and throughout much of the book I look at the ideas of a number of philosophers in their search for truth, meaning and value.

I have been aware throughout of the importance of using gender inclusive language, especially when referring to God and God's actions. However, in a few places I have used the traditional 'him' or 'his' to assist the flow and readability of the text and to affirm the reality that God is personal rather than a neutral principle.

My wonderfully loving and supportive wife Jane has actively encouraged me to undertake this project. It would not have even been begun without her. I am indebted especially to her, to Canon Gordon Oliver, who has spent hours painstakingly reading through the text and discussing it with me; to Prof Michael J. Gilmour, Dr Raphael A. Cadenhead, Dr William B. Sherwood, and the Ven David Garnett for their helpful comments and suggestions; to friends and family; and to the countless people who have upheld me with their love and prayers at this difficult time.

Hugh P.C. Broadbent
Trottiscliffe, Kent
25th April 2020

INTRODUCTION

My aim in writing this book is to show why I believe that love lies at the heart of everything, and is at the very core of God's being. The pattern of divine agapeic love undergirds not only the moral dimension of human life but the cosmos and natural world as well.

The opening chapter outlines the problem of what I call 'The Divided Mind', a problem with which I have been wrestling over many years. It is the tension experienced by people who have no belief in God – who regard the cosmos as the product of meaningless chance, yet who wish to maintain that life possesses objective value and purpose. I am convinced that the problem created by the divided mind can be resolved when seen in the light of God's agapeic love.

I argue that belief in a purposive mind, whom we call 'God', is perfectly reasonable and rational (Chapter 2), but such a belief does not in itself necessarily imply that God is good or loving. Therefore, following a brief discussion on the use of scripture (Chapter 3), I seek to show how 'goodness' is an objective reality and not just a subjective opinion (Chapter 4), and how, having investigated a number of ethical theories (Chapter 5), I am led to the conclusion that the only intrinsic good which can form a unifying basis for all other moral values, is divine, agapeic love (Chapter 6).

The pattern of this same agapeic love, revealed supremely in the cosmic Christ, is reflected both in the moral dimension of human life and in the wider cosmos (Chapters 7 and 8). Belief in agapeic love can be upheld in the face of evil (Chapter 9), and its all embracing power is paradoxically revealed in the cross (Chapter 10). The practical consequences of living in the light of

God's agapeic love are outlined in the concluding chapter (Chapter 11).

'*Where is Love?*' records my own journey to a deeper understanding of God's agapeic love. This journey has inevitably been shaped by external events and by the people I have encountered along the way. To put this book into some kind of context, I therefore begin with a brief account of my life.

My Story

I have been a priest in the Church of England for over forty years, all of them served in Rochester Diocese. Both my grandfathers were clergymen. My father's father was for some years a CMS missionary in Canada, living in a remote settlement which, judging from the old photos, looked a bit like one of those Wild West towns in the movies. I sadly only ever knew him towards the end of his life when he was becoming quite frail. My mother's father I knew rather better. He was a significant influence on my life. He had served as a chaplain with the Eighth Army during the Second World War before becoming Chaplain-General to the Forces. Subsequently in 1951 he was appointed Dean of Ripon Cathedral. I have fond memories of Christmas family gatherings at Ripon. He was great fun to be with. He performed magic for us children at the breakfast table; he played the guitar; he taught me chess, and of course he led services at the cathedral. The cathedral had a profound spiritual impact on me. I have always associated worship as a result with beauty, reverence, and a sense of awe.

My father was an army officer in the Royal Electrical Mechanical Engineers (REME). I have three siblings and we were all born abroad: my older sister in Australia, my brother and I in Germany, and my younger sister in Hong Kong. This nomadic army life affected me in a number of ways.

I became very aware from an early age of the existence of different cultures – of people living very different lives from me and holding very different beliefs. In Hong Kong the Chinese had ancestral shrines on the hillside with pots of ashes, and I saw Ghurkha soldiers sacrifice a bull at a religious festival. It was clear to me that the faith in which I was being brought up was not the only one around! It was not universal.

My father's profession confronted me with questions about life and death. Before we went to Hong Kong he was an instructor at Sandhurst and we attended Sunday services in the chapel. Afterwards we would go into the main building where there were massive paintings of battle scenes hanging on the walls. I was fascinated by them. They helped arouse a keen interest in military history which I still have. I would read the Ladybird books about Julius Caesar conquering Britain, Alfred the Great defeating the Danes, and so on. At prep school I ploughed my way through historical novels by the likes of G.A. Henty, Henry Treece and Rosemary Sutcliffe. Other children had comic super heroes like Batman and Spiderman who always seem to come through their adventures practically unscathed; my heroes nearly all died! I wrote childish, not very good poems about the death of Nelson, soldiers at the battle of Alma, the Texans making their last stand at the Alamo, and the Ninth Legion supposedly wiped out somewhere north of Hadrian's Wall. It all got me thinking: What would I be willing to die for? The good life seemed to go beyond a simple do-as-you-would-be-done-by morality. The truly good was sacrificial.

In order to give some stability to our schooling, my parents decided after our return from Hong Kong to send us children to boarding school. I went first to a small preparatory school in the Malvern Hills called Wells House and then to Sedbergh School not far from the Lake District. Life was tough in both establishments. Corporal punishment was very much in evidence. At the preparatory school there were cold baths and a run before breakfast. At Sedbergh prefects, when I first went there, had the power to use the cane (though I am proud to say that when I and some others became house prefects some years later, we took the opportunity to abolish both the cane and private 'fagging'). Quite a lot of bullying took place, but on the positive side it made me begin to appreciate (really for the first time) the relevance and importance of Jesus' moral teaching and example. He cared for the outcast and unloved, and I found myself wanting to imitate him, to offer a hand of friendship to those who were being mocked, teased, or excluded. I wanted to follow Jesus' teaching, and whilst at Sedbergh I decided to be confirmed on this basis. But belief in God and belief in Jesus as a great moral teacher were therefore at this time two separate things, not really connected. Living amongst the wild, wind-swept fells of the North, I struggled to believe in a personal God. He (or it) seemed more like a force, an impersonal power like the one in Star Wars.

Until I was about sixteen I thought I would follow my father into the army, but the School Cadet Corps put me off. It was boring! I wasn't sure what I wanted to do – least of all in my gap year between school and university. But then, towards the end of my time at Sedbergh, on the suggestion of my grandmother, I applied to CMS (Church Mission Society) for a place on their Youth Service Abroad scheme, and in 1971 I went (totally unqualified) to 'teach' for a year in an Harambee School[1] in western Kenya not far from the border with Uganda. I lived there with a Pentecostal African family in their hut. The father was the school treasurer. We had no running water or electricity; some of the smaller animals like the goats and chickens were brought inside at night because of the leopards. When the crops failed, there was no pay for two months, and not always food on the table at lunchtime. People were really poor. The Kikuyu dominated government were not particularly interested in what happened to us, and I reckoned that if God was only a cosmic force, he (or rather 'it') didn't care much either. I questioned whether, in the context of a vast uncaring universe and a society where life was cheap, human life had any objective value at all, and whether Jesus' teaching was nothing more than a collection of nice ideals artificially imposed upon a harsh, meaningless reality.

A crisis-point was reached one morning when I woke with a raging fever. I had contracted malaria, and the family decided that one of the older boys should accompany me to the small American

---

[1] *'Harambee' is the motto of Kenya and means 'pull together' in Swahili. An harambee school was one which had been set up and run by the local community in the hope that one day it would be taken over and funded by the government.*

mission hospital about three miles walk away. On arriving there I collapsed. They put me to bed. I was extremely ill. At one point, I felt I had somehow become separate from my body and was looking down on myself and the people around me. It was a weird experience which I have never much talked about. However, it took away my fear of death. Despite the fever, I felt a deep sense of calm. A few days later some Australian missionaries, the Van Emericks, who lived not far away in Maseno, heard that there was a msungu (white man) in the hospital, and when I was strong enough fished me out and took me to their home to recuperate. There I read some books by C.S. Lewis which I found really helpful. I began to see Jesus, not just as a remarkable *human* teacher, but as more than that – a window onto what lay at the heart of everything, God himself. God for me was no longer an impersonal force but a personal and purposive mind, a God of infinite unfailing love (See Romans 8:31ff). It was something like a conversion experience. I had come close to giving up and returning home, but now I felt a new strength, a new determination to continue regardless of the cost, and, what was more, I started seriously to wonder whether God might be calling me to some form of full-time Christian ministry.

On my return to England I went to study theology at Selwyn College Cambridge. The course had a heavy emphasis on philosophy which forced me to think deeply and critically about what I believed. This was at times painful and disturbing, but ultimately it was strengthening and enabling. I came to understand how, although faith took me beyond reason into the realm of relationship and trust, it could still be 'reasonable': clear about key concepts, consistent, supported by cogent arguments, responsive to criticisms, aware of and respectful of alternative viewpoints, and open to any practical implications.

I met Christians at university from a wide variety of traditions and backgrounds. It was wonderfully enriching. I was at one time not only a Christian Union college representative but also the college chapel sacristan, a member of a Christian rock band (we toured in a 1950s Humber ambulance), a willing participant on a college chaplaincy expedition to Taizé, and a Franciscan Youth

Camp in Northumberland. A sense of vocation grew stronger, though a vocation to what I was not sure. During my third year as an undergraduate, with the encouragement of David Garnett, the college chaplain, I offered myself for ordination and was accepted. I remained at Selwyn to complete a Certificate of Education before going to Wycliffe Hall in Oxford for a two-year residential ordination training course.

My forty years of stipendiary ministry began at St Stephen's Chatham, where I met and married Jane, the love of my life, whose family lived next door to the vicarage.

Serving as a parish priest was a huge privilege. In addition to the work that one would expect – leading services, preparing sermons, chairing meetings and seeing to various administrative tasks relating to the church, there was also the opportunity to engage with the wider community, often in ways that the regular congregation was barely aware of: in schools, colleges, clubs, groups and care homes. Through the 'occasional offices' (baptisms, weddings, and funerals) I found myself ministering to large sections of the unchurched population, often at quite a deep level.

For fourteen years I worked three days a week at St. Olave's Grammar School in Orpington, Kent, as a chaplain and member of the teaching staff. The school paid the parish half my stipend. My Certificate of Education and 1995 sabbatical research on the interface of science, religion and 'the divided mind' really came into their own here, teaching 'A' level Philosophy of Religion, for example, to extremely bright and eager-to-learn young people. It was truly exciting, helping them to explore some of the big questions of life.

All jobs have their highs and lows. For me, however, two of the most rewarding aspects of my work have been helping someone to come to faith or grow in faith, or secondly, to work through a bereavement or some other trauma. Bringing God to the people and the people to God – making God's love in Jesus a reality through caring and sharing – is what, in common with countless other priests, I have sought to do.

Life is a journey, and during my forty years as a stipendiary priest I have learnt many things:

- From the many people I have encountered, I have learnt how regardless of their background or culture, they all have the same basic spiritual needs, and the gospel of God's love in Jesus is relevant to all.
- From my involvement with the Anglican Society for the Welfare of Animals (ASWA), I have learnt that the gospel is truly inclusive not only of humans but also of animals.
- From a sabbatical I had at Ridley Hall, Cambridge and my subsequent teaching of the Philosophy of Religion to sixth formers at St Olave's Grammar School, Orpington, I have become increasingly convinced that science and the Christian faith can be friends and not foes.
- I have learnt how every gift, and even every hobby, can be harnessed in the service of Christ.
- I have come to appreciate more and more the companionship and support of my beautiful wife Jane who has been very much a partner in my ministry, as well as the joy of being a father to my two wonderful children, Christopher and Sarah, whom I love and admire greatly.
- I have learnt that every day is a gift from God and not a right.

I retired from full-time stipendiary ministry in September 2018. It was my intention to develop my ministry in new and different ways, but as my cancer diagnosis shows, life can be full of surprises.

CHAPTER 1

'The Divided Mind'

This book is about faith in the love of God. Not the overly sentimental kind that has plagued so much Christian 'religion'. Faith has never offered me a comfortable escape from the harsher realities of life. Rather the precise opposite! It has shown itself at its most vibrant when I have stopped running away and have dared to *embrace* reality in the light of God's love.

A few years ago, inspired by Francis Thompson's *'The Hound of Heaven'*, I wrote a poem on this theme[2]:

> O Lord, across the centuries
> Down labyrinthine ways,
> Your love pursues us with a zeal
> Which nothing can erase.
> And though we plumb the darkest depths
> And soar to heights unknown,
> We cannot flee the Hound of Heav'n,
> For all is but your own.
>
> In forest, field, with bird or beast
> No refuge can we find.
> The chase begun – the Hound of Heav'n
> Is always close behind.
> And still your voice we hear above
> His slow, unhurried tread:

---

[2] *Hugh Broadbent, 'The Chase', inspired by Francis Thompson's 'The Hound of Heaven'. Can be sung as a hymn to the tunes 'Vox Dilecti' and 'Kingsfold'.*

'The earth is mine and all therein,
And by my hand you're fed.'

No place to go, we stand at bay,
The Hound of Heaven's eyes
Now penetrate our deepest thoughts
Which we cannot disguise.
He bears the marks of grief and pain;
His message blazoned red:
'With ev'ry creature you have harmed,
I've suffered too, and bled.'

Our fear and guilt all melting in ~
The warmth of Love's embrace.
Redeemed, renewed, we gladly join
The Hound in heav'nly chase.
For through his eyes the wonder of ~
Each creature now we see,
And heed his call to make the world
As it is meant to be.

I often wonder how it must be for those who have no faith in God, yet wish (like most of us) to affirm the value of human life. When a loved one dies, for example, they can find themselves torn between their belief in the dignity and value of that person's life, and their intellectual conviction that this universe, together with everything in it, is just the product of blind chance. Since they regard all values as ultimately a matter of social or personal opinion, the value of the human life, which they quite rightly wish to celebrate, can appear strangely rootless. They may talk about holding their beloved friend or family member in their heart 'for ever', but if they are honest, they know that 'for ever' is at best no more than forty or fifty years – the lifetime of the next of kin. What is more, there are countless people in the world who have no one to remember them when they die. I am reminded of the characters described in Ralph McTell's heart-rending song, '*Streets of London'*, and in particular the forgotten hero seen outside the Seamen's Mission.[3]

What are we to say about the dignity of people like this? Most people without a faith in God would wish to affirm the value of the seaman as a human being, yet to my mind, a belief that the physical universe is merely a product of chance militates against this.

Our society is experiencing the crisis of what I call 'The Divided Mind' – the tension, for example, between what people hold to be of value and what they believe about the physical world.

In this chapter I will explore a number of ways in which the Divided Mind reveals itself within society. We will look at divisions between

> *mind* and *matter,*
> *fact* and *value,*
> *faith* and *reason,*
> *self* and *others.*

We will see how these divisions highlight the need for a unifying principle, a spiritual or moral foundation. My aim in this book will be to show how, for me, this lies ultimately in God's eternal, all-embracing love, brought to us by Jesus, and revealed to us supremely in his cross and resurrection. But for now let us turn to the issue of the Divided Mind.

Mind and Matter

We can trace the origins of modern society's 'divided mind' to the clear-cut division proposed by the French philosopher Renée Descartes (1596–1650). Descartes described a division between mind and matter – the 'res cogitans' (*the thinking 'realm'*) and the 'res extensa' (*the material 'realm'*). Prior to Descartes, the

---

[3] *'Streets of London' is a song by Ralph McTell. He first recorded it in 1969 for his album 'Spiral Staircase'.*

mediaeval picture had been of a Great Chain of Being with the two 'realms' of mind and matter emerging at opposite ends of what was a continuous spectrum. Descartes broke the Great Chain. He saw the separation of mind from matter as a positive step, safeguarding the doctrine of the immortal soul and enabling scientists to maintain a detached objectivity in their observations of matter. Not everyone approved. Those like Descartes' contemporary, Blaise Pascal, who were of a more spiritually sensitive disposition, found the implications of Cartesian dualism horrifying. The old medieval cosmos, of which human beings were an integral part, had been infused with purpose, value, and meaning. Cartesian dualism purged nature of all associations with the human psyche, forcing it to draw back into itself and making itself painfully and "vividly conscious of... being quite different in kind from the natural world which it contemplated."[4]

This feeling of isolation has persisted right up to the present day. Scientist Loren Eiseley reckons that we have become 'cosmic orphans', alone in an uncaring impersonal material universe.[5] People's sense of kinship with the world of nature, expressed most forcefully by St Francis in his familial references to 'brother Sun' and 'sister Moon', has been lost.

The creation of such a wide gulf between the human mind and matter gave further academic credence to the abusive and exploitative attitude already prevalent towards animals and nature. It had been there already in the thinking of Francis Bacon (1561–1626) and in his bid to understand and explain natural events by reference to physical causality rather than spiritual purpose. It had also been there in the hopes of the general public, that the newly emerging science would increase their 'control' over the environment. The claimed objectivity and detachment which science brought had a depersonalising effect. It took us out of the realm of personal 'I-Thou' relationships into the impersonal realm of 'I-It'

---

[4] *Don Cupitt, 'The Sea of Faith' (British Broadcasting Corporation 1984) p.50.*
[5] *Quoted by Lawrence Osborn in 'Restoring the Vision' (Mowbray 1995) p.87.*

relationships[6]. Anything in nature which is reduced to the status of an 'it' can be treated in whatever way we choose, so knowledge became the agent of a potentially exploitative relationship with regard to the natural world.

The Cartesian followers of Descartes were led by their philosophy to conduct the most appalling live experiments on animals.[7] The famous painting of a white cockatoo in an air pump[8], starved of oxygen as part of an experiment whilst two children present look on in obvious bewilderment and distress, captures superbly the cultural outlook of that period. The lecturer conducting the experiment would not have thought that the bird had a mind or soul, or indeed any feelings. As a contemporary observer, Nicolas Fontaine, remarked:

> "[such people] administered beatings to dogs with perfect indifference, and made fun of those who pitied the creatures as if they had felt pain. They said that the animals were clocks; that the cries they emitted when struck were only the noise of a little spring which had been touched, but that the whole body was without feeling."[9]

The continuing reluctance in the 21st century to recognise the suffering of animals through intensive farming is a direct legacy of this Cartesian dualism, and a classic manifestation of the Divided Mind. On the one hand people feel compassion for the animals whom they know intuitively to be suffering, yet on the other hand they often worry over whether, in the cold clear light of reason, their feelings will be dismissed as mere sentimentality. They can be almost embarrassed by such feelings. The issue of animal welfare

---

[6] Martin Buber's book, 'I and Thou' famously drew the distinction between the I-Thou and I-It relationships. It was first published in 1923 and translated into English in 1937.

[7] A fuller account of the impact of Cartesian dualism upon attitudes to animals is given by William C. French in 'Good News for Animals?', pp.24 ff, ed. Charles Pinches and Jay B McDaniel (Orbis Books 1993).

[8] Painting entitled 'An Experiment on a Bird in an Air Pump' by Joseph Wright of Derby 1768.

[9] Fontaine, 'Mémoires pour servir à l'histoire de Port-Royal', 1738.

illustrates the way in which this approach to science encourages an exploitational outlook, a supposedly *rational* attitude in direct conflict with our inherent *moral* awareness of what is good and right.

Fact and Value

The second manifestation of the Divided Mind which we shall explore is the division between fact and value.

This supposed division first proposed by Francis Bacon (1561–1626), between inner *'values'* of the mind and outer *'facts'* of Nature, has proved disastrous. Bacon thought that science could establish incontestable 'facts' by observation, experiment, and inductive 'proof', over against uncertain beliefs and moral values put forward by the different religions which could never amount to anything more than subjective 'opinion'.

By the time Columbus 'discovered' America in 1492, Christians had long been aware of the existence of major religions other than their own, and this made them realise how different the beliefs and values in other cultures could be. The various world religions with which they found themselves coming into contact seemed to them little more than sets of culturally relative convictions, and this made their own religious beliefs internalised, 'privatised' and relativised. Only the baser, materialistic goals of society, goals like economic growth, which were measurable and testable and gave the appearance of being more 'real', were left as the publicly acknowledged ideals for people to pursue.

We may note how the meaning of the word 'economics' has changed. Its roots lie in the Greek word, 'oikonomia', which literally means 'the rule of the home'. This suggests that it was originally concerned with the harmonious running of a household or community (ie the 'political economy')[10]. It was a term which incorporated the personal dimension of relationships.[11] The

---

[10] *Lawrence Osborn, 'Restoring the Vision' (Mowbray 1995) pp. 57–62.*
[11] *In their book, 'The World of the Gift', Jacques T. Godbout and Alain C. Caille adapt Marcel Mauss' idea of a gift-exchange within primitive societies to*

application of the methodological assumptions of classical physics to the field of economics, however, had the effect of remodelling it as a science. Everything of importance now has to be measurable and quantifiable. There is a growing emphasis on cost-benefit analysis, applied extensively even to Education and the National Health Service, where one might have thought more core humane and 'spiritual' values would still hold sway.

Modern Economics wrongly regards itself as an objective, impersonal science and tends as a result to adopt mechanistic models of how everything works. It often assumes that people are motivated by measurable, materialistic self-interest and that the success of a government's policies can and should be judged in terms of an increase in the country's material productivity. The assumption is treated as if it were a universal truth and foisted upon the 'Majority World'[12], despite the fact that it cannot be verified empirically and that there is growing evidence of its disastrous impact upon the environment. Poorer countries are judged by western governments to have 'seen the light', only insofar as they have begun to ape our western industrialised civilisation. The old nineteenth-century imperialism has been replaced by a new economic imperialism, and the firepower of the Victorian gunboats by the subtler but far more effective selling-power of multinational companies like Apple, Facebook, Tesler, McDonalds and Coca-Cola. The economics of modern consumerism has become a quasi-religious missionary 'cult of material acquisitiveness'. As one wit summed it up, "Tesco, ergo sum!"

Every aspect of our lives has been affected by this depersonalising, economic materialism. In the field of education the pressure from industry and commerce to make what is learnt in the classroom relevant to what is done in the workplace, has led to an ever-increasing emphasis on technological training. Training someone

---

show how families function, not on the basis of self-interest and cold market exchange, but through the warmer, more personal exchange of unmerited gifts.
[12] I prefer to use the phrase 'Majority World', as it defines the community in terms of what it is (the majority of humankind) rather than, as in the case of 'Developing World' or 'Third World', by what it supposedly lacks.

to perform a particular task is not the same as educating him or her for life[13]. A good education should of course provide young people with practical skills, but it should also help and encourage them to reflect upon their knowledge and experience and to develop critical freedom and personal autonomy. Training on its own can, if we are not careful, merely prepare them to become cogs in an economic machine. The nightmare scenario depicted by Aldous Huxley in his classic sci-fi novel, *'Brave New World'*, in which a population is genetically and culturally engineered to fulfil pre-ordained roles within society as Alphas, Betas or Gamma-morons, seems at times frighteningly close to what our governments seem actually to desire.

The depersonalising tendency to reduce life to whatever is measurable and economic can be felt at the most intimate of levels. I have been told, on occasions, that even our relationships should be seen as 'emotional investments', and that we should preserve or abandon them on the basis of 'the return' we receive on our emotional 'investments'.

Materialism is a paradox of course. Descartes and the Cartesians looked down on matter; they saw it as little more than a resource to be manipulated, used, and abused (like a slave) in whatever way they thought fit. Materialistic economics, on the other hand, encourages us to venerate material possessions and investments as if they are the be-all and end-all, and this in turn can encourage a dependence upon material wealth which at times almost reverses the roles, turning the slave into our master.

There have been repeated attempts to rebel against materialistic philosophies which insist on the measurable, material, and testable being the only criteria for what is of significance or worth. The nineteenth century Romantic Movement, for example, highlighted the importance of culture. Every nation, it argued, had its own distinctive, irreducible cultural genius. We needed to appreciate our different cultures far more, nurture them, protect them,

---

[13] *For a fuller discussion of the tension between training and education see P.H. Hurst and R.S. Peters, 'The Logic of Education' (Routledge and Kegan Paul 1970) pp.110, 111.*

and protest against their destruction. People were to take pride in their Welsh, Scottish, French or German ancestry.

It was an important movement which has clearly left its mark on western music, art, and tradition. I myself still recall with gratitude the songs which I was taught at school, taken from an *'Oxford Song Book'* or some other similar, romantically inspired collections of folk songs. The movement, however, failed to halt the advance of economic materialism and its accompanying reductionist tendencies. National cultures have survived, but only in truncated and privatised forms. In the United States, for example, immigrants retain elements of their culture in the privacy of their homes or in the areas where they live, but in the wider community they have little choice but to embrace the rationalist ideals upon which the country is built and from which its materialistic economics are derived.

An unhappy division now exists between private cultural beliefs and practices on the one hand, and the impersonal materialism of public life on the other.

Faith and Reason

The third manifestation of the Divided Mind which we shall now explore is that between faith and reason.

Culture is normally seen to include a community's religious beliefs and values, but the advance of the 'new science' elevated Reason to such an extent that at the time of the French Revolution there was even an attempt to impose a secular alternative to the Christian religion, a 'religion' of Reason. A vast church begun by Louis XV in 1744 on the Montagne Sainte-Geneviève, was renamed *The Panthéon*. The hope was that the personified ideals of reason, liberty and fraternity would be worshiped by the people there. In 1793 a Festival of Reason was held inside Notre Dame Cathedral. It was all part of a Europe-wide movement, a swelling tide of atheism which seemed at the time to be unstoppable. Revolutionary leaders in France were convinced that society was about to rid itself of tyranny and superstition once and for all. As

McGrath observed, "The wisdom of the day was as simple as it was powerful: eliminate God, and a new future would dawn."[14]

The Religion of Reason, however, never caught on, and the earlier but closely related deistic 'God of Reason' struck many as being cold and distant and in stark contrast to the warmth, power, and immediacy of the traditional 'God of Revelation'. From the seventeenth century onwards, there emerged a sharp division between adherents to this God of Reason and believers in the God of Revelation or Faith.

The mathematician Pascal (1623–62) found the cold, remote God of the deists totally inadequate. He sought solace, as his writings bear witness, in a warm, emotional, and somewhat pietistic form of Christianity, though he knew in his heart that this was at odds with his more thinking self. From the 17th century onwards people's faith often became more internalised, focused on the warmth of personal experience, and Christ-centred. Hymns to Jesus (as opposed to God) became fashionable. The Bible records very few hymns or prayers addressed directly to Jesus[15], yet this trend towards a more personal, Christ-centred faith has continued to this day. I have been struck by how many contributions to hymn books published in the United Kingdom over the last few years focus on individual believers and their personal relationship with Jesus rather than on the wider world and its creator.

A worrying retreat from Reason underlies the current, global spread of fundamentalism not only within Christianity but across all the major world religions.

Where enlightenment values, advances in science, and rapid modern technological changes have been perceived to challenge traditional beliefs and values, there have arisen deep-seated anxieties and a sense of insecurity. A number of observers like the 20th century political scientist, Leslie Lipson,[16] have observed how

---

[14] *Alister McGrath, 'The Twilight of Atheism – The rise and fall of disbelief in the modern world' (Rider 2004) p.21.*

[15] *The only two prayers to Jesus are Stephen's prayer when he is being stoned: 'Lord Jesus, receive my spirit' (Acts 7:59), and the prayer at the end of the book of Revelation: 'Amen. Come, Lord Jesus' (Revelation 22:20).*

[16] *Leslie Lipson, 'The Ethical Crises of Civilization' (Sage 1993) p.225.*

people have fallen back on the security of more conservative religious traditions and reasserted supposedly 'fundamental' beliefs and absolutes. Fundamentalism has been on the rise, not only amongst Christians proclaiming for example the inerrancy of scripture in a way that would have been totally alien to the early church fathers, but also amongst Hindus in India, Buddhists in Myanmar and Sri Lanka, and Jews and Muslims in the Middle East. India has seen an upsurge in Hindu fundamentalism and violent attacks on Muslim and Christian minorities, especially the dalits, the 'untouchables'. Buddhists in countries like Myanmar and Sri Lanka have been involved in the violent suppression of religious minorities. In the Middle East a number of militant Muslim movements like Islamic State have emerged intent on waging a holy war against the West and imposing shariya law. And Orthodox Jews in Israel, driven by a fervent commitment to the land of their Biblical forefathers, have heightened tensions between Jews and Palestinians in the Middle East.

Humanists like Lipson see this as evidence that the great world religions are outdated and reflect a theistic flight from Reason. But the phenomenon is not confined to believers in God. Some of the more aggressive and overly emotional expressions of atheistic belief, such as those found in the writings of 'New Atheists' like Richard Dawkins, bear many of the characteristic hallmarks of a fundamentalist outlook.

Some thinkers, who hold to a rather more positive view of religion, have seen faith as opening the door onto a level of reality, which technological reason had been inclined to ignore. Sören Kierkegaard (1813–55), for example, did not advocate a fearful flight *from* Reason so much as a courageous leap *beyond* it. He argued that it was a mistake to try and reason your way to faith. A logically proven belief could never constitute genuine faith because faith entails not an inevitable conclusion but an 'authentic choice', the leap into a personal I-Thou relationship with God.

Kierkegaard was part of the romantic protest against the dehumanising effects of the new science upon society. People could sense the importance of spiritual values, but were unable to see how they could be upheld in the purposeless, value-free world which seemed to surround them. Theirs again was a divided mind, and it reminds me of the predicament faced by Puddleglum, a character in C.S. Lewis' Narnia story *'The Silver Chair'*. Puddleglum and two children find themselves in an Underworld where they have been taken prisoner. The witch who controls the Underworld is trying to convince them, with the aid of her magic, that the cold, depersonalising kingdom which she has manufactured is the real world, and that the goodness of the Narnian world above is simply a figment of their imagination, a mass of illusory Freudian projections. In a climactic moment of confrontation Puddleglum exclaims that even if the witch is right and they have only dreamed Aslan's world, all he can say is that "... the made-up things seem a good deal more important than the real ones" and he is going to stand by his 'play-world':

> "I'm on Aslan's side even if there isn't any Aslan to lead it," he says. "I'm going to live as like a Narnian as I can even if there isn't any Narnia."[17]

Puddleglum's words are bold and heroic, but they have a tragic quality about them as well. They echo the underlying sense of meaninglessness found in twentieth century existentialist writers like Camus and Sartre. The gulf between an inner world of personal Faith and an outer world of Reason translated in their secular thinking into highly individualistic philosophies. Each advocated in its own way the basic mantra: 'create your own meaning' or 'do your own thing'.

Self and Others

The fourth expression of the Divided Mind to which we now turn is that between the isolated self and society.

Jean-Paul Sartre (1905–80) was perhaps the most famous of the existentialist writers. He was born in Paris and studied

---

[17] *C.S. Lewis, 'The Silver Chair' (First published by Geoffrey Bles 1953. This edition 1974 William Collins Sons & Co Ltd) p.164.*

philosophy at Sorbonne University. He maintained that, whilst it was natural for people to strive for spiritual beliefs and ideals, they must realise that in the end their striving is doomed to failure. There are no objective values to be recognised and no objective spiritual reality to believe in. We live in a meaningless universe, he argued, and the key to 'authentic existence' is to use our freedom as individuals to create our own meaning and our own values, to decide for ourselves what is good. Values are not *recognised* by human beings. They are *determined* by them. There is no God with a purpose for you already in mind, who brings you into existence in order to fulfil that purpose. In a godless universe, you need first to exist before any purpose can be decided upon. As Sartre so eloquently put it, 'Existence precedes essence.'

Existentialist thinking fosters an isolationist outlook. Everything is subordinated to the individual's egoistic goal of self-fulfilment, and others are used and discarded at the individual's convenience. Ruth Etchells has cited a number of examples of this tendency within twentieth century literature. Stephen Spender's poem *'Song'*, for example, tells of a woman who is willing to abandon any relationship, regardless of the vows and obligations that have been given, if the opportunity for a new and more fulfilling experience presents itself.[18] She has no sense of any obligation towards others.

Existentialist freedom is a freedom which has no positive content whatsoever. The 'authentic act' is defined in purely *negative* terms as an act free from any outside influence or obligation. It is a freedom which stands in stark contrast to the freedom described in the Bible. When the Israelites were rescued from slavery in Egypt, they were not set free to do as they pleased. They were liberated in order to become God's People and to fulfil their God-given destiny.

Biblical theories of rights emphasise our 'responsibilities' *for* others; secular societies prefer to emphasise our individual 'rights' *over against* others. Governments in Western, liberal democracies

---

[18] *Ruth Etchells, 'Unafraid to Be' (IVP 1969) p.83.*

see one of their primary responsibilities as upholding neutral 'tolerance', a seemingly content-less virtue designed to enable individuals or groups to create and pursue their own meanings and values. Tolerance was originally promoted, quite rightly, during the period of the enlightenment, as a response to the horrors of the mediaeval religious wars. Tolerance at its best is a hospitable term which welcomes and celebrates diversity with a willingness to learn from one another. However there can be an anxiety-driven tolerance which is accepting of the existence of difference but is unwilling to engage with it. This has led to a form of 'tolerance' which has unfortunately resulted in a dearth of additional community values, and fostered a society of isolated groups and individuals. You may have noticed, for example, how difficult it can sometimes now be to speak out against blatant social and spiritual evils for fear of appearing 'intolerant'. We may complain at a personal level in conversation with friends, but at a public level our morally neutral culture frequently robs us of any positive framework within which to act or speak.

Countries in the 'Majority World' have tried to use western technology as a morally neutral tool, hoping to preserve their cultural values intact. Generally speaking, however, they have found this extremely difficult to do. The growth of industrial cities and large farming estates has drawn people in from the countryside, often disrupting family life, creating slums and shanty towns and, where jobs are not forthcoming, spreading street crime and sex work, destroying village life and leading people to abandon their traditional customs and festivals. Once a country in the 'Majority World' has opted to accept the benefits of science, the people of that country acquire a taste for it and begin, quite understandably, to want more. To pay for the demand, they are drawn into the global network of western trade and commerce with all the side-effects that this implies. Attitudes and expectations change, and science transports all issues from the realm of the moral to the realm of the feasible. The focus is no longer on what *should* be done but on what *can* be done. And what *can* be done almost invariably determines what *is* done. As Bryan Appleyard has eloquently put it: "'Ability' supersedes 'obligation'; 'No problem!' supersedes 'love'."[19]

No country which has opened its doors to western science and technology has managed to keep its original culture unaffected. It is almost impossible to keep apart the two worlds of personalising value and depersonalising objectivity once they have been brought together in a particular society.

The Need for a Unified Spiritual or Moral Foundation

The dilemma we face in our modern Western society should by now be clear. The world as we see it has split into two worlds: an inner spiritual world of *personalising* beliefs and values; and a public, science-based world of *depersonalising* objectivity and neutrality. It is the dilemma of the 'divided mind', of two worlds each at odds with the other. In many people that I meet it is tearing them apart. They face a constant inner struggle between the personalising and depersonalising influences at work in their minds.

There are three possible responses to the divided mind open to us:

- we can keep our two worlds separate and try to live with the tension;
- we can unite the two worlds by making science the foundation upon which all other levels of understanding are built; *or*
- we can look for some spiritual or moral foundation to provide the necessary, unifying, interpretative framework which will bring the two worlds together.

From what has already been said, it is clear that the first response of trying to keep the two worlds separate does not work. We now consider the second response, illustrated by Scientism, Marxism and Humanism, which also, to my way of thinking, fail to satisfy.

---

[19] Bryan Appleyard, *'Understanding the Present'* (Picador 1992) p.9.

Scientism

In endeavouring to make science the foundation for all other levels of understanding, a number of thinkers have been encouraged by the undoubted success of science to predict that it will one day provide *the* ultimate, one and only explanation of reality and a basis from which everything else can be understood. Stephen Hawking at the end of his book, '*A Brief History of Time*', speculates that it will eventually furnish us with a single, ultimate explanation, a 'Theory of Everything'.[20] The belief that scientific methodology can *on its own* furnish us with a *complete* knowledge and understanding of the world is known as 'Scientism'. It does not simply see Science as one discipline among many and one source of knowledge among many. It proposes a reconciliation of the two worlds I have described by means of a take-over bid: by maintaining that the *only* genuine knowledge is what we obtain by scientific methodology and describe with scientific terminology.

Now if by 'scientific methodology' we are referring to knowledge which is empirically verifiable, this is clearly far too limited. We may label the Big Bang Theory and the Theory of Evolution as scientific, for example, but the Big Bang has never been 'observed', and the Theory of Evolution relies on historical data as much as data from repeatable experiments. Truths of logic and mathematics cannot be verified empirically, and nor indeed can the claim that 'all meaningful propositions ought to be empirically verifiable'. Science is extremely important, but it is clearly not our only source of knowledge. Other disciplines like history and mathematics also have a part to play.

Marxism

Karl Marx (1818–83) argued for a form of scientism. He regarded his theory of economic determinism as 'scientific'. Just as causal chains of events can be observed and predicted at the material

---

[20] *Stephen Hawking, 'A Brief History of Time' (Bantam Press 1988. Reprinted 1993) p.175.*

level within physics, chemistry, and biology, so also, he argued, can they be predicted at a social level. Marx predicted the inevitable collapse of capitalism, a revolution of the proletariat and the eventual establishment of an economic utopia. All ideas were in his view the product of material realities. If you wanted to change the way people thought, for example, you needed to change the world in which they lived. Values and religious beliefs were rooted in society's class structures and hence in the 'science' of economics.

> "...It is not the consciousness of men that determines their being," he wrote, "but, on the contrary, their social being determines their consciousness."

Marx was motivated by a genuine compassion for the poor, but his theory was flawed. It was grounded upon a naively optimistic belief in scientific 'progress' which was widespread in the nineteenth century. He saw scientific progress as a disturbingly fatalistic process. Believing in it allowed him and his followers to play down the importance of personal freedom and justify later attempts by Communist regimes to 're-educate' opponents by crude and cruel methods of 'brain-washing'. It led to the horrors of Stalin's purges, the 'Cultural Revolution' in China, and the 'Killing Fields' of Cambodia. George Orwell's book, '1984', provides perhaps the classic, enduring indictment of this particular form of scientism.

Humanism

Humanists maintain that the tools of scientific reasoning brought to us by the Enlightenment must, as a matter of practical necessity, replace those resources once offered by traditional world religions. Leslie Lipson argues in his book, 'The Ethical Crises of Civilisation', that the other-worldly concerns of religion distract worshippers from the serious problems facing us and cannot therefore provide the necessary impetus with which to tackle them. The West, he believes, suffers from a 'split personality', torn between 'this-worldly values' of the kind espoused by Confucianism in China and 'other-worldly visions' such as those which permeate India.[21]

There is a certain amount of truth in Lipson's argument. Spiritual otherworldliness has certainly been a problem within the major world religions. I can think of Christians, for example, who might well be described with some justification as being 'so heavenly minded as to be of no earthly use'. But his criticism is too broad. He fails for instance to understand the dynamic interaction within mainstream Christian thinking, between the *vision* of God's future kingdom and the *signs* of that future kingdom in the here and now. The Lord's Prayer highlights the tension very clearly:

> "Your kingdom come... *on earth* as it is in heaven." (Matthew 6:10)

Jesus sees the heavenly *future* breaking into the earthly *present*:

> "... if I drive out demons by the finger of God", he declared, "then the kingdom of God has come to you." (Luke 11:20)

It is precisely the transcendent nature of this now-and-future kingdom which provides the moral direction and impetus for Christians which Lipson rightly recognises as being needed.

The humanist programme which Lipson proposes as an alternative offers perhaps the most promising way of putting scientific methodology in the driving seat. But it is far from problem-free. Humanists place great faith in the powers of human reasoning, yet the Romantic Movement's reaction against the Enlightenment is a stark reminder of the dis-ease which was, and is, still felt over the limitations of scientific reasoning: of the way it can ignore our non-cognitive experiences of life, analyse problems without seeing them in their broader cultural context, focus on technical 'means'

---

[21] *Leslie Lipson, 'The Ethical Crises of Civilization' (Sage 1993) p.17.*

whilst losing sight of the 'ends'; and foster through detached objectivity an exploitative attitude towards the environment.

Rationalist arguments often degenerate into reductionist explanations which are self-inclusive. Marxists, for example, dismiss the bourgeois views of their opponents as being nothing more than the product of social upbringing, yet they fail to see that their own views are open to being rejected on precisely the same grounds. Some behaviourists suggest that our beliefs and values are all wholly determined by social or genetic factors, whilst again failing to see that, if they are right, their own beliefs and values are open to the same explanation. John Polkinghorne[22] spells out the chilling effect which the reductionism of these "nothing-butters" can have:

> "Reductionists will try to explain away non-scientific aspects of human experience (aesthetic, moral and religious). There is no place for them in the cold, hard, lifeless world of the reductionist account. For this account, music *is* just vibrations in the air; the 'Mona Lisa' really *is* just a collection of specks of paint of known chemical composition. Ethical intentions and religious intimations *are* just strategies for survival, programmed into us by the selfish genes. It is hard to exaggerate the implausibility of this limited view of reality."[23]

History has destroyed the humanist faith in science as the panacea for all our ills. Solutions which once seemed 'rational' have failed again and again to meet human need. The clearance of untidy slums, for example, and the erection in their place of neat tower-blocks was a social disaster. It led to the isolation of families who had previously been living together in a community. The rationalisation of time and labour, epitomised by the factory assembly line,

---

[22] *John C. Polkinghorne is a mathematical physicist and Anglican priest. He was Professor of Mathematical Physics at Cambridge University until 1979 and ordained priest in 1982. He was awarded the Templeton Prize in 2002.*
[23] *John Polkinghorne, 'Quarks, Chaos and Christianity' (Triangle 1994) p.60.*

makes economic sense, but can result in boredom and frustration and subsequently strained, unhappy industrial relations.

The final nails were hammered into the coffin of humanist optimism with the advent of the First and Second World Wars. In the horrors of those conflicts the limitations of rational science were finally exposed. They produced not only the positive, wonderful cures of medicine, but also the unimaginably powerful instruments of nuclear destruction and the ultimate rational obscenity that was Nazi Germany. The terrible medical 'experiments', carried out by Nazi doctors on Jewish men, women and children in particular, were performed with cold rational objectivity, and their findings solemnly presented to the scientific community for their approval. The utter evil of the Holocaust:

> "was industrial and performed with cold rationality. The Jews were a disease. And Germany was the nation of Leibnitz, Kant, Beethoven, and Einstein. The cradle of the Enlightenment had become the Kingdom of Hell."[24]

Reason had somehow lost touch with humanity. In a dry comment in 1919 on the foundering of the Nietzschean dream, Irving Babbitt[25] wondered despairingly whether people should have sought simply to become more human before striving to be superhuman.

Thoughtful humanists like Lipson acknowledge the inadequacy of technology and science and the need for something more; a this-worldly altruism. But I remain to be convinced that clear, objective ethical values can be held secure within the purely secular context of a universe which is believed to be meaningless and absurd; and to my mind it seems that many modern writers would concur. It is why some of the most profound religious education classes I ever attended at school were English lessons. One of our set texts in English was William Golding's famous

---

[24] *Bryan Appleyard, 'Understanding the Present' (Picador 1992) pp.119-120.*
[25] *Irving Babbitt was an American academic and leader of a literary movement known as the 'New Humanism' or Neohumanism.*

novel, *'Lord of the Flies'*. It tells of a group of schoolboys who are stranded on a desert island after an air crash and who degenerate into savages. It reflects post-war memories of the depths to which humanity can sink and points to the fundamental questions raised by such memories. If the veneer of civilisation is so paper-thin, do 'goodness' and 'God', pattern and purpose, have any real meaning? Is it not truer to speak of the 'monstrous mindlessness of the cosmos'? [26]

The feeling of despair and meaninglessness is a recurring theme in modern literature. The *'Theatre of Cruelty'* and *'Theatre of the Absurd'* are two examples, but there are many others. There is a yearning for genuine spiritual and moral values and a deep sense that they are there to be found. But there is also a fear that society's values could be rootless 'pseudo-values' artificially imposed upon us and ultimately inadequate.

Friederich Nietzsche (1844–1900), who to my mind is one of the most persuasive and consistent of atheist writers, declared the old values of Western culture no longer tenable. God was 'dead' and the time had come for a new 'superman', an heroic atheist, to take his place.[27] The knowledge acquired through science had provided us with the ability to do this, because knowledge had given us the power to impose our own meaning on the unintelligible flux of 'Becoming'. It had nothing to do with any transcendent moral truth. Nietzsche accused Enlightenment philosophers like Kant of being cowardly, for seeking to defend the objectivity of ethical values. Unlike most of his atheistic contemporaries, he saw himself as a courageous thinker who was prepared to take seriously the implications of 'the death of God'. He had some harsh words to say, for example, about the writer George Elliot. Such people, he commented, who, "are rid of the Christian God...

---

[26] *Ruth Etchells, 'Unafraid to Be' (IVP 1969) p.29ff.*
[27] *Out of fairness to Nietzsche it is important to note that he did not envisage the Aryan 'superman' of Nazism, even if the latter did arise historically from his thinking.*

now believe all the more firmly that they must cling to Christian morality."

Leamas, the British Secret Service agent in John Le Carré's book, *'The Spy Who Came in from the Cold'*, was asked at one point by a Communist officer what motivated him. He did not really know. He was not a Marxist; he was not a Christian; he had no real philosophy of life and he saw no real need to have one. All he could say in reply to the Communist officer's questions was that he thought the Communists were 'bastards'. But did that justify the taking of human life, the bomb in the crowded restaurant? Leamas did not know and did not much care either.

Most people in our society survive like Leamas by not thinking too deeply. They are aware of the divided mind which lies at the heart of their existence: the tension between their moral sense of right and wrong on the one hand (the wickedness, for example, of secret agents like Leamas killing without justification) and the apparently meaninglessness of the world they inhabit on the other. They are also perhaps dimly conscious of the undermining effect which this has upon their personal spiritual development and upon the life of the community. But they are confused, and frightened that if they peer too far over the parapet of their castle, they might expose themselves to forces which will overwhelm even the small domain of private meaning that is left to them.

Conclusion

The discussion in this chapter has covered a wide range of writers and philosophers. But wherever I have looked, it seems that attempts to make scientific rationalism the foundation upon which all other levels of understanding are built, have failed. A number of avenues which I have explored have terminated in futility and despair, and even the most promising one, humanism, for which I have the greatest respect, has to my mind fallen short through an overly optimistic evaluation of the powers of human reason, and a commitment to objective moral values floating somewhat uncertainly upon a vast sea of cosmic meaninglessness.

The time has come, therefore, to consider the third of our three possible responses to the Divided Mind. We must look for a spiritual or moral foundation which can provide the necessary, interpretative framework for our understanding of the world.

Humanists tend to see human beings as moral agents in a morally indifferent universe, nobly and heroically committed to goodness for its own sake. Why however should they regard such a moral commitment as being so important? An increasing number of people are beginning to suggest that, if there is an answer, it must lie in some form of transcendental humanism which sees the moral as rooted in a reality which transcends the material world. Then human beings could be viewed, not as, "accidental by-products of an indifferent physical process, but as beings whose essential nature transcends the physical... and whose final destiny lies beyond the physical."[28] It is to the possibility of this 'mind behind the matter' that we now turn.

---

[28] *Keith Ward, 'Religion and Human Fulfilment' (SCM 2008) p.24.*

CHAPTER 2

'The Mind Behind the Matter'

In this chapter I consider the possibility of a mind behind the matter. It will be a reality which brings together the two worlds of our 'Divided Mind': the inner spiritual world of *personalising* beliefs and values, and the public, science-based world of *depersonalising* objectivity, and neutrality. It will be a spiritual or moral reality which provides a coherent, unified basis for understanding the world in which we live.

But how shall we begin? Instead of asking whether 'mind' with its attendant values has emerged from matter, we will consider the possibility (or even the likelihood) that matter has in some way emerged from mind, and whether this way of looking at things avoids many of the problems and pitfalls which we have been encountering. Could it be that this universe springs from a purposeful, creative, loving mind?

The thesis will be examined in two main stages: first by looking at the evidence for a purposeful mind undergirding our modern, scientific understanding of the universe; and then by asking whether such a mind, if it exists, could be the objective source of our moral awareness.

We begin with science and its current understanding of the origins of the universe. The findings of modern science need to be taken seriously. If we genuinely believe that God is the God of Truth, we must be open to all truth, however painful or disturbing its implications may seem.

Fundamentalists who adopt a literal interpretation of the Genesis creation story and maintain that God brought the universe into existence in six twenty-four hour days, clearly have difficulty in reconciling their approach to the Bible with the generally accepted theory of evolution which speaks of a process of development lasting millions of years[29]. They protest that the theory of evolution is only a theory and open to debate, but the arguments which they put forward do not cut much ice within mainstream scientific circles.

Readers may in any case be surprised to learn that belief in a literal six-day creation is a comparatively recent development in the history of the church. The third century thinker, Origen, was scornful of the idea:

> "What man of intelligence," he wrote, "will consider that the first and the second and the third day, in which there are said to be morning and evening, existed without sun, moon and stars...? These are figurative expressions..."[30]

Many of the great leaders of the early church such as Gregory of Nyssa, Jerome, Ambrose, and St Augustine, followed the example of early Jewish rabbinic commentators in interpreting the Genesis story along far more symbolic lines.

The Genesis narratives and poems seem to have been brought together around the time of the Babylonian exile in the 6th century BCE. This has tended to lead modern scholars to view the points that the Genesis creation story makes in the context of contemporary near-eastern cultures like that of the Babylonians. In the Babylonian myth there are many gods vying for power and the world is the accidental by-product of a battle between two of them, Marduk and Tiamat. Genesis, in stark contrast, speaks of a uni-verse and a single creator who brings everything into being in a positive and purposive manner.

"In the beginning God created ..." (Genesis1:1)

---

[29] A brief outline of my own approach to interpreting the Bible is given in Chapter 3.
[30] Origen of Alexandria, 'On First Principles', written around AD 220–230.

In the Babylonian story, human beings are the playthings of the gods and their lives are strongly influenced by celestial powers (astrology played an important part in Babylonian culture). The Genesis creation story talks of humans made in the 'image of God', called in other words to represent his good and gracious rule on earth (Genesis 1:26). They have a real dignity and purpose whereas the stars are placed in the heavens with no particular power or authority (Genesis1:14-18).

Evolution is often assumed to be incompatible with belief in a purposive God of the kind described in Genesis, because it is deemed to involve a process of pure chance. But although random genetic mutation clearly plays a major role in the evolutionary process, natural selection provides such an effective filter that the overall result is similar to that of playing with loaded dice. It seems to encourage over a period of time certain lines of development. We see this in the well-known phenomenon of 'convergence', where the same organ (such as an eye or limb) repeatedly emerges (albeit in a slightly different form) from quite separate evolutionary pathways of development.

Scientists are concerned with a limited but clearly defined aspect of reality, and quite rightly therefore exclude from their investigations all metaphysical concerns about value and purpose. But the evolutionary process as a whole favours the production of increasingly complex organisms, which in turn give rise to consciousness and other attendant 'goods' such as awareness of truth, goodness, beauty, and love. This process of 'complexification'[31] ties in well with a theist's belief in the existence of a purposive Creator and is strongly suggestive of a spiritual dimension to reality.

It may seem absurd in the context of such a vast universe to consider the emergence of life in general, and human life in particular, as being of any real significance, but size is not necessarily

---

[31] *FR Tennant (1866–1957) coined the word 'complexification' to describe the evolutionary tendency to produce increasingly complex organisms. He was the first theologian widely known to suggest the existence of God as being necessary to explain the purposive quality of the evolutionary process.*

that important. The smallness of a diamond found beneath a huge mountain, for example, does not seem to affect unduly people's appreciation of its value. If the universe needs to be of the size and nature that it is, in order to enable beings like us to emerge, then that is how it must be. We should simply accept that the end necessitates the means. It is not always possible to tinker with the way it has been structured, if the whole thing is, so to speak, 'a package deal'.

The in-built freedom we observe within the creative process is a problem to many, but it need not be for Christians. God's providential control over people and events is looser than we often suppose. A God of love would never treat his creatures like robots, any more than a loving parent would wish to control or determine his or her child's every thought or action. In Jesus' famous story about the prodigal son (Luke15:11–end), the father (who clearly represents God) allows the son the freedom to make his own mistakes – to leave home and squander the family inheritance. The son eventually decides to make amends and return home, but the power which brings this about is the gentler, persuasive lure of love, not brute force. The cross for Christians is the supreme revelation of divine power but the power it discloses is not power as the world sees it (1 Corinthians1: 22-25). God's lordship over creation could be likened to the control that an ultimate Grand Master has over a game of chess.[32] The Grand Master (God) cannot (and would not wish to) control or pre-determine his opponent's *moves*, but he can nevertheless remain 'in control of the *game*' as a whole, always able to respond with a

---

[32] *Peter Geach employs the analogy in 'Providence and Evil' (Cambridge University Press, 1977). He seems to believe however that the Grand Master's knowledge and expertise will enable him to predict the precise square on the board where checkmate will be delivered. The American philosopher and psychologist William James (1842-1910) employed the same analogy in 'The Dilemma of Determinism', an address given to the Harvard Divinity Students, published in the Unitarian Review for September 1884. He does so, however, in a looser, more open way which I personally find more convincing. The Grand Master's victory is assured, but the precise way in which it is achieved cannot be known from the start.*

superior counter-move to whatever his opponent may do, and confident that he can bring the game to a successful conclusion.

The modern anti-evolution Creationist movement began in the United States at the start of the 20th century. It was in its origins a commendable *moral reaction* to the growing influence of *social Darwinism,* and to the claim that the oppression of the weak by the rich and powerful was the inevitable outworking of a natural evolutionary struggle for survival. A Democrat candidate for the presidency called Bryan campaigned against the teaching of evolution on these grounds.[33] His campaign however led unfortunately to the teaching of evolution being outlawed in Tennessee, and this in turn resulted in the notorious Scopes Trial of 1925 in which the law was challenged.

When Darwin first published his theory of natural selection in his book, *The Origin of Species*, the Church and scientific community were equally divided in their reaction to it. There was no neat division of opinion between clergy on the one side and scientists on the other. There were clergy like Charles Kingsley, author of '*The Water Babies*', who accepted evolution quite happily and respectable scientists who had serious doubts and questions. Darwin himself oscillated between belief and agnosticism.

There were a significant number of clergy in those days working at the forefront of scientific enquiry. The famous Oxford debate in 1860 between Samuel Wilberforce, Bishop of Oxford, and Thomas Huxley, is often caricatured as a debate between rational science and irrational religion. In fact it was held as part of the annual meeting of the British Association for the Advancement of Science, and Bishop Wilberforce, being a former vice-president, was simply an obvious person for the organisers to invite to participate in the debate.

Today there are many scientists (some of them quite eminent) who are committed Christians, and many more who, whilst not

---

[33] *'Social Darwinism' was also linked to the theory of eugenics popular at this time, which fuelled rejection of evolutionary theory by some Christian groups, especially in Europe.*

necessarily subscribing to belief in a Christian God, are nevertheless inclined towards the idea that there may be a God or 'something akin to a mind' behind it all. The God-hypothesis has in fact much to commend it. Consider, for example, the so-called 'Big Bang' theory about the origins of the universe. Talk of a 'big bang' originated in the late 1940s, when a debate was raging between scientists like Fred Hoyle (1915–2001) who believed that the universe was eternal and that it had remained basically the same throughout its history (the 'steady state theory'), and those like George Gamow, a Russian scientist, who argued that, because the universe is expanding, there must have been a beginning, a moment when it was a single solid mass.

During a radio talk Hoyle referred dismissively to Gamow's theory as involving 'some sort of big bang'. His description of it stuck, and as supportive evidence from the field of radio astronomy grew, people began to speak of it as an established scientific (or perhaps, more accurately, 'historical') fact.

Many assume that the Big Bang account of the origins of the universe renders belief in God redundant; in actual fact a good number of theistic scientists see it as providing some remarkably strong evidence in support of their belief.

John Polkinghorne illustrates the extraordinary significance of the Big Bang by inviting us to imagine that God has lent us his universe-creating Machine. On it there are a large number of knobs, dials, and switches with which to determine the basic structure of the universe. We begin to play with it. What forces do we want? How strong or weak shall we make them? How big do we want our universe to be? Having adjusted the knobs, we pull the lever. What sort of 'Creation' have we produced? Many of us assume that the result would be a variation on a similar theme, the evolution of different kinds of substances, structures and living organisms, such as we might encounter in a science fiction novel. But we would be wrong. Unless we have adjusted the 'knobs' very precisely indeed, and in a way similar to how they have in fact been adjusted by God, our 'Creation' would contain nothing of interest whatsoever. It would have been fruitless.

Suppose the explosive force from the 'Big Bang' had been a little bit greater? The universe would have expanded too quickly and have become too dilute for anything significant to develop. Suppose that the gravitational force of attraction had been much stronger? The universe would have collapsed back in on itself before life had had time to evolve.

We worry about how small and seemingly insignificant we are in such a vast universe, but there is really no need for us do so. If it were not this big, we would not be here.

"Only a cosmos at least as big as ours could endure for the fifteen billion years necessary for evolving carbon-based life. You need ten billion years for the first-generation stars to make the carbon, then about five billion years for evolution to yield beings of our sort of complexity. It's a process that just can't be hurried."[34]

The possibility of carbon-based life (which is the only kind we know) depends on a very delicate balance within the fundamental forces of nature.

"If the weak force were weaker," for example, "and the decays (of particles) in consequence went slower, then there would be all helium and no hydrogen. In such a world, without hydrogen, there would be none of the water which seems so essential to life. If the decay went faster, then for more complicated reasons super-novae explosions (distributing the first-generation heavy elements so as to be available in the environment of potentially life-evolving second-generation stars and planets) would probably be impossible. In that case the carbon and iron needed for life would be locked away useless in the cores of dying stars."[35]

---

[34] John Polkinghorne, 'Quarks, Chaos and Christianity' (Triangle 1994) pp.30–31.
[35] John Polkinghorne, 'One World' (SPCK 1986) pp.56–57.

The fundamental forces established at the Big Bang singularity (the strong and weak nuclear forces, electromagnetism, and gravity), all appear to be remarkably 'fine-tuned' and set at just the right level for life to evolve. This is a striking phenomenon and one which has so impressed scientists of all persuasions that they have given it a name, the anthropic principle. How can such a feature have come about?

Those who resist the conclusion that it is the product of a purposive mind are forced to seek an alternative explanation. They have suggested, for example, that there must have been an infinite number of 'big bangs' with an endless series of universes expanding and collapsing, until the present one finally produced the right conditions for life to evolve. The problem with this suggestion, however, is that, according to current evidence, our universe appears to be on a path of *continual expansion*. There will be no future 'big crunch'. The universe we inhabit is not going to collapse in on itself. So if there have been a series of universes prior to our own, it is remarkable that the fruitful one happens to have appeared at the very end – on the last 'throw of the dice', so to speak.

A more promising explanation from an atheistic point of view is the theory that there may exist a great many universes, perhaps even an infinite number, a multi-verse. Most of these universes would be barren perhaps, but with so many at least one would be bound to be fruitful, and we know about it because we live in it.

The 'multi-verse' theory is popular. But it is not the knock-down argument that some atheists imagine it to be. Even if it were accepted as true, it would not rule out theism. We could easily conceive of God creating more than one universe. But the existence of a multi-verse is in any case highly speculative. Not all scientists are convinced by the arguments put forward in support of it. Sir Roger Penrose, a former collaborator with Stephen Hawking who shared with him the prestigious Wolf Prize, refers to the idea of a multi-verse as "overused ... [and] an excuse for not having a good theory." To begin with, he points out, the idea is untestable. These 'other universes' cannot be visited; they are by definition separate from our own. We know neither what they are like nor whether they are even there.

Where more than one explanation can account for the facts as we know them, scientists generally favour the simpler one. The notion of a single purposive creator-God is far simpler and more straightforward than the idea of an infinite number of unknowable universes, and what is more, it seems far more rooted in the 'real world'.

Particle physicists like Polkinghorne speak of the 'fine tuning' of the *physical* cosmos because that is their area of expertise. When we turn to the *biological* evolution of life the picture is more complex. The emergence of life on earth is shrouded in mystery. So difficult have some scientists found it to explain it, that they have speculated on it having arrived (in bacterial form) in a rocket from outer space (Crick) or embodied in comets or meteorites (Fred Hoyle). Of course, this does not explain how it evolved elsewhere in the universe. Nor does it account for the emergence of 'higher' forms of life.

The original Darwinian mechanism of 'chance mutation' combined with 'natural selection' (survival of the fittest) is clearly part of the story, but other factors are also almost certainly at play.[36] On its own it would seem inadequate to account for the dramatic, and at times extremely rapid, development of complex life-forms and possible non-human cultures.

Some evolutionary developments, for example, would seem to suggest that a rudimentary appreciation of beauty is at work in the process of selection at least as much as that of mere survival. The horns of the Irish elk, for example, weigh nearly a quarter of a ton, and are far too cumbersome as weapons, whilst those of the mastodon are so curved that they are useless for attack and can at best only serve as buffers. The enormously long tail of the lyre bird makes it difficult for the creature to walk and fly. And the peacock's fan, impressive as it must be to the female of the species, is absurdly 'over the top' if survival is the *only* factor at work.

---

[36] *The basic idea of evolution is not in question here, only the classic Darwinian theory of how the evolutionary process operates.*

Science and religion are not implacably opposed to each other. There are perfectly reasonable grounds for postulating the existence of a purposive creator. There are those who do not like this fact. They would dearly love to dismiss faith in God as an irrational and irresponsible 'leap in the dark'. Richard Dawkins[37] in a lecture delivered at the Edinburgh International Science Festival in 1992 dismissed it as intellectually irresponsible:

> "Faith," he said, "is the great cop-out, the great excuse to evade the need to think and evaluate evidence. Faith is belief in spite of, even perhaps because of, the lack of evidence... Faith is not allowed to justify itself by argument."

Dawkins and others like him believe (and I use the word 'believe' advisedly) that the natural sciences provide a complete, simple and coherent account of the world we live in and that talk of a 'spiritual', non-material dimension is an unnecessary complication. The universe has no objective purpose or value; it is in their view comprised entirely of mindless matter.

Now if materialists like Dawkins are right, the implications are far reaching. It means for example that, in principle at any rate, we ought to be able to give a *complete* account of our mental activity purely in terms of blind, meaningless, and irrational physical causality. Any thought which we suppose to be rational will have to be judged as illusory, and all aesthetic and moral values will need to be seen as simply arbitrary personal or social opinions.

The vast majority of people, I suspect, would reckon that this is going too far. Our experiences of beauty and goodness are much more 'real' than that. Great artists and moral reformers, for example, are inspired by visions of beauty or goodness which seem to come from 'beyond' or 'outside' of them, to take hold of

---

[37] *Richard Dawkins is an ethologist and evolutionary biologist. He was at one time Professor for Public Understanding of Science at Oxford University. He is an outspoken atheist, arguing for the incompatibility of science and religion.*

them on occasions almost in spite of what they might naturally wish.

People's views and tastes may differ, but there is nevertheless a significant degree of agreement as to what is aesthetically or morally good. When governments designate certain parts of our countryside as 'areas of outstanding natural beauty', for example, they highlight areas which everyone recognizes as possessing an objective value; it is more than just their personal opinion. And when certain actions are condemned as 'war crimes,' it is because people across the globe, regardless of background or nationality, recognize such behaviour as being objectively unacceptable.[38]

People who believe in objective aesthetic and moral values do not necessarily believe in God. But they do believe in minds, because values presuppose a valuer, and a valuer implies the existence of a mind which is capable of valuing something. Atheists believe that the only minds which exist are those which have evolved in creatures such as ourselves. But are they right? The possibility of a 'Cosmic Mind' (or in other words 'God') has a strange habit of creeping in by the back door as the inadequacy of alternative accounts becomes more apparent.

Atheists often treat their experiences of truth, beauty, and goodness as if they exist as objective realities. But how can these values just float around rootless in the ether? Would it not make more sense to suppose that they spring from something akin to a mind, a reality perhaps in which everything is grounded? To entertain such a notion seems to me to be perfectly reasonable. A cosmic mind could account very well for these important aesthetic and moral aspects of our experience, far better in my judgement than any atheist alternative.

When we engage, as we are doing now, in the great God-debate, there is no single knock-down argument whereby the case can be 'proven' one way or another. For theists like myself the evidence is *cumulative*. We are like the jury in a court case, who must hear all the evidence and decide which 'story' or hypothesis

---

[38] *'Objectively' is of course always a demanding word to use, even in the context of corporate perceptions.*

is the most coherent and convincing – which best accounts for everything we know. There is no argument *for* design, as people once thought there might be; only an argument *from* the initial hypothesis of design. The theist considers the whole picture: the fine tuning of the fundamental forces of the universe to just the right strength to make the emergence of life possible (the anthropic principle); the directional tendency within the evolutionary process to produce more and more complex structures, organisms and creatures; the intelligibility of the universe (its openness to rational investigation); and the emergence of conscious minds with their yearning for rational understanding and their awareness of beauty and moral goodness. It is when all these things are looked at *together* that the strength of the case for theism becomes most apparent.

When God is put forward as the explanation for everything, it is often objected that causal chains are infinite and that to say 'God created the universe' simply begs the question as to who created God? It is an interesting point to make. But there are a number of good reasons why theists suppose it reasonable 'to stop at God'.

First we have the issue of explanatory scope. Suppose by way of example that a child finds a tennis ball on the ground and asks you to explain its presence there. You might initially tell him about the existence of the tennis court close by and about the game of tennis. But the child could take it a stage further and ask why the game of tennis exists. You would then be forced to broaden the scope of your explanation and talk about our enjoyment of sport. Pressed still further to explain our enjoyment of sport, you might well find yourself expanding the explanatory scope yet again, and entering upon issues relating to human nature and even the purpose of life. Every answer you gave, in other words, would of necessity extend the explanatory scope until eventually, you felt obliged to invoke the notion of an infinite, all-encompassing God in whom we live and move and have our being. Then you would have reached a point where there is no wider explanatory scope available and questions, by force of logic, would have to cease. It seems reasonable to me to stop at God as an explanation for the universe on similar grounds. There is simply no wider explanatory scope available.

Secondly we should consider the principle associated with 'Occam's razor'. William of Occam (1290–1349) was originally a pupil of Duns Scotus (1265/6–1308) and one of the great medieval scholastics. He famously invented his 'Occam's razor' in an attempt to put an end to all the laboriousness of scholasticism.

"It is vain," he said, "to do with more what can be done with fewer."

By which he meant that, if there are two or more theories which can account equally well for the data available, the simplest theory ought properly to be preferred. Scientists like the late Stephen Hawking have been spurred on by this idea to seek a single, simple 'Theory of Everything' (TOE) which will combine and include within itself all other theories currently relating to the fundamental forces of the universe: the theories of gravity, electromagnetism and the stronger and weaker nuclear forces. It could be argued, however, quite persuasively in my view, that the 'theory' of a single creator-God fulfils this role rather well, for the concept of God includes within itself an explanation for everything that exists at every level – physical, moral, and spiritual. And if we have arrived at a single theistic Theory of Everything, we can go no further in terms of simplification. It is time to stop.

Thirdly, we turn to the question of personal agency. Suppose a body has been found by the police. They will investigate the cause of death. Questions will be asked: 'Why did this person die?' Initial enquiries may reveal physical causes: that the person died perhaps as a result of blood loss, and that this in turn was the result of several vicious stab wounds to the chest. But such causal explanations will not in themselves satisfy the police. The question as to why the person died will only have been answered to their satisfaction, when the rational agent who initiated the terrible chain of events has been discovered. Similarly, with regard to agency and the origins of the universe, once we have discovered the rational divine agent who initiated it all (God), and not just the physical causes, our enquiries can legitimately cease.

Personal agency can in such situations mark an appropriate stopping point for what might otherwise be an endless chain of questions. It is the idea of personal agency which lies at the heart of William Lane Craig's 1979 version of the Kalam Cosmological Argument for the existence of God[39]. He begins by drawing a distinction between 'potential' and 'actual' infinites. You cannot, he says, add to an actual infinite, so if the universe was 'actually infinite', the present moment would not exist to be added to. The present moment however does exist to be added to, so the universe must be finite and only *potentially* infinite.

Now a finite universe must have had a beginning and what begins must have a cause, since things cannot simply cause themselves. There are only two types of causality of which we are aware, the physical and the personal; so it is reasonable to assume that the beginning of the universe came about either by a natural occurrence or by an agent's act of free choice. Since the laws of nature did not exist before the beginning of the universe, the universe could not have been the result of a natural occurrence, so the only possible explanation for the universe is that it was the product of free choice by a personal being whom we call God.

Whether or not we find philosophical arguments of this kind persuasive, the faith we share in a creator-God takes us far beyond the rational conclusion to an intellectual debate or line of philosophical reasoning.

Faith begins as a particular way of looking at the world. It functions like the working hypothesis of a scientist only at a metaphysical level. St Augustine said that his faith was like a door which opened up a whole new way of looking at things and a whole new range of possibilities. It was like seeing everything in colour for the first time, or in 3-D instead of in simply two dimensions.

---

[39] *William Lane Craig and Quentin Smith, 'Theism, Atheism and the Big Bang' (Clarendon 1995) p.3ff.*

"Credo ut intelligum," he wrote: "I believe that I might understand."

When a scientist puts forward a hypothesis, he does not know whether or not it is true. In the early stages it is more the product of intuitive insight than of evidence or rational argument. But the point I want to make is that it is none the worse for being that way, because reason always employs assumptions. Believers in God are simply those who begin with the perfectly reasonable assumption that the universe's beauty, order, openness to rational inquiry and so on, reflect the purposive mind of God. They then proceed on the basis of this, to find that, when they look at the world in this way, the world makes sense – much better sense in fact than it ever did before.

The famous 18th century philosopher David Hume reckoned that we should only believe something in proportion to the evidence available. But we cannot always do this, and going beyond the evidence is not necessarily irrational and irresponsible in any case.

There are practical considerations to take into account as well as intellectual ones. It is all very well debating from the comfort of a philosopher's armchair the probability of a particular belief being true or false. But risks and uncertainties are a part of everyday living. Imagine that we are journeying through the Amazonian jungle and arrive at a rickety rope bridge which spans a deep rocky gorge. We know perhaps that the local people have occasionally used it, but we can also see that the rope is frayed and a number of the planks are cracked or apparently missing. We examine the bridge carefully and come to the conclusion that there is a seventy to eighty percent chance of crossing it safely. The odds are not bad. But do we take the plunge? At the end of the day it is a straight choice: either we cross or we move on and seek an alternative route. There is no half-way house; no 'proportional response'. And if the group as a whole decides to cross (influenced perhaps by the fact that a member of their party is seriously ill and needs to be taken to hospital as quickly as possible), there will be no *practical* difference between those with a seventy percent belief in the bridge's safety and those with an eighty percent belief.

Evidence which might help to justify a certain course of action may sometimes only become apparent *after* the 'step of faith' has been taken. If the travellers in the Amazonian jungle decide to cross that rope bridge, for example, they may discover as they do so that the rope is not as frayed as they had initially thought, that the cracked planks of wood which they had been worried about were thick, seasoned timber – much stronger than they had appeared to be at a distance, and that the apparent gaps in the planking were an important and necessary part of the structure. Faith in this way can become a potential source of new knowledge and fresh insights.

This is particularly true when we reflect upon our knowledge of other people. We come to know them at a deep level only when we take a leap of faith and begin to trust one another. It is the same with God. Faith is not primarily about our believing certain propositions to be true, "believing three impossible things before breakfast," as the Queen of Hearts once declared in Lewis Carroll's classic tale of *Alice through the Looking-Glass* (1871). It is about relationships of trust: trusting other people and trusting God.

When Abraham felt the call to leave the city Haran in which he had always lived (Genesis12:1–5), I am sure he would have thought and prayed about it and discussed it with his family and friends. I am sure too that there would have been plenty of rational discussion. But at the end of the day, he had to make a decision: Should he stay in Haran or should he set out on this journey? There was no half-way house, no 'proportional response'; either he went or he stayed. It was all or nothing. He knew the dangers and the fact that he would be taking a calculated risk. But in that respect he was no different from the great pioneers, explorers, and discoverers of more recent times. All such people, in one way or another, take calculated risks with their journey into the unknown. Abraham took this first step of faith, and as he did so, he found that it brought him new insights and fresh knowledge.

His relationship with God began to grow and his trust to deepen as new evidence of God's faithfulness and love was given to him.

Faith need not be an irrational leap in the dark as critics sometimes claim. But if it does not have to go *against* reason, it must at some point take us *beyond* reason.

The faith which has taken hold of me and inspired me during the course of my life, the faith which I am struggling to describe and express in this book, is a faith in God as an eternal, cosmic mind, a God who creates and sustains the universe and who upholds in his 'agapeic' love the dignity and value of every single human and every living creature.

Let me close this chapter with a brief but important footnote on the word 'agapeic'. It is a word of crucial importance which I will be using frequently. C.S. Lewis in his classic book, *'The Four Loves'* (1960), analyses four Greek words which we commonly translate as 'love': *philos*, which is the love between two friends bound together perhaps by a common interest or concern; *storge*, which can refer to the affection of a parent for his or her child; *eros*, which describes the romantic or sexual attraction of two lovers; and *agape*, which is the word used by Jesus and the early Christians to describe the ongoing commitment of a person to care for someone and to seek their wellbeing, regardless of how they themselves feel (ie to care for them, even if they are their enemies). When I speak of the love of God, it will almost always be in this agapeic sense of the word. It is God's agapeic love for us and for the whole of creation which constitutes the good news I wish to celebrate and proclaim.

CHAPTER 3

'Interpreting the Bible'

In order to formulate a distinctively Christian understanding of God's agapeic love for the world, we must take careful note of how we read and use the Bible. Before proceeding any further, therefore, I propose to spend a few moments explaining my approach to the scriptures.

A plausible, coherent account of the Christian faith must, in my view, give equal weight both to reason and revelation – to what is discovered about God and creation from the sciences, history and other academic disciplines, and what is learnt from the Bible. Christians who ignore reason or play it down can tend towards an inward-looking fundamentalism, whilst Christians who ignore the Scriptures can end up in a vague, rootless, and even faithless liberalism.

The Hebrew Scriptures (or what Christians refer to as the Old Testament) were important to Jesus and to his first disciples, and have always played a central role in the life and worship of the Church. But why should Christians take the Bible seriously? What is the rationale? And what entitles a book in the Bible to a place amongst the canonical[40] books of the Church? More than one answer has been given to these questions.

As far as the Roman Catholic Church is concerned, a book becomes canonical through the decision of the Church. In 1546 the Council of Trent listed the books which for the Roman Catholic Church form the Old and New Testaments, and as far as

---

[40] *The canonical books are those which are regarded by the Church as being authoritative.*

Roman Catholics are concerned there is really nothing more to be said. The authority of the Church is absolute.

In Reformation churches the situation is very different. They chose to break away from the Church of Rome, so basing anything on its tradition or authority is the one thing they cannot do. It is sometimes said that the Protestant Churches simply replaced an infallible Church with an infallible book, but this is not entirely fair. Most of the reformers were well aware of the critical history of the books of the New Testament, and fully prepared to give that critical history full place in their evaluation of a book. The Reformers were not at all fundamentalist in the modern sense of the word, insisting that every word of scripture was equally inspired and equally authoritative. Martin Luther (1483–1546) for example had a rather low opinion of the epistle of James, describing it as 'an epistle of straw'.

The reformer John Calvin (1509–64) judged the authority of a book, neither on the basis of ecclesiastical tradition nor on apostolic authorship, but on the intuitive witness of the Holy Spirit within him responding to the witness of the same Holy Spirit within the book. Martin Luther judged a book by the extent to which it bore witness to Jesus, the Word incarnate, and that perhaps comes nearest to the approach I take.

To understand the central role that the Bible plays in the lives of Christians, it is instructive to compare it with the Muslim holy book, the Qur'an.

The Qur'an is believed by Muslims to contain the very words of God spoken to the prophet Muhammad by the angel Gabriel. This is why no translation from the Arabic is ever regarded by Muslims as truly authoritative, and why they can take so much trouble to learn the text by heart in its original language. It also explains why there is a generally much lower level of critical historical analysis of the text by scholars than that to which we have become accustomed in relation to the Bible. The Qur'an is for Muslims quite literally 'the Word [of God] written'.

Now the focus of revelation is for Christians not a book but a person. They look upon Jesus as the key to understanding God's nature and purpose, and they speak, not just of 'the Word *written*', but of 'the Word made *flesh*' (John 1:14). Although they often refer to the text of the Bible as 'the Word of God' (and some within more conservative traditions view it as having come almost direct from heaven in a way not dissimilar to the Muslim Qur'an), strictly speaking it is only the primary witness to the Word of God, who became 'incarnate' amongst us in the life, death and resurrection of Jesus.

The Bible is essential to anyone who sees Jesus as the key to understanding the nature and purpose of God, and who wishes therefore to understand and follow him.

The first part, which Christians call the Old Testament (literally 'the old covenant' or agreement), prepares the way for the coming of Jesus, and the second part, the New Testament, bears witness to the Christ-event and the experience of the first generation of Christ's followers.

The writing within the Bible contains many different literary forms and it is important to recognise this when reading it. It is not all straightforward factual history. Even the history was written in a different way then from how it is now. There is law; there are collections of wise sayings (eg in Proverbs), poetry (eg in the Psalms), myths, parables, gospels (which literally mean 'good news') and even love songs.

Critics of Christianity like Richard Dawkins love to highlight passages from the Old Testament in which God appears vengeful and full of wrath. The God described in these passages appears morally dubious and unworthy of worship, so how should Christians respond to such criticisms? It is interesting to note that there were Christian leaders within the early Church who felt equally challenged and disturbed by such passages. Marcion (89–160), for example, thought that the God of love and mercy revealed by Jesus was so radically different from the deity described in the pages of the Old Testament that they were effectively two different gods, and that the God of the Old Testament should therefore be discarded. The Church, however, rejected this suggestion. It would be like 'throwing the baby out with the bathwater'. All the key concepts and ideas which Jesus used to define his own identity ('Son' of God, suffering servant-king etc), and to explain his mission (ushering in the 'Kingdom of God') were derived from the Old Testament. He was a Jew and the Hebrew scriptures were, for him and his contemporaries, their 'Bible'. He frequently quoted from them. His commands to 'love the Lord your God' and to 'love your neighbour as yourself', for example, were both quotations from the Hebrew scriptures, the first from the book of Deuteronomy and the second from the book of Leviticus. If we abandoned these texts, we would find it very difficult properly to understand Jesus and his significance for us.

Regarding the 'hard sayings' and difficult passages highlighted by people such as Dawkins, Christians in their approach to the Bible tend to fall into two main camps. Those of a more conservative and fundamentalist persuasion treat it like an instruction manual in which every book, chapter and verse is given equal weight and taken in almost *every* instance quite literally and at face value. A description of God in the Book of Joshua or a law in the Book of Leviticus is regarded, for example, as being just as authoritative and insightful as an equivalent description or saying of Jesus in the gospels.

Others, including myself, interpret the Bible as basically the story of a growing relationship with God and a deepening understanding of his nature and purpose for the world. Within this 'story' Jesus is for Christians the fullest and clearest disclosure of God. He is also the key to interpreting the scriptures and the relative significance of earlier laws, sayings, events and descriptions of God's nature. Many of the 'hard' sayings and 'events' found in parts of the Old Testament and elsewhere can be explained, by those who adopt this approach, as reflecting an earlier and less developed relationship and understanding.

It is interesting to note that in the great 19th century debate over slavery, defenders of the slave trade (including some church leaders) quoted Old Testament laws about how slaves should be treated and pointed to the fact that some of the patriarchs had slaves. There was no shortage of scriptural passages to support their viewpoint. But Christian reformers like William Wilberforce (1759–1833) argued for Scripture being the story of ongoing revelation and deepening understanding, and pointed to the way in which the story was clearly moving in the teaching of Jesus and St. Paul towards the emancipation of slaves and equality for all. In Galatians Chapter 3, verses 26–28 Paul writes:

"…There is neither Jew nor Gentile, male nor female, slave nor free, for you are all one in Christ Jesus."

And in his letter to Philemon he urges the latter to take back an escaped slave called Onesimus, not as a slave but as a 'brother' (Philemon16).

It seems from all this that biblical Christians are not those who believe that every law in the Bible is eternally binding, all ethical statements equally authoritative, and every historical account infallibly accurate. Rather, biblical Christians have faith in the God of Love revealed in Jesus Christ and recognise the Bible as the essential primary witness to that revelation. Their faith enables them to see texts in this context and appreciate their true importance. Keith Ward puts it well. We read the Bible, he says,

"in such a way that it allows God to address us personally, as we read it in the context of the Church's worship and of *the Christ-illumined key* to interpreting each part of the Bible."[41]

To be a biblical Christian is to respond to the living God whose living word it is.

---

[41] *Keith Ward, 'By Faith and Reason: The Essential Keith Ward', ed. by W.M. Curtis Holtzen & Roberto Sirvent (DLT 2012) p.197.*

Chapter 4

'Moral Realities'

Following our brief diversion into the realm of biblical interpretation, we return now to the main discussion. We had previously been looking at reasons why Christians such as myself are led to believe in God – an infinite, eternal, purposive mind, who creates and sustains the material universe in which we live.

A key element within the discussion was the emergence of conscious beings like ourselves with a capacity for moral thought and behaviour. This now needs to be looked at again in rather more detail. We need to confirm that the moral dimension actually exists as an objective reality. If it is simply the product of individual or social imaginations, then the *objective* value and dignity of human and non-human beings, not to mention a God of Love, must be called into question.

We will explore in this chapter the way in which a number of key thinkers have understood what we conceive to be 'the good', and why to my mind they all fail to satisfy.

David Hume (1711–76)

Eighteenth century empiricists thought that knowledge is acquired solely through the senses. When they came to examine ethical beliefs concerning what is 'right' or 'wrong', 'good' or 'bad', they sought empirical data with which to equate these terms.

None, of course, were to be found in the observable 'outside' world. If you give someone a box of chocolates to show how much you love or care for them, your love and care are not visible properties of the chocolates. We cannot even observe your love

46

and care in your act of giving, as the act could always open to other more sceptical, cynical, and less endearing interpretations. 'Goodness' and 'badness' are not empirical properties. They seem, rather, to be related internally to how people feel. The eighteenth-century philosopher, David Hume, described the situation thus:

> "Take any action allowed to be vicious: wilful murder, for instance. Examine it in all lights, and see if you can find that matter of fact, or real existence, which you call 'vice'. In whichever way you take it, you find only certain passions, motives, volitions, and thoughts. There is no other matter of fact in the case. The vice entirely escapes you, as long as you consider the object. You never can find it, till you turn your reflection into your own breast, and find a sentiment of disapprobation, which arises in you, towards this action."[42]

The inevitable outcome of this empirical line of thinking was to equate moral judgements with human feelings. But did these feelings constitute moral 'knowledge'?

Logical Positivists[43]

Twentieth century Logical Positivists like A.J. Ayer followed in the footsteps of empiricists like Hume. They side-stepped the issue of moral 'knowledge' by maintaining[44] that moral judgements have nothing to do with *knowing* anything. They simply express a moral *attitude*, a moral feeling of approval or disapproval. Of course, people voice approval or disapproval of many things which have nothing to do with morality. We say, for example, "This is an excellent kitchen knife," or "That football team is

---

[42] David Hume, 'Treatise of Human Nature', Book III, Part i (1).
[43] I spend some time looking at the Logical Posivists, not because their ideas carry much weight amongst today's philosophers, but because they are still so prevalent within popular culture.
[44] The chief exponent of this view was A.J. Ayer in 'Language, Truth and Logic' (1936).

lousy". But what distinguishes our moral 'judgements' from these other statements of approval or disapproval is that they express attitudes or feelings which we would wish everyone to share. In other words they are universalised. We want others, for example, to express with us revulsion over some horrific murder, or admiration for a remarkable act of charity or heroism.

It is easy to see why the Logical Positivist argument has been so appealing, and why it continues to linger in popular culture. It fits neatly into our current 'scientific' way of thinking – the emphasis, for example, on empirical observation and verification, and the desire for an explanation, which will sound 'scientific' rather than 'religious' or 'mystical'. What is more, it highlights the fact that the moral dimension is not something which can be observed dispassionately. It involves experiences which touch our inmost being and stimulate the profoundest thoughts, feelings, and attitudes.

Logical Positivism is, in philosophical circles these days, a spent force. Even A.J. Ayer, one of its founding fathers, came eventually to admit that it was fundamentally flawed. One major problem with the theory is that it fails to do justice to the objective reference implicit in our ethical discussions. When we seek moral guidance from a friend, we do not look for subjective expressions of approval and support; or if we do, the approval or support is not the same as what we mean by *moral* guidance. To seek moral guidance is to seek what is objectively 'right', regardless of our feelings.

Let us consider the situation in which a friend and I hold strong but conflicting views on an important moral issue. The Logical Positivist theory will look upon these views as simply two contrasting expressions of opinion which we must learn to accept. But there are matters over which we hold very strong moral convictions, and which we cannot lay to one side, however hard we try, as simply 'matters of opinion'. When a terrorist kills an innocent child, we do not just say,

> "My own personal opinion is that he shouldn't have done that… but, of course, I am happy to accept that others – the terrorist included – may feel differently."

Most of us would want to say, "The terrorist is wrong, even if he thinks he is not!"

There is an implicit belief here in a shared, objective understanding of 'right' and 'wrong', which takes us beyond the mere expression of a personal moral attitude or feeling.

Logical Positivists say that moral judgements are neither true nor false. But if they were right in this, the role of rational argument in our moral discussions would become highly problematic. How can an ethical viewpoint be supported or refuted by any argument, if that viewpoint is merely the assertion of a personal opinion or feeling? Giving reasons for a moral viewpoint becomes meaningless. The expression of a feeling is simply an expression of a feeling, and that is all there is to it, unless its purpose is to sway people by the emotional impact of what is said. The Logical Positivist position fails to do justice to the importance we attach to reason in our moral discussions.

Logical Positivists maintain that the only statements which can be judged as 'true' are 'scientific' statements which have been tested and verified empirically. This enables them to dismiss moral statements as conveying nothing more than meaningless personal opinions. But whilst moral scepticism can be maintained at a philosophical level, sceptics will *in practice* almost certainly live as if there are objective moral truths. Logical Positivists talk about the importance of testing and verifying statements, for example, and in so doing reveal a passionate concern for 'Truth'. But on what grounds can they claim that 'Truth' is important? It is a non-empirical value which they recognise and adhere to on *non-empirical* grounds.

The Naturalistic Fallacy

Logical Positivists who espouse the so-called 'emotivist theory' equate 'what is right' with 'what we express approval for'. But in this they are guilty of what G.E. Moore (1873–1958) called 'the naturalistic fallacy'.[45] Goodness, Moore argued, is irreducible.

---

[45] G.E. Moore, 'Principia Ethica' (1903). (cf David Hume also noted the problem in 'A Treatise of Human Nature' (1739) at the end of Bk 3, Part 1, Section 1).

'The naturalistic fallacy' occurs whenever a person tries to explain goodness in terms of something other than goodness. The 'Good', for example, has at various times been defined as that which evokes approval of the self or others, as a utilitarian pursuit of happiness, as whatever aids human survival, or as that which promotes social development and increases social stability. But all these explanations of the 'Good' suffer from the same fatal error. They all start from an empirical statement about what *'is'* the case and try to deduce from this what *'ought'* to be the case. Logically this is impossible. To give just one example, if we are told that bull fighting *is* a part of Spanish culture and has been for hundreds of years, this does not prove that it *ought* to be a part of Spanish culture in the future. We cannot deduce from a statement of fact about what *is* the case now, what *ought* to be in the future, or indeed what ought to have been in the past.

Karl Popper (1902–94)

The Logical Positivists sought, by their insistence on empirical verification, to rule out all moral and religious claims to knowledge. In practice, however, it did far more than that. History, Geography, Geology, and Cosmology, to name but four major disciplines, all fell foul of the Logical Positivist criterion, and even science, the very cornerstone of their argument, was found wanting. The philosopher David Hume demonstrated long ago that the scientific process of 'induction', 'the method of basing general statements on the accumulated observations of specific instances', could never lead to certain knowledge. The fact that I have observed the same occurrence repeatedly thousands of times, does not 'prove' that the next time something different may not happen. We may come to expect that it will, but that is another matter. Karl Popper, arguably the greatest 20th century philosopher of science, wrestled with the problem of induction and came to the conclusion that the Logical Positivists' understanding of the task of Science was seriously flawed. Scientists should not try to 'verify' their theories, for that is not only logically impossible but dangerous too. It can tempt researchers to look only for evidence which will support their theory, whilst ignoring important data which would help them to modify or change it. Rather than seeking to 'verify' their theory, Popper believed that scientists should do their best to 'falsify' it. Scientific knowledge, however well established, must always, he argued, carry with it an air of the provisional.

Many of us will have been taught in school that water boils at 100° centigrade and we will doubtless have accepted it as a proven fact, a scientific law. But supposed 'facts' like this are never conclusively 'proven' no matter how many times they are tested. They may hold true in most situations, but it is always possible that circumstances will arise when the so-called 'law' is broken. Water in closed vessels, for example, does not boil at 100° centigrade. If we were scientists first making this discovery, we would have to revise the original theory. But then again, a little further down the line, we might discover that the boiling point changes at high altitude. Once more we would need to alter our findings. The process is intrinsically open-ended, and progress is only made when we accept the provisional nature of scientific theories and genuinely seek through testing to 'falsify' rather than to 'verify'.

Intuitionists

The Logical Positivists' belief in empirically verified, certain knowledge is generally recognised as untenable. There is a clear need to revise such ideas about what can count as knowledge, and broaden our understanding of 'a priori', 'intuited' knowledge. Everyone who enters into an ethical discussion will bring to it certain moral assumptions as to what is 'right' or 'wrong', 'good' or 'bad'. As A.C. Ewing points out in the introduction to his book on Ethics:

> "There seems to be no possibility of validly deducing ethical propositions by some sort of logical argument from the nature of reality without first assuming some ethical propositions to be true; or at least if there is, the way to do so has not yet been discovered by anybody."[46]

---

[46] A.C. Ewing, 'Ethics' (English Universities Press, 1953 and 1962) p.1.

It is often claimed that our knowledge of 'right' and 'wrong' is acquired through the upbringing we received from parents, teachers, and the community in which we live. We do not receive it 'direct from heaven'. We do not intuit it through some distinct religious sense perception. So is it simply the product of social conditioning?

Our social environment certainly affects the way we think and see things, and there is no doubt that much of our moral education comes through parents and teachers. But two points need to be made here. First, the status of a piece of knowledge is not logically *dependent* upon the source from which it is acquired. I do not have to know someone to be infallible before I can accept that what they are teaching me is true. Secondly, if you believe in the possibility of positive social reform, you cannot go along with the theory that what is right is determined by 'what the majority of society believes to be right'. 'Right' and 'wrong' can indeed be mediated *through* society, but they can also on occasions stand in judgement *over* society. Reformers like Wilberforce and his friends, who campaigned against slavery, were initially a minority challenging the majority opinion within society, but we deem them to have been right just the same. They were, for whatever reason, more sensitive and open to the demands of the moral dimension of reality than others of their day.

Variations in sensitivity and openness (which may, perhaps, be analogous to people's varying musical sensitivity and the existence of some folk with an 'exceptional ear' and perfect pitch) remind us that 'intuitions' are not infallible. Nor are they a substitute for careful thought and reflection. The intuitive insights of the great scientists only occurred against the background of study and thought, and the same principle applies to the great moral reformers. Reason may highlight inconsistencies which require us to modify our perceptions. It may also draw our attention to relevant ethical considerations which support or militate against a certain course of action. But when all is said and done, it still seems that we possess an intuitive awareness, however distorted and inadequate, of at least some a priori moral truths.

The supposedly widespread differences in ethical belief within our world seem, to many people, to constitute a decisive stumbling block to the acceptance of an objective moral dimension to reality. But with regard to this, a number of points need to be borne in mind:

First, we may note that wide differences of belief can also occur amongst people over questions of ordinary fact. It may simply be that some propositions are 'true' and others 'false', that a certain military commander, for example, is mistaken in saying that his fortress is impregnable, or a certain politician is correct in his analysis of the social causes underlying a particular breach of the peace.

Secondly, we will often find that ethical differences have arisen through differences in belief about fact. Some, for example, may oppose abortion on the grounds that it entails the murder of a human being, whilst others may favour it on the grounds that it is part of the woman's body, to do with as she pleases. Both sides agree with the moral principle that it is wrong to murder a human being. The debate in this particular instance concerns the factual question of what constitutes a human being.

Thirdly, we need to note the way in which different situations can make different kinds of behaviour appropriate. A normal rule of thumb, for example, is that it is wrong to eat human flesh. However, many of us would accept the need (notwithstanding our emotional revulsion) to modify that rule in the famous case of the 1972 plane crash in the Andes, when passengers felt obliged to eat the flesh of dead comrades in order to survive.

Fourthly, we noted earlier how intuitions can be positively refined by 'thought' and 'reflection'. To this we must now add the factor of 'experience'. Genuine ethical differences may arise because some people, for whatever reason, have lacked certain experiences which would have helped them to gain a particular insight. Again, some may not have had the time or perhaps the inclination needed for necessary background thought and reflection.

A fifth point, which must be made, is that people can actually prefer to hide behind their ignorance and prejudice, rather than expose themselves to an uncomfortable moral truth which will require them to change or do something they find unappealing. Many meat-eaters, for example, can dislike being shown pictures illustrating modern intensive farming because it calls into question the morality of a diet which supports such a blatantly cruel system. Tea or coffee drinkers can react in a similar vein to documentaries depicting poor conditions of people working on tea and coffee plantations, because it reminds them of the price paid in human suffering for certain brands of cheap tea and coffee.

If these points which I have mentioned may not resolve every difficulty, this should not overly disturb us. There are unresolved problems in all accepted branches of knowledge, including the sciences. What is important to hold onto is the fact that, when all possible reasons for moral differences have been taken into account, we may be surprised at the level of agreement which is reached. Amongst moral philosophers, for example, there are significant similarities in ethical judgement. Where they tend to disagree is at the secondary stage, of finding theories to explain these judgements. D.D. Raphael probably overstates the case for global agreement, but the general thrust of his argument holds good.

"Different societies and different groups," he writes, "do differ in the relative weight attached to values that can compete with each other. And, of course, they do not all have to face the same dilemmas; a modern Western society does not live near the margins of subsistence, as the ancient Spartans did, so that the preservation of handicapped children does not have to be set against any real risk of the non-survival of the society as a whole. If we put aside the differences in judgement in the relative weight given to possibly conflicting principles, and if we simply consider the principles themselves which have some value in the moral codes of different societies, the underlying similarities are quite striking. All societies think that it is wrong to hurt members of their own group at least (or to kill them unless there are morally compelling reasons); that it is right to keep faith; that the needy should be helped; that people who deliberately flout the accepted rules should be punished."[47]

Some more 'advanced' religions and philosophies may go further than others in the help and guidance which they offer. Just as individuals can be more open and sensitive to the moral dimension of reality than others, so also (not surprisingly perhaps) can communities and groups.[48]

Enough, I believe, has been said to establish the moral dimension of 'right' and 'wrong' as an objective reality and our common sense awareness of it. We can of course build on this. It is a natural human desire to search for a deeper understanding of the world in which we live. With science we start from 'common-sense' perceptions and proceed to generalise. We advance, for example, from the single observation of an apple falling from a tree to the more general observation that all apples fall. We then move on to the theory that there is a force of attraction pulling apples to the ground, and from that to the idea that other things besides apples are also attracted by the same force. Finally we arrive at the notion that everything, including the planets, may be subject to this force. As our understanding broadens, some 'common-sense' assumptions, which we originally adopted, may have to be modified or even abandoned, but they still remain our essential starting-point.

In the ethical realm, the process of understanding works in a similar fashion. We start from particular 'common-sense' perceptions and then proceed to generalise. We move from the incidence of a theft, perhaps, to the belief that stealing in general is wrong, and from there to a more subtle understanding as to what constitutes stealing, and how, if we are Christians, we should view our 'property' and 'possessions'. I myself, for example, used to believe very strongly in 'private property' and the idea that what I had was mine to do with as I pleased. Nowadays I try to look upon

---

[47] D.D. Raphael, 'Moral Philosophy' (Oxford University Press, 1981 and 1994) p.16.
[48] For a useful discussion of New Testament ideas about 'Natural Law', see William Lillie, 'Studies in New Testament Ethics' (Oliver & Boyd 1961) Ch. 2.

everything as belonging to God. God is the creator of all: I am a steward of his bounty, called to use what I have in God's service and to God's glory.

I remember one cold winter's night how we were just coming to the end of a house group meeting at the vicarage during which we had been exploring the Bible passage about entertaining angels without knowing it (Hebrews 13:2), when the doorbell rang. It was a homeless person requesting food and drink. I made him some soup and gave him a cup of tea and piece of cake. But when the meeting finally ended and everyone had gone, I was faced with a dilemma as to what to do next. I could not bring myself to send him away. We lived in a small village miles from any hostel and there was snow on the ground. I was on my own; my wife was in hospital awaiting the birth of our first child. But I felt that I had to offer him shelter. I gave him some bedding and he slept on our hallway floor. After breakfast the following morning he went on his way. Although I took the precaution of locking various doors, what I did that night was undoubtedly risky and I certainly felt quite anxious about it. Some might say I was foolish. But my home was something of mine that night which I felt I had to share.

As we incorporate experiences like this and wrestle with the conflicting ethical generalisations we have formed, so our understanding broadens, and we find our perceptions of what is 'right' and 'wrong' need to be modified or changed completely.

As my own moral understanding has grown, so I have become more and more convinced that the moral dimension of reality is rooted in the ultimate reality of God – a purposive, creative, cosmic mind who has created the universe and who continues to sustain everything that exists.

I believe God to be a God of agapeic love. And in contrast to those who favour a Kantian or utilitarian ethic (we will explore their views in the next chapter), I also believe that divine agapeic love is the single, unifying principle which underlies our moral experience. It is a love which draws us, if we allow it to do so, into a radically new orientation towards the earth and towards a recognition that everything in it is sacred and belongs not to us but to the Lord (Psalm 24:1).

CHAPTER 5

'The Search for a Unifying Moral Principle'

Scientists like Stephen Hawking have sought to discover a single unifying 'Theory of Everything' which will account for all other theories about the fundamental forces of the universe.

In the ethical field philosophers have tried to do something similar. They have searched for a single 'good' under which everything can be subsumed, and by which a coherent, unified account of the moral dimension of reality can be established. In this chapter we will look at some of the most popular candidates for the role of unifying moral principle (such as John Stuart Mill's intrinsic utilitarian value of 'happiness'). I will then seek to show why I believe they are all found wanting and why the Christian notion of agapeic love offers the most promising way forward.

When we describe people, objects or actions as 'good', we can do so in two different ways. Either we may deem them to be 'good' as a *means* to a particular end, or else we may look upon them as intrinsically 'good' *in themselves*. A surgeon, for example, can be said to make a 'good' incision, not because cutting up patients is good *in itself*, but because it is a *means* of promoting a good end, namely the patient's health and wellbeing.

The distinction between what is good as a means and intrinsically good in itself is not always, of course, as clear or as simple as the illustration I have just given might suggest. A means may lead to an end, which then becomes a means to a higher end. A painter may use his equipment to produce a work of art (an intrinsic good), but this work of art may then be sold as a means of raising money for the needy, as an instrumental means in other words of achieving a higher end. It remains an intrinsic good for the beauty it conveys and the pleasure it gives, yet when it is sold it is also used as a means of raising money – an instrumental good.

Our devotion and commitment to something can of course only ultimately be justified in terms of what we regard as intrinsically good and an end-in-itself. We turn, therefore, to consider some of the major theories put forward by philosophers concerning the nature of these ultimate ends.

Utilitarians

Hedonistic utilitarians argue that the only intrinsic 'good' in life is pleasure. An action is 'right' insofar as it is useful in promoting pleasure or reducing pain. If we have to choose between two actions, both of which will produce a degree of pleasure, then the 'right' course of action will be to choose the one which will produce the greatest amount of pleasure.

Egoistic hedonists argue that we are selfish by nature and should only consider our own pleasure in calculating the effects of a particular action. Surprisingly, their outlook need not necessarily lead them to behave as selfishly as we might expect. Jeremy Bentham, a famous nineteenth century philosopher (1748–1832), was an egoistic hedonist (at least to start with) yet he was also known for his philanthropy. Caring for others, he said, brought him pleasure. He liked doing it. It 'made him feel good'. Furthermore, being kind and considerate was a good, practical policy, because it enhanced relationships, and personal happiness depended to a very large extent on warm, harmonious relationships.

G.E. Moore (1873–1954) has argued that egoistic hedonism is inherently self-contradictory. If every individual in the world said that his or her 'good' was the *only* good, and we deemed them correct to say so, we would have millions and millions of 'only goods', which is impossible! Of course the egoistic hedonist may retort that, whilst there may exist many other goods in the world besides his own, his own good is the only one which he has a moral obligation to pursue. But this position is fraught with difficulties. Once you have admitted the existence of other genuine goods, it is hard to see how you can remain wholly indifferent to them. A 'good' is something which, by definition, you recognise to be of value.

Egoistic hedonism is only one branch of hedonistic utilitarianism. Most philosophers who have aligned themselves with this theory have included the pleasure of everyone in their ethical calculations (universalistic hedonism). If, for example, we face a choice between spending money on a personal luxury which will give us a small amount of pleasure or donating it to a charity which can help restore someone's sight or save a life, the hedonistic utilitarian would calculate that the second option is the 'right' one, because the amount of pleasure created and the amount of pain removed would be infinitely greater.

Universalistic hedonism sounds more plausible than the egoistic version, but its notion of 'pleasure' as the ultimate good-in-itself is still too narrow. Most of us would wish to say that pleasures have a measurable *quality* as well as *quantity*. Suppose, for example, that a group of sadistic bullies found their chief delight in tormenting a small child, and that the sum of their various experiences of pleasure outweighed the pain suffered by the victim, would their action be justified? Of course not! Or suppose a vandal amused himself by upsetting people and spraying their cars with black paint. Would the fact that the car he sprayed was about to be taken to the dump and that the owner was not especially upset mean that the vandal's action could be judged 'acceptable'? Again I would answer 'no'. Most of us would say that 'pleasures' can be qualitatively 'high' or 'low', and that in the two cases I have cited of the bullies and the vandal, it is qualitatively speaking extremely low.

John Stuart Mill (1806–73), another utilitarian, took issue with Bentham over the way in which pleasures can vary in quality. It is better, he contended, to be someone like the great philosopher Socrates, who was dissatisfied and devoid of pleasure, than a fool satisfied. Socrates' commitment to the truth gave him, in Mill's opinion, a spiritual happiness which far outweighed the trivial, hedonistic pleasures of the fool.

Bentham, of course, might also have favoured Socrates' state of mind over against that of the fool's. He might have argued, for example, that the fool's pleasures do not last as long as those derived from more creative and intellectual skills like philosophy, art or music, and that the greater benefits which a philosopher like Socrates would bring to society would also give him greater pleasure.

But Mill's objection can be pursued still further. If pleasure varies only in quantity and never in quality, there is little to choose between a contented philosopher, a contented fool, and a contented sheep. Indeed, as the philosopher Smart points out, the most certain way of increasing the amount of happiness and contentment in the world would be to reduce the human population and replace it with millions of contented sheep![49]

One might object that the passive contentment of sheep is not the same as the positive fulfilment of human desires. But if this is so, the distinction between 'higher' and 'lower' desires still remains. Smart invites us to imagine a brave new world in which there has been invented a happiness-machine. People are able to plug into this machine whenever they like, by attaching various electrodes to their heads, "one to give the physical pleasure of sex, one for that of eating, one for that of drinking, and so on." Would we wish to live in such a world, where creative and intellectual abilities are despised, stifled or by-passed? Smart finds it profoundly disturbing, and so do I:

> "... Is this," he asks, "the sort of life that all our ethical planning should culminate in? A few hours work a week, automatic factories, comfort and security from disease, and hours spent at a switch continually electrifying various regions of one's brain? Surely not. Men were made for higher things, one can't help wanting to say, even though

---

[49] *J.J.C. Smart and Bernard Williams, 'Utilitarianism for and Against' (Cambridge University Press, 1973) p.16ff.*

one knows that men weren't made for anything, but are the product of evolution by natural selection."[50]

Concern about the quality of different pleasures has led to what is known as Ideal Utilitarianism expounded by philosophers such as H. Rashdall (1858–1924) and G.E. Moore (1873–1958). Ideal utilitarians recognise values like love, truth, and beauty, which are intrinsically good but which do not always directly or immediately result in happiness or pleasure. They rightly point out how, once we admit to a hierarchy of 'higher' and 'lower' pleasures, we must also recognise the existence of a separate set of criteria – *additional* intrinsic goods – by which we can prioritise these pleasures. Ideal utilitarians still maintain that the rightness or wrongness of an action should be judged by its consequences. The 'good' however is for them more than simply pleasure or happiness, and 'evil' is more than pain or misery.

An action may be deemed 'right', even if the outcome proves disastrous. A person, for example, can only be expected to weigh up probable outcomes. He or she cannot be blamed for unforeseen or improbable occurrences which mar what would otherwise have been a sensible course of action. An ambulance driver cannot be blamed for taking a 'short cut' to the hospital, if the short cut turns out to be blocked by an accident, because he could not be expected to have foreseen the problem. The fact that the patient is delayed in getting treatment is not his fault. On the other hand, a person deserves to be blamed if he or she fails to take a course of action which is almost certain to produce a considerable amount of good, because they are afraid that a highly improbable (but technically possible) disaster might occur. Utilitarians, they argue, must be careful here to distinguish between two different kinds of 'ought', the *non-moral* kind which speaks from hindsight (e.g. "I shouldn't have said that; I didn't realise the situation.") and the *moral* kind, which dictates what you ought to do in the light of the probable consequences. A slightly lesser good, which is more likely to prove

---

[50] *J.J.C. Smart and Bernard Williams, 'Utilitarianism for and Against' (Cambridge University Press, 1973) p.19.*

attainable, should outweigh a higher good, which you could gamble on obtaining, but which will probably elude you.

The utilitarian idea of 'adding up' the 'pleasures' and 'goods' resulting from an action sounds straightforward. But it becomes quite complicated when you consider the way in which 'pleasures' or 'goods' sometimes inter-react with one another. The consequence of an action must be viewed as a whole and not simply as a sum of the separate 'goods' which it produces. When two goods are combined, they may either cancel each other out or produce a sum greater than their parts. 'Knowledge' is good and 'pleasure' is good, but if your knowing someone to be suffering is accompanied by a feeling of pleasure, that will be bad – the mark of a sadist. Conversely, the sun and rain each have their own natural beauty, an aesthetic 'good'. But when they combine to produce the beauty of a rainbow, that beauty is even greater than the sum of its constituent parts.

There is an important point to note here, which we shall return to later when we consider the Christian notion of divine agapeic love. The supreme good lies, not *in* isolated values, people, animals or objects, but in the matrix of relationships which exist *between* them. Towards the end of my working life as a full-time stipendiary minister, my parish became involved in a major fund-raising project to repair one of its churches, a beautiful grade one listed building. We were tasked with raising hundreds of thousands of pounds – a tall order. But one of the most heart-warming outcomes of our fundraising efforts was that we not only succeeded in raising the amount we needed to repair the church building, but we also discovered in the process how much good will and support there was within the wider community. Staff in a local shop, for example, who were not regular worshippers, organised various events and collected a four-figure sum for the project. Money for the church building was raised, but, in the process, *positive relationships* with the wider community were also fostered in unexpected ways. Nurturing right relationships at every level is, of course, of supreme importance within the pattern of agapeic love.

Utilitarianism in its various forms is an understandably popular theory of ethics. It draws our attention to the importance of consequences in considering the 'rightness' or 'wrongness' of an action, and it offers a relatively simple, unifying rationale to the bewildering maze of ethical values which we embrace.

However, it will not do. One major problem is that it ignores the personal and unique vocational responsibilities we can have. If I found myself for example on a sinking ship, I would of course have a moral duty to help everyone on board as best I could. But if I also happened to be a parent I would have *an additional* responsibility, which I would call the 'vocational' responsibility of parenthood, to see to the welfare of my own children. Or again, if I were a teacher responsible for a particular group of young people on the ship, I would have an *additional* 'vocational' responsibility as their teacher to ensure their safety as best I could.[51]

Special vocational responsibilities cannot be ignored. Suppose someone has been hurt or upset, the individual who has caused the problem should, quite rightly, feel himself or herself under a particular obligation to do what they can to alleviate the pain and hurt. The duty to promote happiness and relieve suffering is not evenly distributed in the way that utilitarians suggest. There are special relationships and special responsibilities.

Linked in with the tendency of utilitarianism to ignore the deeper, personal network of relationships, is its tendency to treat people and animals as means to supposedly higher ends. The potentially exploitational attitude which this can foster is best revealed by the narrowness of the utilitarian approach to justice. Laws are justified by utilitarians on the grounds that the happiness of the community as a whole (eg peoples' general sense of peace and security) should never be undermined by the anti-social pursuit of happiness by the few.

Anti-social behaviour must be deterred. So the pain inflicted by the punishment, utilitarians argue, must be such that the deterring

---

[51] Note how a 'vocational' responsibility for one's family comes as an _additional_ responsibility and not an alternative to caring for fellow human beings and non-human creatures in general. The Mafia's insistence that loyalty to the 'family' should take precedence over any broader commitment to the wellbeing of society at large contravenes the all-embracing nature of God's agapeic love.

fear of punishment weighs heavier on the minds of would-be offenders than any possible happiness which they might hope to derive from their crime. The problem with deterrence, however, is that it can lead to punishments which are out of all proportion to the crime. A law which says, for example, that thieves will have their hands chopped off will almost certainly reduce the crime rate. But would it be a fair or just law? Suppose a teenager had his hand chopped off for stealing a school rubber. The punishment might be successful in deterring future offenders, but most of us I suspect would regard it as excessive. It is wrong to 'use' a defendant simply as a means to an end, to ensure the maintenance of social peace and order.

Any number of injustices could in fact be justified on utilitarian grounds. It could be decided, for example, that the handicapped and elderly should be 'removed', to avoid the trouble and expense of caring for them and to increase the overall peace and tranquillity of the community. The 'punishment' of an innocent individual could be advocated on the grounds that it avoids the even greater suffering of others who are not innocent. I am reminded of the high priest Caiaphas who was worried that Jesus' ministry, however good in itself, was causing trouble with the Romans, and that his innocent death would therefore be in the interests of the population as a whole.

> "You do not realise." he said, "that it is better for you that one man die for the people than that the whole nation perish."(John 11:50).

The intrinsic value of the individual is clearly under threat in such circumstances. But this is hardly surprising, when we consider the way in which so many utilitarians focus on 'pleasure' as if it were the only intrinsic good. Their view is simply too narrow. We are not just sentient creatures who feel pleasure and pain. Our feelings are important, yes, but so are our thoughts and actions. Ideal utilitarians, who recognise the value of our free will and powers of reason as well as our emotions, have placed alongside the 'self-evident' good of happiness other 'goods' such as knowledge (exercising our powers of reason) and moral virtue (exercising our free will).

However, this has had the effect of transforming a basically empirical theory into a modified form of Intuitionism[52]. When utilitarians put forward the idea of 'promoting happiness' as a *self-evident* moral truth, we find Intuitionism creeping into the utilitarian way of thinking by the back door.

As more and more 'self-evident' goods are introduced in this way, so the suggestion that utilitarianism is succumbing to intuitionism begins to sound more and more plausible. The single principle of 'promoting' happiness, for example, covertly splits into two principles, first that of *producing* the maximum amount of happiness and secondly that of *distributing* it as evenly as possible. The utilitarian argument is developed by reference to the 'logical consequences' derived from these principles, conveniently forgetting that the laws of logic are themselves a priori.

Having seen how utilitarianism tends inevitably to incorporate elements of intuitionism, we now move on to consider the strengths and weaknesses of intuitionism.

Intuitionism

Intuitionists maintain that there are a number of moral principles which are self-evident and known to be true by *'rational intuition'* (i.e. intuitions which undergird and permeate our rational thought). They do not deny the importance of moral instruction by parents and teachers, nor do they claim that people have an automatic knowledge of 'right' and 'wrong'. Rational intuition is not *mystical intuition*. It is perfectly compatible with the idea that we learn about 'right' and 'wrong' through the community in which we live. However, we reach a stage when we intuitively recognise the validity of certain ethical principles for ourselves. These intuitive insights cannot be dismissed as merely the products of our social upbringing. If they were, we would never be able to challenge or question

---

[52] *Intuitionists maintain that basic moral propositions are self-evident, and that moral properties are non-natural.*

what goes on in our society. When Wilberforce and others began their campaign against the slave trade, they were in a minority and going against values and practices prevalent at that time. As I have said earlier, society can both mediate values and be judged by them.

Different philosophers have different ways of stating baseline ethical principles, and, not surprisingly, we can observe a number of variations and even discrepancies between them. But there is a remarkable measure of unanimity. Amongst the self-evident principles we frequently find in their lists of ethical principles are:

a)   the promotion of happiness in others,
b)   the just treatment of others,
c)   the duty not to harm others,
d)   telling the truth,
e)   keeping promises,
f)   behaving virtuously, and
g)   expressing appreciation and gratitude.

Intuitionism is a helpful safeguard against the reductionist tendencies of utilitarianism, but on its own it cannot wholly satisfy either. There is something inherently unsatisfactory about a list of seemingly unconnected moral values, which are devoid of any guiding principle to indicate how they fit together.

I will describe later how I believe divine agapeic love can perfectly fulfil the role of this missing principle. But before I do that, we must turn our attention to one other major approach to ethics – Kant's notion of the categorical imperative.

The Categorical Imperative

Kant (1724–1803) took a very different approach from that of utilitarians. He introduced into the ethical debate the notion of the 'categorical imperative'. He drew a sharp distinction between what he called the *'hypothetical imperative'*, which was conditional and prudential (eg, "You ought to leave now, *if* you want to catch the train") and the *'categorical imperative'*, which is unconditional, universal and moral (eg, "You ought to do this, irrespective of what you want or what may happen to you").

The categorical imperative, he said, operated in accordance with a three-fold principle of moral action (ie three maxims). The first maxim focused on the *act* and its universally binding nature:

> "Act as if the maxim of your action were to become by your will law universal."

The thief, Kant argued, is immoral, because he expects others to refrain from stealing his possessions whilst allowing himself to be an exception to the rule. He intuitively recognises that the moral law against stealing is universal, yet he fails to act in accordance with it.

The second part of Kant's three-fold principle of moral action centres on the *object* of the act:

> "Act so as to treat humanity both in your own person and in that of every other man always as an end and never only as a means."

Of course, there are many occasions when we treat others as a means to an end: when a shopper asks a taxi driver to drive him home, for example, or when a teacher asks a child to take a set of books to the school office. People can help us to achieve our ends. But the point Kant is making is that we must never treat other people *only* as a means to an end. We must always recognise them as 'ends' in themselves, as having intrinsic value as human beings. We must take into account their own wish for happiness and respect their own personal decisions. Kant quite rightly reacted against the utilitarian tendency to use people as a means to an end. That tendency, he argues, leads to exploitation and domination.

The third part of Kant's three-fold principle of moral action concerns the *agent* and the way in which he is linked to the object of his action (who is also a morally free agent), through the idea of

> "the will of *every* rational being as a universally legislating will."

Kant's idea of a community of autonomous moral agents under-girds the constitutions of a number of western democracies like France and the United States of America: liberty (everyone can decide for himself), equality (everyone is equally free and responsible), and fraternity (everyone must be respected as an 'end' and not just as a 'means').

Kant's emphasis on the morally free agent leads him to emphasise free will. Utilitarians have usually upheld happiness as the only intrinsic good, but Kant challenges this. Happiness may be good in itself, but only when it is accompanied by a 'good will', by someone actively choosing to promote that happiness out of a sense of moral duty. Happiness is not good in all circumstances, nor should it be sought at any price. The utilitarian idea that the amount of happiness which an action produces determines its rightness or wrongness is totally misconceived. There are times when we must stand up for what is right even if the result is persecution and suffering. A person, for example who is living under an oppressive régime can feel morally obliged to speak out against cruelty and injustice, even if the power of oppression is such that the most probable outcome will be his own death, torture or imprisonment.

In 1972 I was in Kenya teaching in an harambee school close to the Ugandan border. Whilst there, the news came through that the Ugandan president Obote had been ousted and General Idi Amin had taken over. Amin was at first welcomed, but his rule quickly turned into a nightmare of oppression, torture, and ex-judicial killings. I remember meeting up with some fellow teachers during the summer holiday and hitch-hiking into Uganda. The Asians had not yet been thrown out, but people were being lynched and bodies were being found in the dam. Missionaries we stayed with told of how, driving home after collecting their children from school, their car was stopped at gunpoint and stolen. Later I learnt how the Archbishop of Uganda, Janani Luwum, had bravely challenged Amin to halt the torture and killings, but Amin had responded by having him arrested, tortured, and killed. Janani Luwum was not driven by a desire for happiness, He was motivated by a Christian sense of duty, to stand up for what was right and to speak out against cruelty and injustice.

Kant's stern emphasis on 'duty' leaves little room for emotion. We should obey the categorical imperatives, he says, out of 'respect for the moral law'. Emotional love and sympathy have a value of sorts, but someone who is governed by their feelings is not behaving morally.

Kant is sometimes accused of ignoring consequences, but this is not entirely fair. He recognises the connection between 'right' action and positive effects. His point is that we must beware of always determining what is 'right' or 'wrong' from the effect an action can have.

The primary weakness in Kant's position lies in the enlightenment culture in which he had become immersed. He seems to have believed in a remote and largely irrelevant deist God, who has handed over his role as a guide and moral legislator to us as rational autonomous human beings. Notice the first of the maxims in his analysis of the categorical imperative:

"Act as if the maxim of your action were to become *by your will* law universal."

We have become our own legislators. God is redundant, and the purpose of divine revelation has, in Kant's view, been reduced simply to illustrating or confirming what reason has already told him.

Kant's enlightenment philosophy suffers from a number of defects. First, the idea of the human being as a legislating, rational agent suggests that we are in control: we are the subject, and we are the ones '*grasping*' the truth. This does not accord well with our experience of *being grasped* by a moral imperative, of feeling that a certain course of action is 'right', whether we will it or not. We do not control the moral imperative. It controls us[53].

Secondly, rational principles of the kind described by Kant are too cold and rigid. He maintains, for example, that lying is always

---

[53] *The Apostle Paul alludes to this experience perhaps when he talks of being 'grasped' by a higher authority in 2 Corinthians 5:14, 'For Christ's love compels us...'*

wrong, that there is a universally binding duty to tell the truth, and that we must tell the truth, even if in doing so we endanger someone's life. The enquiring Nazi search party, for example, would on Kant's view have to be told where any Jews are hiding. A 'white lie' is not permissible.

There is a lack of warmth in this rational approach. We noted earlier the failure of utilitarianism to account for special responsibilities, such as a parent's responsibility for his or her own children. Kant's categorical imperatives fail in the same way.

The enlightenment was notorious for its lack of feeling towards the so-called 'savages' living in the jungle as well as towards wild and domestic animals. Kant's philosophy does little to rectify the matter. When he says that *rational* beings are 'ends' in themselves, this logically implies that those labelled as non-rational (i.e. animals) can be exploited as 'means' and need not be respected as 'ends'. A growing number of people in our society would wish to expand the category of 'ends' in some way, so as to accommodate respect for animals and oppose their abuse and exploitation.

Kant places an important emphasis on the moral act as an act of the will against the response driven by the emotions. But having conceded this point, we are still left wondering whether the solitary, 'iron will' of the autonomous, rational being is up to the task it has set itself. What motivates the will? What gives it that inner strength to do what is right? Psychologically, I find St John's belief that, "we love because he first loved us" (1 John 4:19) more persuasive; that goodness becomes possible because of our experience of God's goodness towards us. Can we really find within ourselves the motivational desire to do what is good and right, until we have experienced goodness and love in our lives? The fact that some people from disturbed or deprived backgrounds can find it hard to do so would suggest otherwise.

The third and final objection which may be levelled at Kant's rational a priori categorical imperatives, is that they suffer from the same difficulties as the intuitonists' list of principles. When two 'universal' imperatives clash, such as the imperative to tell the truth and the imperative to preserve life, one of them has to give way.

The choice between the two appears, on Kant's view, to be arbitrary. There is clearly a need for a higher principle by which the conflict may be resolved and the two categorical imperatives prioritised, but the fact that he has to make a choice at all sits uneasily with his claim that the categorical imperative is binding in every circumstance *without exception*. If we can conceive of occasions in which it needs to be laid aside, then clearly there are exceptions.

Prima Facie Duties

David Ross has tried to soften Kant's imperatives and to make them more flexible by speaking of a 'prima facie duty', "an obligation that only holds subject to not being overridden by a superior obligation."[54] But when two prima facie duties conflict, there are again no guidelines for resolving it and no higher principle to which one can appeal. We are effectively confronted with the same mishmash of principles that we were when we examined Intuitionism.

Harmony

A.C. Ewing suggests, very tentatively, that 'harmony' could be a candidate for becoming the single unifying good:

> "The mind has commonly been classified as having three aspects, that of feeling, that of knowledge and that of will and action...[55]."

Feeling is drawn towards the utilitarian good of 'happiness'; *knowledge* towards the intrinsic value of 'truth', and *the will* towards the Kantian value of 'moral virtue'. 'Harmony', suggests Ewing, could perhaps be seen as the governing factor in each of these three areas. 'Happiness' could be defined in terms of a

---

[54] W. David Ross, 'Foundations of Ethics: The Gifford Lectures' (Oxford University Press, 1939).
[55] A.C. Ewing, 'Ethics' (English University Press, 1953) p.72.

feeling of harmony with yourself and with the environment; 'truth' as harmony with reality; and 'virtue' as fostering harmony with other people.

The idea is an interesting one, but Ewing himself admits that it may not do justice to those situations where we must face up to moral conflict and refuse to accept a false harmony and shallow peace. Would we feel comfortable, for example, living in harmony and friendship with thieves and murderers? He seems furthermore a little uncertain as to where the religious dimension fits in. He clearly wants to include it, but it is tacked on rather awkwardly at the end with a comment about being at peace and in harmony with God.

The most suggestive insight, which he offers in a throw-away remark never pursued, is that aesthetic values, religious values, and love (which do not fit neatly into his three-fold description of the mind) may perhaps relate to "all three sides of our nature at once." When we turn to the Christian concept of agapeic love, we will see just how right he is.

Theological Ethics

The lists of virtues and intrinsic goods produced by the utilitarian, intuitionist and Kantian theories we have looked at, all seem in different ways to be somewhat rootless. They need grounding in a cosmic mind, or in other words 'God'. We are entering the realm of theological ethics.

Agapeic love, which I defined at the end of Chapter 2, is clearly a theological concept central to Christian ethics. But before considering it in detail, I need briefly to distinguish it from two other kinds of theological ethics which I would not wish to espouse.

The first of these equates what is morally 'right' with 'what God commands'. A classic discussion of the difficulties associated with divine 'command ethics' can be found in one of Plato's dialogues, 'The Euthyphro'. Euthyphro faces a dilemma which can best be summarised by the following question: Is something good because the gods command it, or do the gods command it because it is good? Neither option seems particularly palatable to the theist. If we equate what is good with what the gods or God command us to do, what are we to say about those situations when the gods or God command us to do something which we know to be immoral, such as slaughter innocent men, women, and children? There are passages in the Old Testament which appear to involve dubious instructions of this kind. But on the other hand, if we insist that God or the gods only ever choose to command what is good, then this seems to imply that they have submitted to a higher, independent standard of goodness and are no longer the ultimate moral authority. Human beings who are seeking moral guidance, could simply ignore the gods or God and go straight to this independent standard of goodness.

At first sight Euthyphro's dilemma seems irresolvable. But for Christians, Socrates' distinction between our awareness of God and our awareness of the good, whilst understandable perhaps within Greek culture at the time of Plato, when the gods were fickle and frequently immoral, is a false one. Our experience of what is good is *part and parcel* of our experience of God.

The second kind of theological ethics from which I would wish to distinguish my approach is that which venerates mother Earth as if she were a goddess. The agapeic pattern of divine love which we will explore is certainly all-embracing – inclusive of all animals and humans on this planet. But it is not pantheistic. In recent years there has been a growing interest in the New Age concept of 'Gaia'. Gaia was originally the name of a classical goddess, the earth mother. James Lovelock, a scientist who worked for NASA and Hewlett-Packard and also served as president of the Marine Biological Association, used the name to develop his famous 'Gaia hypothesis'.[56] The basic idea was that the earth should be regarded as a single, self-adjusting, living organism. At the level of scientific theory the hypothesis has been extremely helpful in drawing people's attention to the inter-connectedness of

---

[56] James Lovelock, 'Gaia: a new look at life on Earth' (Oxford University Press, 1979).

life and the possibility of self-regulatory patterns within the eco-system.

However, the use of the word 'Gaia' has had the unfortunate consequence of introducing pagan, religious overtones into debates about the hypothesis. Lovelock, in describing Gaia as a 'living' entity, positively encouraged such a development, and New Age writers like Kit Pedler and Peter Russell have used the concept of Gaia, not as a scientific hypothesis so much as a religious and moral myth, to promote their own distinctive world-view.

At the religious and mythical level Gaia, the Earth mother, implies a pantheistic belief, whereby the Earth is not seen as having been created *by* God; she actually *is* God. I am reminded of a song by Ralph McTell called *'The Ferryman'* which I sometimes used to listen to as a student. It tells of a traveller who, in search of the meaning of his life, comes to a river where he meets an old ferryman. The ferryman tells him that the answers he seeks are to be found in 'the singing river'. He only had to listen. He does so, and, in so doing, discovers that all is one: "The traveller was the river, was the boat and ferryman."[57]

The pantheistic idea that we are all one with God or Gaia, in the way that the religious Gaia hypothesis suggests, has a number of drawbacks. First it implies a static view of the cosmos and the way it operates. A self-regulatory eco-system does not develop or evolve. History (and thus divine providence), is denied. Neo-Darwinist scientists have criticised Lovelock's theory on these grounds. His insistence on the Gaia hypothesis has forced him to speak of a series of very sudden, dramatic leaps forward to new levels of equilibrium.

Secondly, our experience of the moral imperative is future-orientated. It draws us on towards what 'ought' to be. It inspires us with a real sense of potential history and potential moral development. The Gaia concept of God goes against this. The moral *'ought'* of the potential future is collapsed into the *'is'* of the actual present. Gaia *is* the Earth and we, the New Agers tell us, are

---

[57] *Ralph McTell (born 1944) is an English singer/songwriter, an influential figure in the world of folk music.*

already part of the divine being. Our spiritual task is not to respond to the moral call and *become* what God purposes us to be in the future, but to discover by a process of enlightenment what we already *are* in the present.[58]

The end result is fatalism. For as Lawrence Osborn has observed, Gaia fails at this point to undergird the environmental concerns which New Agers quite rightly wish to promote. The effect is the opposite – a passive laissez-faire:

> "It is perhaps worth noting..... an underlying assumption of the Gaian approach to the environment. Gaia, understood as the sum total of all interactions of the biota and abiotic environment, is assumed to be self-regulatory. This is uncannily similar to the underlying assumption of laissez-faire economics: no conscious regulation of individual selfish behaviour is required because the system as a whole is self-regulatory. Behind this lies the Enlightenment's secularisation of providence into the concept of harmony."[59]

The divine agapeic love which I have come to know, does not spring from an *overly transcendent* Euthyphro-like being, who issues commands from a remote heavenly 'head office'.

Nor does it emanate from an *overly immanent* reality, like the Gaia goddess of the New Age movement. The latter allows the world to be so venerated as it *is*, that the future-orientated moral drive towards what 'ought' to be risks being lost completely.

The God of Love whom I proclaim is a God who is both transcendent and immanent, a God whom we encounter at every level of existence through the patterned activity of agapeic love, the supreme good. It is to this pattern of love that we now turn.

---

[58] *Of course supporters of the Gaia hypothesis are subtly different in their time perspectives. The telos of Gaia is to return to the point of sustainable balance. In this sense it could be argued that Gaia has a place for history (re) development, albeit limited.*
[59] *Lawrence Osborn, 'The Machine and the Mother Goddess', an article in 'Science and Christian Belief', Vol.4, No.1, p.33.*

CHAPTER 6

'The Anatomy of Love'

In my discussion of the ethical dimension of reality I tried to demonstrate how the main ethical theories all presuppose the existence of a supreme good or goods intuitively known. We saw how even the empirically-minded utilitarians talk of 'pleasure' or 'happiness' as supreme values which we intuitively recognise, and presuppose a moral dimension to reality which they have neither 'observed' with their four physical senses nor deduced by reasoned argument.

I have also shown how the moral 'truths' thus intuited are not merely insights which we grasp; they are realities which 'grasp' us. This is an important point. It highlights the close affinity between moral and religious experiences analysed by Rudolf Otto in his seminal book, 'The Idea of the Holy', first published in 1923. Our sense of being grasped by another, which Otto refers to as the sense of the 'numinous', manifests itself, not only in the basic religious experience of creaturely fear and awe, but in the 'higher' moral awareness of 'the holy'. The holy as 'a category of value' is not simply,

> "'fear' in the face of what is absolutely overpowering, before which there is no alternative but blind, awe-struck obedience..." [It is a recognition of] "a might that has at the same time the supreme right to make the highest claim to service, and receives praise because it is in an absolute sense worthy to be praised..."[60]

---

[60] *Rudolf Otto, 'The Idea of the Holy' (Oxford University Press, 1973) pp. 51 and 52.*

Martin Buber, in his analysis of our encounter with the other[61], distinguishes between 'I-It' and 'I-Thou' relationships. In our rationalistic culture, he argues, we tend to regard ourselves as 'subjects' and the things which we study or analyse as 'objects'. We adopt the role of a detached observer and the result is an 'I-It' relationship. Such a relationship is of course perfectly valid in the context of a rational enquiry. But Buber is concerned that our pre-occupation with analytical I-It enquiries adversely affects those other situations in which roles are reversed and we find ourselves being confronted and addressed as objects.

We may be surprised by how frequently this happens. The 'I-Thou' encounter (which is what this is) can be sparked off by objects as unexceptional as a tree or a mountain. As John Taylor explains, within the 'I-Thou' encounter,

> "The mountain or the tree I am looking at ceases to be merely an object I am observing and becomes a subject, existing in its own life, and saying something to me – one could almost say 'nodding' to me in a private conspiracy. That, in fact, is the precise meaning of the word 'numinous', which comes from the Latin 'nuo', to nod or beckon. The truly numinous experience is not marked only by primitive awe in the face of the unknown or overwhelming, but occurs also when something as ordinary as a sleeping child, as simple and objective as a flower, suddenly 'commands' attention'."[62]

The 'other' – be it a mountain, a tree, a child, a flower, a painting, or a piece of music – meets us in its own authenticity. We find ourselves not just contemplating a truth *about* it, but being confronted with the truth *of* it. Such a confrontation can have a profound effect upon us and sometimes even compel us to action:

---

[61] *Martin Buber, 'I and Thou' (T. and T. Clark, 1966).*
[62] *John Taylor, 'The Go-Between God' (SCM 1972, 4th Impression 1974) pp.11 and 12.*

"To encounter the truth of Kilimanjaro," Taylor continues, "or the truth *of 'The Death of Actaeon'* (a painting by Titian) or the truth *of* Jesus is to submit to being the object of their impact. From one point of view this is a dangerously subjective way of knowing truth, but from another point of view it is the only way in which truth authenticates itself. It is the truth *of* Jesus which compelled men, and still compels them, to testify that he speaks not as the scribes but as one with authority..."[63]

The Kantian moral philosopher is someone who has been 'grasped' by a sense of 'duty', the utilitarian by an awareness of the value of 'pleasure' or 'happiness', the scientist by his passion for 'knowledge' and 'truth', and the Christian by the reality of divine agapeic love revealed supremely in Jesus two thousand years ago.

It is to Jesus and his revelation of divine agapeic love that we now turn. Our description of agapeic love will inevitably be messier than the other potential 'supreme goods' which we have considered, because it is bound up with the untidiness of history and human development. But as we proceed, its fundamental character will, I trust, begin to emerge. The way in which it helps us to grow and develop echoes Aristotelian virtue ethics in a number of ways, though it takes us well beyond Aristotle's interest in personal development through its concern for our relationship with God, the wider human community and the non-human cosmos.

Agapé's Being and Becoming

In his *'Situation Ethics'* Joseph Fletcher talks of love as the supreme good.

"Only one 'thing' is intrinsically good; namely, love: nothing else at all."[64]

---

[63] John Taylor, 'The Go-Between God' (SCM 1972, 4th Impression 1974) p.13.
[64] Joseph Fletcher, 'Situation Ethics' (SCM 1966 and 1969) p.57.

Things are of objective value, he says, because they are valued by their creator.[65]

Agapeic love could be described simply as a 'property' of God, in the sense that it characterises the eternal pattern of relationships within the Triune Godhead, Father, Son and Holy Spirit. But from our own personal perspective we first become aware of agapeic love through our experience of the creator 'valuing' us and drawing us to engage with his agapeic presence in our lives.

The essentially dynamic nature of agapeic love perhaps explains why the Hebrew culture became the setting for its divine disclosure. The ancient Hebrews focused on active 'becoming', the Greeks on static 'being'. It is a striking contrast. C.H. Dodd draws out the distinction beautifully in his commentary on the fourth gospel:

> "The Greek conceives of knowing as analogous to seeing; that is, he externalises the object of knowledge, contemplates... it from a distance... It is *the thing in itself*, as static, that he seeks to grasp..."

> "The Hebrew on the other hand conceives knowledge as consisting in experience of the object in relation to the subject... Thus it is *the object in action* and in its effects, rather than the thing in itself, that is known."[66]

Transcendent Agency

Agapeic love and its activity amongst us springs from the transcendent agency of God. We noted earlier on the important moral distinction between how things 'are' in the present and how we sense they 'ought' to be. The moral 'ought' orientates us towards the future, 'beckoning' us from beyond. It confronts us in the

---

[65] Andrew Linzey argues in his book, 'Christianity and the Rights of Animals' (SPCK 1987), for 'theos-rights' as an objective basis for animal rights, the rights of a God who values his creation. We will explore such wider concerns later on.
[66] C.H. Dodd, 'The Interpretation of the 4th Gospel' (Cambridge University Press 1953) pp.151 and 152.

here-and-now whilst remaining un-actualised. What 'ought to be' is not yet here. It has a strange transcendent quality about it.

Christians ground this experience in God, who is not only the 'Alpha' undergirding the past and present, but also the 'Omega' who beckons us on towards his goal or end in the future. The moral imperative itself is the call of agapeic love, because it sums up the purposive pattern of God's activity amongst us:

> "... *God* is love," says John (1 John 4:16b).

> "... *God* has poured out his love into our hearts by the Holy Spirit," writes Paul. (Romans 5:5).

It is vital that we recognise the transcendent origin of agapeic love. As Bonhoeffer says:

> "*God* is love; that is to say not a human attitude, a conviction or a deed, but God Himself is love. Only he who knows God knows what love is; it is not the other way round..."[67]

If we start to look upon agapeic love as a merely human phenomenon which we create and control, we will end up equating it with human love. It will be a form of idolatry. As C.S. Lewis rightly observed:

> "Every human love, at its height, has a tendency to claim for itself a divine authority. Its voice tends to sound as if it were the will of God Himself. It tells us not to count the cost, it demands of us a total commitment, it attempts to override all other claims and insinuates that any action which is sincerely done 'for love's sake' is thereby lawful and even meritorious. That erotic love and love of one's country may thus attempt to 'become gods' is generally recognised. But family affection may do the same. So, in a different way, may friendship."[68]

---

[67] *Dietrich Bonhoeffer, 'Ethics' (SCM 1955; 2nd Impression 1971) p.34.*
[68] *C.S. Lewis, 'The Four Loves' (First published by Geoffrey Bles Ltd. 1960; Collins Fount Paperbacks 1977) p.12.*

Human gift-love can look very like divine agapeic love because of its committed and sacrificial, self-giving qualities. However, it is precisely for this reason that it can also become the most wicked and the most dangerous. Lady Macbeth murdered a king out of passionate devotion to her husband. Terrible things can be done in the name of human love.

Agapeic love is certainly sacrificial in its outworking. Its ultimate manifestation lies in the historical reality of the 'Christ-event'. Jesus likens himself to a shepherd laying down his life for his sheep (John 10:11) or a grain of wheat dying in order that the harvest might come (John 12:24). In the words of Bonhoeffer:

"Jesus Christ... is the only definition of love."[69]

Jesus is the supreme revelation of the divine pattern of agapeic love. "For even the Son of Man did not come to be served, but to serve, and to give his life as a ransom for many" (Mark 10:45), to die for us on the cross (Hebrews10:5–7).

All-Embracing

Agapeic love is all-embracing. Christians see the coming of Jesus as reflecting God's love for the whole world (John 3:16). The entire cosmos is important to God, not just the human race. Jesus speaks of a creator who is concerned for the fate of even the tiniest sparrow (Matthew 10:29).

Early Christian writers like Origen and Athanasius describe Jesus as the embodiment of the divine 'word' through whom the whole created order is brought into being and sustained (John1:1–14), and envisage the entire material world being caught up in the redemptive process. The epistles hint at a cosmic redemption by a cosmic Christ (Colossians 1:19, 20; Ephesians 1:9, 10; Romans 8:21).

There is a debate over whether *individual* creatures will be saved, or whether their salvation will somehow be on a more

---

[69] *Dietrich Bonhoeffer, 'Ethics' (SCM 1955; 2nd Impression 1971) p.35.*

general level. I am inclined to side with theologians like Andrew Linzey and Keith Ward. God's justice demands that,

> "*all* sentient beings will be redeemed in a way that compensates them for the injustice and suffering that they have had to undergo."[70]

Christ's resurrection is a sign of God's desire to redeem all suffering and transform grief into joy (John 16:20–22):

> "If there is any sentient being which suffers pain, that being – whatever it is and however it is manifested – must find that pain transfigured by a greater joy. I am agnostic as to how this is to happen, but that it must be asserted to be true follows from the doctrine that God is love..."[71]

A Free Agency

If God is likened to an impersonal cosmic force like the force in the *'Star Wars'* films, then God is an 'it' that simply does what it does unthinkingly. Agapeic love however is the expression of a purposeful mind, a free agent, a Kantian 'good will'. An agent who is not free, whose actions are strictly determined either by instincts within or circumstances without, will never express agapeic love. The creation of the universe was in Christian thinking a 'free' act, a pure gift. God was not obliged to create. As C.S. Lewis observed in symbolic language which we may find startling,

> "This primal love is Gift-love. In God there is no hunger that needs to be filled, only plenteousness that desires to give..."

> "If I may dare the biological image, God is a 'host' who deliberately creates His own parasites; causes us to be that we may exploit and 'take advantage of' Him. Herein is love.

---

[70] *Andrew Linzey, 'Creatures of the Same God' (Winchester 2007), p.155.*
[71] *Keith Ward, 'The Concept of God' (Oxford: Basil Blackwell 1974) p.223.*

This is the diagram of love Himself, the inventor of all loves."[72]

God's redemption of Israel is described in similar terms, as a free and unmerited act of divine will. When the Israelites were 'chosen', it was not because they were better than anyone else – that they somehow deserved to be chosen. In the words of Deuteronomy:

> "The Lord did not set his affection on you and choose you because you were more numerous than other peoples, for you were the fewest of all peoples. But it was because the Lord loved you and kept the oath he swore..."
>
> (Deuteronomy 7:7, 8)

Respect for Freedom

Agapeic love desires the wellbeing of the 'other', either as an object of love, or else as a being with whom one can ultimately enter into an agapeic relationship. This is why a God of love, in the very act of creation, must for the sake of love grant a measure of freedom and autonomy to the world. Without such freedom and autonomy they would simply exist as an extension of his own Being, like an arm or a leg.

Freedom and autonomy must be allowed within each successive layer of interacting complexity and each successive layer of life. The cosmos is not a machine in which each and every cog moves together in a frictionless, unchanging cycle of motion. It is open to a purposive future and to the dynamic emergence of new levels of complexity, which will lead inevitably to 'clashes' and 'conflicts' between different biological structures and levels of existence.

Unless you believe in an *historical* 'fall', by which creation was changed out of all recognition to allow for such biological processes as birth, growth and death, these 'clashes' and 'conflicts'

---

[72] C.S. Lewis, 'The Four Loves' (First published by Geoffrey Bles Ltd. 1960; Collins Fount Paperbacks 1977) p.116.

which we call 'natural evils' must be in-built. There are avoidable 'natural' disasters which we bring upon ourselves. Pollution can cause all kinds of illness. Poor farming practices can lead to the erosion of top soil, the silting up of rivers and subsequent flooding. But alongside these, there are other life-threatening phenomena like earthquakes and volcanic eruptions over which we have little or no control. Life in this universe is far from risk-free, and in willing the agapeic end or goal, God must of necessity will the means and (however reluctantly) permit these natural evils [73].

> "Austin Farrer once asked himself what was God's will in the Lisbon earthquake. His answer - hard but true - was that the elements of the Earth's crust should act in accordance with their nature. God wills neither the act of a murderer nor the incidence of a cancer, but He allows both to happen in a world to which he has granted the freedom to be itself." [74]

The more intimately harrowing tragedies such as the birth of a badly deformed baby or the suffering of a terminally ill cancer patient (like me) are a focus for similar thoughts by the Anglican theologian and biochemist Arthur Peacocke:

> "The chance disorganisation of the growing human embryo that leads to the birth of a defective human being and the chance loss of control of cellular multiplication that appears as a cancerous tumour are individual and particular results of that same interplay of 'chance' and 'law' that enabled and enables life to exist at all." [75]

Observations such as these about the harsher side of life are sometimes labelled as 'unbiblical'. But the Bible itself offers numerous

---

[73] *There is an important distinction to be made here between God's <u>active will</u> (what God wishes to happen) and God's <u>permissive will</u> (what God reluctantly allows to happen).*

[74] *John Polkinghorne, 'Reason and Reality' (SPCK 1991) p.84.*

[75] *Arthur Peacocke, 'Theology for a Scientific Age' (SCM 1990, 2nd Edition 1993) p.126.*

counterbalances to an over-sentimental view of nature. When the psalmists praise God as creator, they do so in a way that recognises the power of the storm wind and other destructive forces (eg Psalm 97:2–5) as well as the existence of predatory animals like the lion (Psalm 104:21). The Lord's answer to Job (Job 38–41) focuses mainly on the mystery and power of the natural order. It is a strong corrective to any narrow anthropocentrism.

> "Where were you when I laid the earth's foundation?...
> Have you ever given orders to the morning, or shown the
> dawn its place...? Can you bind the beautiful Pleiades? Can
> you loose the cords of Orion? Can you bring forth the
> constellations in their seasons...? (Job 38:4,12,31-32)

There are frequent references to God's power and ultimate control over the course of history, but there is also an increasing emphasis on freedom. Adam willfully disobeyed God. Joshua at Shechem invited the people to *choose* between serving the Lord and worshipping the gods of their forefathers (Joshua 24:21, 22). And Jesus explicitly rejected at the time of his temptations the tactic of coercion – the acquisition of political power, the use of military force, or the crude demonstration of miraculous power – to establish God's kingdom (Matthew 4:1–11). He wanted people to respond of their own accord rather than to be cowed into submission.

When we come to examine more closely the significance of the cross with its humble, vulnerable appeal of love, we will see the supreme demonstration of this divine strategy:

> "Jews demand miraculous signs and Greeks look for
> wisdom, but we preach Christ crucified: a stumbling-block
> to Jews and foolishness to Gentiles, but to those whom God
> has called, both Jews and Greeks, Christ the power of God
> and the wisdom of God." (1 Corinthians 1:22-24)

God does not force himself upon us. God looks for a free response of faith. When a Christian is 'filled' with God's Holy Spirit, he or she is never 'possessed'. In stark contrast to the notion of being 'possessed', oppressed, or taken over by depersonalising forces of evil (Luke 8:26–37), Christians see the outpouring of God's Holy Spirit as *enhancing* their freedom, and the apostle Paul talks of the Spirit-filled life bringing greater 'self-control' (Galatians 5:23), a heightened sense of autonomy – freedom and responsibility.

In Jesus' classic story of the Prodigal Son (Luke 15:11–32) God is compared to a loving father. The father is concerned for his younger son's welfare and remains unfailingly committed. But he nevertheless allows the boy, on reaching an appropriate age, to make his own mistakes, even when doing so endangers his life. The clear implication is that a loving God, like a loving parent, will resist the temptation to control and manipulate their child, however painful the consequences might be. Instead we encounter once again the important distinction between God's active and permissive will. A good God, like a good parent, may, out of respect for their child's autonomy, *passively* permit him to make mistakes and to suffer as a result of his foolish, selfish or arrogant actions, but that does not mean God *actively* wishes or wills these things to happen.

Expression of Grace

Agapeic love is an expression of what Christians call grace – God's free, unconditional, unmerited goodness. Jesus' use of a parental image for God (eg Matthew 7:9–11) is highly significant. Children do not 'earn' the good parent's love by achieving something or becoming somebody; they receive it from the moment they are born. They do not forfeit the love of the good parent by being naughty; any sanctions for poor behaviour are, or ought to be, an expression of the parent's continuing love (Hebrews12:7–11).

Jesus, who for Christians is the perfect human exemplar of God's agapeic love, taught us to care for everyone unconditionally, not just those who have 'earned' our love in some way. We are called to love even our enemies (Matthew 5:43–48). At the time in which Jesus lived, Jews and Samaritans were alienated from each other by a wall of suspicion and hatred. Jesus' parable about the good Samaritan (Luke10:25–37) who stopped to help a wounded

Jewish traveller, shows how agapeic love transcends the barriers and limitations which we impose upon our neighbourliness. Jesus was 'the friend of sinners' (Mark 2:15–17), the companion of those who, in the minds of his opponents, were society's outcasts and did not deserve to be loved.

I do not think we always appreciate the radical nature of Jesus' agapeic love. The great Chinese philosopher, Confucius, advocated kindness but rejected the idea of loving enemies on the grounds that to do so would be unreasonable and unjust. Judaism taught the message of loving your neighbour (Leviticus19:18) but 'neighbours' were generally equated with fellow-countrymen, members of one's own family or social group. Jesus' understanding of love went much further. He rooted it in the infinite, transcendent being and activity of God who bestows the blessing of rain freely on the good and bad alike (Matthew 5:45).

God's agapeic love is free and unconditional. It is given regardless of what the beloved may do in return. God may yearn for a response and rejoice when there is one, but none is ever guaranteed. One of the important distinctions which Christians make between someone freely receiving God's 'Spirit of love', and someone *possessed* or oppressed by an 'evil spirit', is that God respects the individual's freedom and dignity whereas the evil spirit seeks to undermine or destroy it. Compulsion, like possession, is alien to agapeic love.

Jesus proclaimed a vision of God's kingdom, which could never be imposed by military or political power. What was required was a free response of faith. When Jesus was preparing for the start of his public ministry following his baptism in the river Jordan, the Spirit led him into the desert to be tempted. There he found himself reflecting upon the methods he should use (Mark 1:12), and it is significant to note how he expressly rejected the option of seizing political power (Matthew 4:8–10) or presenting himself as some kind of supernatural wonder worker (Matthew 4:5–7). On the first 'Palm Sunday' he rode into Jerusalem on a humble donkey, a symbol of peace, rather than on a war horse. He had no intention of brow-beating people into submission.

Constant and Committed

In seeking a free response, agapeic love is inherently vulnerable to rejection. When Hosea's wife, Gomer, proved herself unfaithful, the prophet saw in his own experience of betrayal something of the pain which God was experiencing in the face of Israel's rejection of his agapeic love (Hosea 1:2, 3).

The possibility of rejection highlights another remarkable characteristic of agapeic love, namely its ability to remain constant and committed despite rejection. Hosea came to see how, just as he could never give up on his unfaithful wife, so God could never abandon his people. God's love would never let them go:

> "The Lord said to me, 'Go, show your love to your wife again, though she is loved by another and is an adulteress. Love her as the Lord loves the Israelites'...." (Hosea 3:1)

Jesus was nailed to a cross. The people's rejection of him could not have been plainer. Yet he continued to care for them and to pray for their forgiveness:

> "Father, forgive them, for they do not know what they are doing."(Luke 23:34).

His love remained constant and committed.

There is a consistency about agapeic love. It persists whatever happens. It never wavers. Christians refer to it as covenant-love:

> "... he is the faithful God, keeping *his covenant of love* to a thousand generations." (Deuteronomy 7:9)

> "Give thanks to the Lord, for he is good; his love endures *for ever*." (Psalm107:1)

> "This is my blood of *the covenant*, which is poured out for many ..."
> (Mark 14:24).

In the Bible, God's relationship with the people of Israel centres upon a series of covenants. Each of these is a representation in time of the covenant of God with the whole of creation which will eventually lead, in the symbolic language the Bible uses, to, "a new heaven and a new earth" (Revelation 21:1ff). The Bible describes covenants with Noah (Genesis 8:21–9:17), Abraham (Genesis 15) and Moses (Exodus 24). God's devotion to them is compared to that of a father, mother or marriage partner. God cannot simply abandon them on a whim (Isaiah 54:4–8). God's commitment to the wellbeing of his people and the environment is constant. God's purposes are unalterable (Numbers 23:19, Psalm 33:11). God's faithfulness is sure (Deuteronomy 7:9, Psalm 105:8).

God who is love never willingly abandons or rejects anyone. Judgement is something which we bring upon ourselves. As Jesus said:

"This is the verdict: Light has come into the world, but men loved darkness instead of light because their deeds were evil." (John 3:19).

Paul, in his letter to the Romans, tells how God in his wrath, "gave them over" to the shameful, immoral, and dehumanising consequences of their idolatrous sin (Romans 1:24–28). 'If that is the way you want it, then that is the way you can have it'. God can appear to abandon us in the sense of allowing us the freedom to reject him, but no-one is abandoned as a 'lost cause'; no-one is ever beyond forgiveness, unless or until *they* exclude *themselves*, perhaps by rejecting God's life-giving power of Love, the Holy Spirit (Mark 3:29).

People have an innate yearning for faithful, committed, unwavering love. Anything less is somehow false. One of the three marks of 'false love' described by Vanstone in his spiritual classic, *'Love's Endeavour, Love's Expense'*, is what he calls "the mark of limitation". People will test the genuineness of another's love, to see if it is limited:

"In a deprived child, the testing of love often consists of erecting the barrier or limit of outrageous behaviour on his own part – of offending to see if he is still accepted, of running away from home to see if he is sought."[76]

In relation to the natural world, patterns of agapeic love imply consistency rather than random intervention, and this indeed is what we find. It is not like the unpredictable capriciousness of the old pagan deities or the gods of primal religions.

We noted earlier how significant it was that modern science began to take off in western Europe where belief in a single, loving creator-God had replaced the old allegiance to an unpredictable pantheon, and led to the idea of an ordered and purposive cosmos. Scientists like Isaac Newton were encouraged by this belief to look for patterns within nature:

> "The whole of science works on the presupposition that results can be replicated, that what holds good in Washington from a physical point of view applies in Moscow too...
>
> We can go from the known to the unknown, from what we have experienced to what lies beyond experience. This encapsulates the problem of induction which empiricist philosophers, like Hume, have always found insuperable. This is because it cannot be solved within science... It has to be taken for granted that the world as investigated by science is ordered and structured... The applicability of mathematics to the physical world itself illustrates how an underlying rationale appears to be built into the fabric of the world..."[77]

The unwavering constancy and 'faithfulness', which lies at the heart of agapeic love, is the reason why we are able to discern 'patterns' or 'principles' within the moral and physical dimensions of reality. These 'patterns' or 'principles' are not rigid 'rules' any more than the so-called 'Laws of Nature'. Rather they reflect the purposive and faithful patterns of the agapeic love which brought them into being.

---

[76] *V.H. Vanstone, 'Love's Endeavour, Love's Expense' (DLT 1977) p.43.*
[77] *Roger Trigg, 'Rationality and Religion' (Blackwell 1998) p.81, 82.*

There is of course an in-built balance here between order and freedom:

> "... One who is faithful must show reliability in his relationship with his world. He will not be an arbitrary intervener in its processes, but they will have about them a consistency which reflects his character. On this view the laws of nature are a sign of God's fidelity. The one who is love will grant a generous measure of independence to his world, for love is grounded in the free interchange between lover and beloved. The God of love can be no puppet-master, pulling the strings of a world which is totally subservient to him.'[78]

Order and disorder are subtly intertwined. It is a world of orderliness but not of 'clockwork regularity', 'potentiality without predictability'.

Restoring and Renewing

God's agapeic love reaches out to the broken and lost. God's love for the Israelites is first revealed when they are slaves in Egypt (Exodus 3:7–10), a small and politically insignificant nation (Deuteronomy 7:7). The biblical story of salvation tells of a long and sometimes painful process of development, with God continuously building, repairing, restoring, and renewing what has gone before. Only in the story of the flood is God portrayed as despairing of the world and desiring to make a fresh start, and even here it is emphasised that this is abnormal and will never happen again (Genesis 9:12–15). Healing, renewing, and restoring were central to Jesus' ministry. As he reminded his critics:

> "... It is not the healthy who need a doctor, but the sick... I have not come to call the righteous, but sinners." (Matthew 9:12, 13)

---

[78] John Polkinghorne, 'Science and Creation' (SPCK 1988) p.51, 52.

The agapeic pattern echoes the process which we observe in the natural world. The poet Gerard Manley Hopkins points to the incredible resilience of nature in the wake of a storm or environmental disaster – its capacity for renewal and development:

> 'Generations have trod, have trod, have trod;
>   And all is seared with trade; bleared, smeared with toil;
> And wears man's smudge and shares man's smell: the soil
>   Is bare now, nor can foot feel, being shod.
>
> *And for all this, nature is never spent;*
>   *There lives the dearest freshness deep down things;*
> And though the last lights off the black West went
>   Oh, morning, at the brown brink eastward, springs –
> Because the Holy Ghost over the bent
>   World broods with warm breast and with ah! bright
>   wings.'[79]

Love of the Real

Agapeic love is found in Jesus in the concrete and specific. The love he reveals is not a vague, abstract principle, everywhere in general but nowhere in particular. God is the creator of all and God's pattern of agapeic activity is present everywhere. But the Christ-event shows how it must necessarily become present in a particular place and at a particular time in a very concrete and visible way.

God's agapeic love is directed towards what is 'real', towards people and situations as they actually are, and not people or situations as we (or anyone else) would perhaps like them to be. Jesus tells the story, for example, about a publican and a Pharisee who go up to the temple to pray (Luke18:10–14) The publican who is trying to be as open, honest and 'real' as he can about himself, prays: "God have mercy on me, a sinner." The Pharisee, who is struggling to preserve a false and artificial 'public image',

---

[79] *Gerard Manley Hopkins, 'God's Grandeur' (1877).*

boasts of his achievements. It is the publican, says Jesus, who goes away justified. He and not the other has been 'real' with God.

'The covenant of forgiveness' established through the cross (Matthew 26:27, 28) encourages people to be 'real', to come before God as they are, with all their weaknesses and failings. No sin is beyond his forgiveness or healing love.

> "But now in Christ Jesus you who once were far away have been brought near through the blood of Christ." (Ephesians 2:13)

So declares the writer to the Ephesians. And the same message is reiterated throughout the New Testament:

> "... (Christ) has appeared once for all at the end of the ages to do away with sin by the sacrifice of himself." (Hebrews 9:26)

> "He himself bore our sins in his body on the tree, so that we might die to sins and live for righteousness..." (1 Peter 2:24)

> "(Jesus) is the atoning sacrifice for our sins, and not only for ours but also for the sins of the whole world." (1 John 2:2)

Each writer expresses the effect of the cross in his own way but there is no changing its liberating effect. It constitutes a central and universal aspect of the Christian Gospel. It is the historical focus of Agapé's concern for the real. Sinners are invited, through the cross, to approach God *as they are*, to receive forgiveness and to embrace the opportunity for a fresh start within the agapeic pattern of God's will and purpose.

Agapeic love can only effectively work with what is real. It deals in reality because it springs from reality. Its source is God, the ultimately real. The flow of Agape is 'real-to-real'.

Its fullest and clearest manifestation was of course in Jesus. He is for Christians the most 'real' or authentic person who has ever lived. St John described him as "the *true* light" (John 1:9), "the *true* bread" (John 6:32), and "the *true* vine" (John 15:1), because the reality of his human life enabled him to mediate the ultimate reality of God. C.H. Dodd comments in his *'Interpretation of the Fourth Gospel'* on how:

> "... The term in this gospel rests upon common Hellenistic usage, in which it hovers between the meanings of 'reality', or 'the ultimately real', and 'knowledge of the real'. On one side at least, the knowledge of God which is life eternal is an apprehension of ultimate reality – that reality which stands above the world of phenomena, and is eternal while they pass away. This eternal reality is manifested in Christ..."[80]

God's agapeic commitment to what is real is seen most powerfully in the way Jesus homes in on particular individuals – the single lost sheep or the specific lost coin (Luke 15). Divine Agapé is not a vague ideal, of the kind alluded to by Linus in the Peanuts cartoon when he declares "I love mankind... it's people I can't stand." God does not love a rootless, intellectual abstraction. God is not simply in love with the idea of love. God is committed to real people, real animals, and real situations *as they are* in the real world:

in the cosmos

> "God saw all that he had made, and it was very good" (Genesis 1:31);

in society

> "I led them [Israel] with cords of human kindness..." (Hosea 11:4);

and in the individual

> "God... called me by his grace." (Galatians 1:15)

Enlightenment critics, who have been brought up with universal, rational principles, can find this hard to understand. They dislike

---

[80] *C.H. Dodd, 'The Interpretation of the Fourth Gospel' (Cambridge University Press, 1953) pp.177, 178.*

the way in which God's love revealed in Jesus of Nazareth 'homes in' on real or particular groups of people or individuals and treats each one differently. They call it 'the scandal of particularity', a failure to deal with everyone equally the same.

But if God is a God of agapeic love who respects and fosters the freedom of every creature, we would expect a more varied and directly individualised approach. Each relationship would need to be unique. A particular individual or group might be 'called', for example,[81] to fulfil a particular agapeic purpose, which no-one else would be capable of fulfilling, to meet a specific need at a specific time. I think, for example, of Mother Teresa committing her life to the poor in Calcutta, or Archbishop Desmond Tutu deciding to make a stand against apartheid in South Africa. As soon as we begin to cite such examples, we start to appreciate how wide is the range of differing responses and relationships which can arise, and the importance, within this more flexible moral framework, of more personal vocations.

Vocations

The classic ethical systems which we examined in Chapter 5 all speak of principles and moral obligations which are *universally applicable*. This is fine as far as it goes, but none of them, as far as I can see, properly consider the more personal but equally important 'vocation' we can have to perform a *specific task*. Oliver O'Donovan tries to distinguish personal callings from the more general moral obligations which are applicable to everyone:

"It would be wrong," he argues, "to say of any action which I might find myself 'called' to do that such an action was 'morally obligatory'."

---

[81] *Biblical examples of 'election' are numerous. They include such passages as:*
Genesis 12:1 "The Lord has said to Abram, 'Leave your country....'."
Malachi 1:2, 3 ".... I have loved Jacob, but Esau I have hated."
Hosea 11:1 "When Israel was a child, I loved him, and out of Egypt I called my son."

"As Kierkegaard unforgettably demonstrated," he continues, "there may be a conflict between the vocational and the
ethical, between God's call to Abraham to sacrifice Isaac
and the moral principle forbidding it."[82]

Such a dichotomy seems to my mind unsustainable. The 'call'
which results in a personal vocation, and the more general moral
requirement, which is applicable to all, both arise from the purposive mind of the one God. To suggest that they can be incompatible with each other would be to imply that an internal inconsistency
can exist within the mind of God. That is surely unacceptable. We
know that sacrifice was part and parcel of the culture in which
Abraham lived and that this needs to be taken into account in
trying to understand the test of faith faced by the patriarch. But
God is ultimately above and beyond transient human cultures.
The Alpha and the Omega is the same yesterday, today and for
ever. So if someone claimed that they had been 'called' by God to
sacrifice their son in the same way as Abraham (Genesis 22:1–19),
I would be contacting the appropriate safeguarding authorities. I
could not possibly accept their 'call' as genuine. There must
always to my mind be a strong sense of harmonious compatibility
between what is perceived to be God's *general* will, applicable to
all, and what is God's *specific* will for a particular individual.

Every Christian with any sensitivity has, I suspect, struggled
with the Abraham and Isaac story. The biblical scholar Von Rad,
for example, referred to it as a divinely "incomprehensible self-
contradiction"[83]. The level at which the story makes most sense to
me is as a 'call' to replace human sacrifice with animal sacrifice.
But be that as it may, the distinction between our general commitment to agapeic love and our more specific, vocational acts of
service is a blurred one. It is only a matter of degrees, and when
we come to consider Jesus' particular breaches of the (general)

---

[82] *Oliver O'Donovan, 'Resurrection and Moral Order' (IVP 1986 and 1994)
p.43.*
[83] *Gerhard Von Rad, 'Old Testament Theology' (Oliver & Boyd Ltd. 1968
reprint) Vol.1, p.171,*

law, we will see how dangerous it is to try and create a gulf between the two. General duty and personal vocation are opposite ends of a single spectrum. Each at its own level is a 'call' to share in the pattern of agapeic love, which God is seeking to weave with us in free and joyful cooperation.

Life as the End or Goal of Agapeic Love

God's end or goal is the flourishing of creation at every level. Jesus talks about the physical, emotional, mental, and spiritual wellbeing of humans and his ministry of healing amongst them is an important sign of God's kingdom (Luke 7:22; 11:20):

> "I have come that they may have life," he says, "and have it to the full." (John 10:10; see also John 5:40)[84]

Everything is 'good' in the eyes of God (Genesis 1:31), something to be cherished and nurtured. Even creatures which live in the wild and have no obvious use to humans are cared for:

> "Who provides food for the raven when its young cry out to God and wander about for lack of food?... Who let the wild donkey go free? Who untied his ropes? I gave him the wasteland as his home, the salt flats as his habitat."
> (Job 38:41, 39:5, 6)

Life is the gift of a loving God. The universal drive to procreate is a positive blessing (Genesis 1:22,28). Where human or non-human creatures are sick or in any kind of trouble, it is God's will to help and heal them. The good shepherd looks for the lost sheep; the righteous man cares for the needs of his animal (Proverbs 12:10).

Agapeic love will often create or draw out qualities in a life which were completely hidden or non-existent. As the

---

[84] *There are close similarities here with Aristotle's goal in Virtue Ethics: eudaimonia – flourishing as the fulfilment of our human nature.*

hymn-writer, Samuel Crossman, wrote, God's "Love to the love-less [is] shown, that they might lovely be".[85]

Jesus and his first followers liken the process of entering life in its fullness to a 'new birth' (John 3:3; John 1:13; 1 Peter 1:23, 2:2; 1 John 3:9,4:7 etc). Paul speaks of it as the emergence of a 'new self' (Ephesians 4:24, Colossians 3:10) or a 'new creation' (2 Corinthians 5:17, Galatians 6:15). The believers' awareness and attitude is radically transformed. There is a whole new orientation and energy. The Christian moves from a life centred on the self to a new life totally surrendered to the will of God. The submission comes as a free and glad response to the love of a God who is totally committed to our wellbeing. God wills nothing for himself. God's will, says Küng, "aims at man's wellbeing at all levels"[86] and, I would add, the wellbeing of the environment and of all living creatures too.

God in Jesus came to bring 'life' (John 20:31), life which is 'eternal' both in the sense of quantity (continuing beyond death) and quality. The Old Testament anticipated many of the themes associated with the Christian concept of 'eternal life', but for the most part these were in seminal form only. There was, initially at any rate, no clear concept of immortality (e.g. Psalm 39:13, Psalm 49:12, Ecclesiastes 3:19-20.). The most that people could hope for was a longer than usual earthly existence. During the Inter-testamental[87] period there developed the idea of two 'Ages': The Present Age and the Age to Come. A believer's participation in the Age to Come still did not imply a belief in the soul's immortality, which was a Greek notion, but it did involve the idea of a new quality of life (4 Ezra 7:12-13, 8:52-54).

In John's gospel Jesus accepts the idea of the two ages, and of life after death as a separate event in the future. Jesus' words to Martha just prior to the raising of Lazarus allude to this (John 11:20–24). However, he also speaks of an overlap. We can begin

---

[85] *From Samuel Crossman's hymn 'My song is love unknown' (1664).*
[86] *Hans Küng, 'On Being a Christian' (Fontana 1978) p.251.*
[87] *The inter-testamental period is the period between the Old and New Testaments in the Bible.*

to experience the new quality of life associated with the Age to Come in the here and now. On a number of occasions he refers to 'eternal life' in the present tense:

"... whoever hears my word and believes him who sent me *has eternal life*..."

(John 5:24)

"Whoever eats my flesh and drinks my blood *has eternal life*, and I will raise him up at the last day." (John 6:54)

If God's agapeic love is life-promoting, we would expect to find the whole cosmos infused at the physical level with a 'drive for life', and indeed it is. The so-called anthropic principle which we looked at earlier suggests an in-built bias in favour of life under-girding the evolutionary process at both the cosmological and biological levels.

This drive is frequently characterised as a violent, competitive and 'selfish' struggle for survival, totally incompatible with belief in divine agapeic love. Holmes Rolston III notes some typical descriptions given by biologists in his 1997 Gifford lectures:

"There is 'aggression' in ants, honeybees, hamsters, crusta-ceans, birds, carnivores, primates... Gorillas and wrens 'lie to one another' and get 'cheated'... Lions, guppies, salaman-der larvae, even termites are 'cannibals'; not just langurs but even wasps practice 'infanticide'... 'Hyenas are truly mur-derous'... Despite the reservations that these are behav-ioural and not moral descriptions, the overtones are clear."[88]

But Holmes Rolston III also argues that such negative portrayals of nature 'red in tooth and claw' are misleading. Organisms are simply 'self-actualizing' in both competition and symbiosis with other organisms. There is nothing wrong with self-maintenance

---

[88] *Holmes Rolston III, 'Genes, Genesis and God' (Cambridge University Press 1999) p. 82, 83.*

and self-propagation like this. They are not evils. Without them life would simply not be possible.

Dawkins' well-known claim that genes and organisms act 'selfishly' has been heavily criticised. A number of philosophers and biologists point to behaviour which would be characterised far better as a form of co-operation. Genes frequently combine to produce a particular physical effect or type of behaviour, and

> "Every organism, plant or animal, lives in a biotic community. Nothing lives alone. There are insects and fishes that simply hatch and live on their own; still they are more or less together with many siblings. Plants live together with other plants. Animals, undeniably, are often social and cooperate. They mate in pairs and rear their offspring, hunt in packs, nest in colonies, give alarm calls, lead each other to food sources."[89]

The relationships thus promoted all help to cultivate the potential for spiritual and moral growth, and to feed into the development of fresh patterns of agapeic love.

New Value and Dignity

One of the most striking and immediate effects that agapeic love has had upon people, is to affirm the value and dignity of humans and animals which have previously been despised or ignored. No-one and nothing is neglected. Even the tiniest sparrow is precious in God's eyes (Matthew 10:29).

Within the early Church, the recognition of God as heavenly Father meant that slaves and nobles were to treat each other as 'brothers' and 'sisters' in Christ. At the time of the Roman Empire this presented a serious challenge to the hierarchical pagan society in which Christians found themselves:

---

[89] *Holmes Rolston III, 'Genes, Genesis and God' (Cambridge University Press 1999) p. 86.*

"You are all sons of God through faith in Christ Jesus,"
wrote St. Paul. "There is neither Jew nor Greek, slave nor
free, male nor female, for you are all one in Christ Jesus."
(Galatians 3:26,28, see also Colossians 3:11)

Romans shared the opinion of Aristotle, that the household was a
paradigm of the natural social order. Everyone had their place.
Some were destined to rule (free males, owners, and fathers), others
to serve (women, children, and slaves).

> "Upset the order of the home... and the whole of society was
> in trouble," Meeks explains.

> "... When converts were initiated into the Christian group
> they might hear the strange proclamation that with their
> clothing they had 'stripped off the old human' who was
> divided in those ways, 'putting on' in his place the 'new
> human, Christ,' in whom there is no slave nor free, no Jew
> nor Greek, no male nor female."[90]

This Christian challenge to the existing social order was a major
reason for the early Church being persecuted. Even Christians
themselves could find some of the changes, which agapeic love
was calling them to make, quite difficult. There is clear evidence in
the apostle Paul's letters that some were reverting back to lists of
conventional virtues – albeit virtues with a Christian gloss –
plucked from Stoic writers who believed in a hierarchical society
embedded in the natural order of the world (eg Colossians 3:18-
23). The spiritual adjustment to the new vision was hard and did
not happen overnight. It took time, courage, and perseverance,
and indeed is something which needs to be rediscovered and
renewed in each generation.

---

[90] *Wayne Meeks, 'The Moral World of the First Christians' (SPCK 1987) pp.
112, 113.*

Social and Environmental Dimensions

The fullness of life which God's pattern of agapeic love seeks to promote has profound social and environmental implications. Jesus did not simply come to save individual souls but to usher in the rule of God:

> "The time has come," he said. "The kingdom of God is near…"
>
> (Mark 1:15)

The 'kingdom' of which he spoke was a social and environmental concept. It entailed the establishment of new, caring relationships at every level – of God's righteous rule within the life of the individual, community and whole created order.

These 'right relationships' could never fully be brought about by military force or government legislation. The God-given task of governments within a 'fallen world' is principally to protect citizens from outside attack, uphold justice, maintain a level of order and security so that people can go about their business in peace, and provide a social and medical safety-net for the poor and vulnerable. Insofar as governments fulfil these tasks, they demand our fullest support (Romans 13:1–7; 1 Peter 2:13–14). But there are governments which believe they can do more than this – that they can bring about all the necessary inner spiritual change by means of political legislation. They are sadly mistaken. Their efforts, however well-meaning, have all too often resulted in oppression and the unwarranted violation of people's freedom. There can be exceptional occasions when legislation is required to try and alter people's inner attitudes. Laws relating to problems of climate change are perhaps a case in point. But the outward coercion required for the enforcement of laws bears no comparison with the inward inspiration of people motivated by faith and spiritual vision. Governments will always be limited in what they can achieve. George Orwell's classic novel, *Animal Farm* (first published in 1945), records an abortive attempt by farm animals to overthrow the oppressive rule of a farmer. The political changes which they are able to bring about are rapidly undermined and destroyed by the spiritual greed and selfishness of the pigs who in the end replace the farmer as the animals' new oppressors. Outward political change has limited value if it is not accompanied by an inward spiritual change in people's hearts.

The right relationships in the Kingdom, which God's agapeic patterns of love will always strive to promote, is inextricably bound up with justice:

> "Love and justice," says Fletcher, "are the same, for justice is love distributed, nothing else... To say that love is between individuals and justice between groups, and that a union cannot 'love' a corporation or a city cannot love the nation, is to sentimentalise love and dehumanise justice."[91]

Justice ought to be a primary concern of Christian politicians and leaders. But Fletcher goes too far in *equating* love with justice. To equate love with justice is to deny those vocational responsibilities (eg to one's family) which rightly affect the otherwise equal 'distribution' of love. *Justice* tells us that we should care for everyone equally, regardless of their status or background. *Love*, whilst certainly including this more general care, also leads us on occasions to focus on a particular individual or group, and perhaps to respond in widely differing ways to the particular needs of an individual or group. Justice, therefore, is a subset of agapeic love. It operates at a more general social or environmental level.

Life as Love

We have seen how the end or goal of agapeic love is life in its fullness, eternal life – quality as well as quantity. But of what does 'life in its fullness' consist? It seems that those who respond to God positively, manifest patterns of activities and relationships which we associate with agapeic love. And this suggests that 'life

---

[91] *Joseph Fletcher, 'Situation Ethics' (SCM 1966, 1969) pp. 89 and 90.*

in its fullness' entails the creation of an agapeic pattern of love. Agapeic love is, in other words, not just the *means* to an end – the way we must follow in order to attain eternal life; it is the *end* itself. The love of God which is there from the beginning is realised in us his creatures at the end, as we are drawn deeper and deeper into God's pattern of agapeic love. The words of God in St John's vision come to mind:

> "... It is done. I am the Alpha and the Omega, the Beginning and the End..."
>
> (Revelation 21:6)

The end (or Omega) is anticipated in Jesus whose life was lived in perfect conformity to the agapeic pattern. New Testament writers variously describe him as the 'image' of God (eg Colossians1:15, Hebrews1:3), the eternal 'Son' in whom the Father can be 'seen' (eg John 14:8–10), and the one who is standing at God's 'right hand' (Acts 7:55). God is the creator, not a creature, but he becomes present in space and time through his activity, activity which in its pattern of behaviour is characterised by agapeic love. He was in Jesus as fully 'present' as it is possible to be, because his pattern of Agapé was perfectly manifested in him. God was present through the concrete life of perfect agapeic love. As John's Gospel has it:

> "No-one has ever seen God; but if we love one another, God lives in us and his love is made complete in us." (1 John 4:12)

Because God's pattern of agapeic activity was seen by the early Christians as perfectly revealed in Jesus, they naturally tried to imitate the qualities which seemed most central to his life: his willingness to serve (John 13:15), for example, his generosity (2 Corinthians 8:9), his humility (Philippians 2:5–11) and his patient suffering (1 Peter 2:18–25). In imitating and following Jesus, they sought to align themselves with the agapeic pattern of God.

"Be imitators of *God*, therefore, as dearly loved children and live a life of love..." (Ephesians 5:1)

"Be perfect, therefore, as your heavenly Father is perfect." (Matthew 5:48)

In St John's Gospel we encounter Jesus making the famous three-fold pronouncement,

"... I am *the way* and *the truth* and *the life*..." (John 14:6).

We could consider the three elements of this saying separately, but in the context of our analysis of agapeic patterns of love, it is worth noting a possible relationship between them. Each of them corresponds quite neatly with the three major elements we have outlined within the pattern of agapeic love.

'The way' reminds us of the nickname, 'followers of the way', given to the early Christians (eg Acts 9:2; 19:23), and of Jesus' call to his followers to pursue the narrow road or way which leads to life (Matthew 7:14). Following in 'the way' obviously involves an act of will by a purposive mind. We have to *choose* to go down the narrow road rather than the broad one. 'The way' emphasises the importance of the free response within the pattern of agapeic love.

'The truth' relates quite straightforwardly to the 'object' of God's agapeic love and the fact that God deals with what is real – with the world and all creatures as they are, not as perhaps they would like themselves to be.

'The life' corresponds to the 'end' or 'goal' of agapeic love, 'eternal life' or life in its fullness, and Jesus is the way, the truth and the life because these three elements together make up the pattern of God's agapeic love – God's perfect presence and activity.

The Supreme Good

We see now how agapeic love is the one, supreme, universal good. It is the summum bonum which contains all other goods within itself. It is no longer just one quality or virtue among many. It is the ultimate good, before which everything else must, in the last analysis, give way. There cannot be more than one, supreme, universal moral principle. St Augustine was exactly right when he wrote:

> "Dilge et quod vis, fac." ("Love with care, and then do what you will".)

Love, says Fletcher, is "the hinge principle upon which all other 'virtues' hang".[92]

During the course of his ministry Jesus repeatedly subordinated the demands of the law to the pattern of agapeic love and its chief goal – our wellbeing. As Irenaeus observed in the early 2nd century, "the glory of God is humanity fully alive." When defending his disciples' from critics who were complaining that they had picked and eaten ears of corn on the Sabbath, for example, Jesus urged them to remember the reason why the laws were there in the first place: "The Sabbath was made for man, not man for the Sabbath," he said (Mark 2:27). Obedience to the demands of the law should never be blind or unthinking, and it should always allow room for the call to celebrate agapeic love and the generous, overabundant life which God seeks to bring us.

Jesus relativised the Sabbath observance; he relativised the food laws (Mark 7:15); he relativised rules about touching lepers (Mark 1:41). Humphrey Carpenter, a professed non-Christian, offers us an interesting comment on Jesus' attitude to the law from an historian's viewpoint:

> "The whole point of his teaching... is that fixed laws do not work. By simply obeying the law you cannot be certain that you are carrying out God's commands to the full. Observing the law may be good, but it is not enough."[93]

---

[92] *Joseph Fletcher, 'Situation Ethics' (SCM 1966) p. 78.*
[93] *Humphrey Carpenter, 'Jesus' (Oxford University Press 1980) p. 47.*

The idea that 'loving your neighbour' lay at the heart of the law was not uncommon amongst the rabbis in Jesus' day. What was new and different was the way in which Jesus *brought together* the two commands (Matthew 22:34–40): "Love the Lord your God with all your heart and with all your soul and with all your strength" (Deuteronomy 6:5) and "... love your neighbour as yourself" (Leviticus19:18). He wanted to highlight the fact that we cannot truly claim to love God if we do not also love one another. And we will never truly be able to love our neighbour, except by loving God and knowing his love for us.

Jesus' famous summary of the Law, 'Love the Lord your God..., and love your neighbour as yourself, was not a 'compendium', a summary of a code which had to be kept in every detail, but a 'distillation', the essential spirit or ethos of the law, which had been "distilled or liberated, extracted, filtered out, with the legal husks, or rubbish, thrown away as dross."[94]

Early Christians clearly understood the implications of Jesus' attitude to the law. Pride of place, for example, was given to the love-command, and the law was interpreted, even by the most conservatively Jewish Matthew, in the light of it. When debates arose amongst the first Christians as to what food could legitimately be bought, eaten, and regarded as kosher, the apostle Paul had only one overriding consideration: 'What would be most helpful to his fellow Christians? What would be the most 'upbuilding? What would be most loving?'

> "'Everything is permissible' – but not everything is beneficial. 'Everything is permissible' – but not everything is constructive. Nobody should seek his own good, but the good of others." (1 Corinthians10:23, 24)

He adopted the same flexible attitude towards circumcision, allowing at one particular time a mission partner, Timothy, to be circumcised (Acts 16:3), whilst on another occasion strongly

---

[94] *Joseph Fletcher, 'Situation Ethics' (SCM 1966) p. 71.*

opposing it (Galatians 2:3–5). Everything was subordinated to the goal of agapeic love, the promotion of life in its fullness:

"Neither circumcision nor uncircumcision means anything," he wrote; "what counts is a new creation."(Galatians 6:15)

Every law, every principle, every virtue and every deed was to be judged and evaluated in the light of this new, God-given pattern of agapeic love:

"... if I have a faith that can move mountains, but have not love, I am nothing. If I give all I possess to the poor and surrender my body to the flames, but have not love, I gain nothing." (1 Corinthians13:2, 3)

The Christian life is the life of agapeic love, no more, no less.

"Without norms," writes Küng, "... without a minimal consensus on norms of political, economic, social, and individual action, no society would be viable. But Jesus' instructions are not norms, not abstract, universally binding rules of human behaviour and human fellowship, the limits of which are exposed by the concrete base. And in particular the much quoted 'commandment' of love is not so much a commandment as the quintessence, the main issue, the whole meaning, and according to Paul the 'fulfilling' of the law. Understood from Jesus' standpoint, love is not simply one virtue among others, not one principle among similar principles. It is really the basic criterion of all virtues, principles, norms, forms of human behaviour. The commandment always exists for the sake of love and not love for the sake of the commandment."[95]

The liberating power of agapeic love was opposed by the legalistic tendencies of the religious authorities in Jesus' time, and it is still

---

[95] Hans Küng, 'On Being a Christian' (Fontana 1978) p. 560.

often undermined by the Church even today. Roman Catholics, for example, have sought to spell out the implications of loving God and neighbour through detailed rules and regulations, but the resulting 'casuistry' has led to the bending of rules and the twisting of interpretation. Many Protestants have reacted against the catholic position by adopting what on the surface appears to be a more straightforward biblical approach. But this has not entirely freed them from legalism either. If anything, their lack of casuistry had led to an even greater dogmatic rigidity which on occasions has all but buried compassion beneath a blanket of unbending judgementalism. Pentecostal Christians emphasise in their teaching the freedom of the Spirit, but in practice they can be just as hidebound. People crave rules. Rules provide security which limit the need for responsible thought and reflection. Agapeic love is, by contrast, both open and demanding. It can lead us into situations of vulnerable uncertainty, and prompt almost limitless self-giving.

The freedom within agapeic love does not imply, of course, a 'do-as-you-please' 'antinomian' philosophy. Agents of agapeic love may in fact be contrasted with Antinomians (literally 'people who are against law') in a number of ways.

First, they are 'care-ful'. They think things through; they 'test the spirits' (1 John 4:1). They search for what is 'real' and 'true'. Antinomians are profoundly anti-intellectual, relying either on inner 'enlightenment' (gnosis) or else on the direct, spontaneous guidance of the Holy Spirit.

Secondly, antinomians despise principles and guidelines derived from the past. Like Sartre and the existentialists, they are concerned only with the present. Agents of agapeic love recognise the 'patterns' which agapeic activity tends to foster, and are keen to learn from the past.

Thirdly, divine agapeic love never allows its flexible patterns and 'principles' to become rigid unalterable laws. It lies beyond both legalism and antinomianism. It is freer and less complicated than the first, but firmer and more thoughtful than the second. There is an air of simplicity about it, the simplicity of a single, transcendent creator and his unified will. Bonhoeffer once commented on the essential simplicity of life in union with God (over against the complicated existence of the Pharisees who must wrestle with every jot and tittle):

"There is only one will of God. In it the origin is recovered; in it there is established the freedom and the simplicity of all action."[96]

The dynamic nature of agapeic love which I am trying to describe here has sometimes been likened to the 'dance' of the Trinity. This has been beautifully captured in a famous icon by the 15th century Russian artist Andrei Rublev. The painting depicts the three angels who came to see Abraham near the great trees of Mamre (Genesis 18:1–8), though typically it is regarded as an icon of the Holy Trinity. Each of the figures holds a rod in their left hand to show their equality; each of them wears a blue cloak, the colour of divinity; and the face of each is identical, signifying their oneness. There is a beautiful circular movement in the way that they gaze upon each other and a deep sense of unity, harmony, and mutual self-giving love.

The Father blesses the Son to show he is pleased with the sacrifice he is about to make. The Son, who is in the middle, wears both the blue of divinity and the reddish purple of royal priesthood. He blesses the cup of suffering he is about to drink, to show his readiness to offer himself as a sacrifice. His head is bowed in humble submission to the Father. The Spirit is on the right, wearing a cloak of green over his blue tunic to symbolize life. He rests his hand on the table next to the cup, as a sign that he will be with the Son to strengthen and support him in the task that lies ahead.

He inclines his head toward the Father and the Son, but gazes also towards the open space at the table, perhaps as an invitation to us as outside observers to come and join them in this dance of agapeic love initiated by the Father, embodied in the Son, and accomplished through the Spirit. The icon is not so much an object to be observed, as an activity with which to engage. We are given, not a rigid set of rules but a flexible pattern of principles;

---

[96] *Dietrich Bonhoeffer, 'Ethics' (SCM 1955, 1972 2nd Impression) p. 15.*

and we are led, not so much towards intellectual enlightenment as into a new and life-changing relationship with the living God and his amazing world.

Agapé as the Key Ethical Concept

If agapeic love is accepted as the 'supreme good', the summum bonum, many of the problems and inadequacies which we have encountered in the other main ethical theories seem to resolve themselves. I shall draw this chapter to a close by briefly highlighting some of them.

a)   Agapeic love combines or includes within itself three main goods proposed by moral philosophers: Kant's emphasis on the importance of moral freedom and responsibility; Plato's concern for what is real and how things really are; and the utilitarian recognition of the importance of an ultimate goal in the promotion of fullness of life.

b)   Agapeic love brings coherence and unity to what would otherwise be quite arbitrary and unrelated lists of ethical principles. It links them together and, in doing so, provides a higher over-arching framework which can help resolve issues when two or more moral principles clash.

c)   Agapeic love affirms the importance of the Kantian 'good will' and the moral self-discipline which this implies. It undergirds the biblical emphasis on virtues like 'perseverance' and 'endurance'.

The weakness of the Kantian 'good will' is that it tends to rely solely upon human will-power. It lacks the inner motivation we need to live the good life. Paul highlights the problem in his letter to the Romans when he speaks of his struggle with the law of Moses and his repeated failure to do what he knows he ought to do (Romans 7:7–25). The gospel provides a means of escape. It not only offers us forgiveness when we fall short; it also empowers us with a deep love for God as revealed to us in Jesus and strengthens us to act in accordance with his will through the indwelling of the

Holy Spirit (Philippians 2:13). The gospel gives us both the motivation and the ability to respond.

Those who have never experienced God's agapeic love and who have had to struggle on alone in a seemingly meaningless world of chance, can come under enormous pressure to abandon their struggle. When they see everyone else living selfishly, they can find themselves wondering why they should remain moral and unselfish. What should be their motivation?

> "Suppose", says Keith Ward, "that you believe it is right not to tell lies but to be honest. Suppose too that everybody else in your society is being dishonest. Unless you are also dishonest, in much the same way, you will lose out consistently, all along the line. Might you not then be tempted to say: 'Well, I know that honesty is a value all right. But in this society it would be silly to stick to such absolute moral standards. I may try to be honest on the whole; but I will have to enter into the general run of dishonesty if I am not to be walked over.' There is a great conflict between these moral ideals, which we all know to be intrinsic values, and the way the world actually is."[97]

The agapeic love of God in Christ shows that the path of virtue is not a cul de sac, a rootless human ideal, but rather the reflection of a divine purpose which lies at the heart of the universe. We are 'called' and held in God's love, and given a fresh strength and desire to weave for ourselves his patterns of love.

> "We love," says St John, "because he first loved us." (1 John 4:19)

  d) Agapeic love affirms the Kantian insight that individuals should be respected and cared for as 'ends' and not just 'means' (ie as having intrinsic value). One of the failings we noted in utilitarian theories was that they can encourage

---

[97] *Keith Ward, 'The Living God' (SPCK 1984) p. 42.*

the exploitation of an individual for the benefit of the majority. If the amount of happiness generated by an action is all that matters, then an innocent individual could potentially be abused on the grounds that the happiness created for the majority outweighed the misery caused to that particular individual. God's agapeic love upholds the intrinsic value of individuals and minority groupings.

Utilitarianism fails to take adequate account of the more vocational side of morality, such as a parent's special calling to care for the children whom he or she has brought into the world. Agapeic love makes up for this deficiency.

e) God's agapeic love promotes fullness of life at every level and offers, therefore, qualified support to the utilitarian emphasis on pleasure or happiness as part of the end or goal we must pursue. A person's life, which is filled with joy and happiness, is obviously a 'fuller' life than one filled with pain and misery.

However, utilitarians never adequately distinguish between 'higher' and 'lower' pleasures. Patterns of agapeic love suggest an inbuilt preference for 'higher', morally responsible, creative levels of existence. They provide the rationale as to why we should generally speaking value, for example, creative activities more than aimless pleasures.

f) Agapeic love speaks of God's kingdom. It has a profoundly social dimension and takes full account of the Kantian 'realm of ends' and his concern for social justice.

g) Agapeic love's allowance for in-built freedom within the cosmos explains why there are not always any clear-cut answers to the moral dilemmas we face or a single correct course of action. There can on occasions be genuine choice, genuine creative freedom, and times when we simply have to weigh up the relevant factors as best we can and 'step out in faith'.

h)   Agapeic love has been seen to undergird both the moral
and physical dimensions of reality. This link between the
world of moral values and the world of nature is, as we
shall see, of fundamental importance. It opens up the possibility of uniting the two divided realms and of undergirding them under the one summum bonum of agapeic love.

CHAPTER 7

'Queen of the Sciences'

At the beginning of this book I sought to show how human (and non-human) minds are not just an accidental by-product of impersonal matter but rather the expression of an eternal, purposive mind. I also demonstrated in Chapters 5 and 6 how effectively agapeic love can function as the 'summum bonum' of the moral dimension, and how it can hold together all the key elements highlighted by the main ethical theories. What though of agapeic love's relationship with the Sciences and the natural world?

In the Middle Ages, theology reigned supreme as the 'Queen of the Sciences' and the acceptability of all new knowledge was judged in the light of her doctrines and formulae. In the 17th century the enlightenment forced the abdication of the so-called 'Queen' and brought about the enthronement of science in her place. The roles were reversed. The 'Queen' became the servant. Her beliefs, values and doctrines were accepted or rejected in the light of science and reason.

This revolution has for the most part been extremely welcome. Theology is not a science, and there have been times in the past when it has interfered unhelpfully and inappropriately in the important work which scientists do. But as we have seen, the revolution also had some quite serious negative effects. It has led to a reductionist view of life and the dis-ease of the divided mind – the destructive conflict between people's inner, *personalising* beliefs and values on the one hand, and their outward *depersonalising*, pseudo-scientific ideas about reality on the other.

We cannot, of course, put the clock back or behave as if the scientific revolution never happened. Nor would we wish to do so.

The behaviour of the old-style mediaeval scholastics who resisted new knowledge is not what we would wish to see amongst those who profess to serve the God of truth. It is vital that we recognise and appreciate the contribution which the various disciplines (the sciences in particular) have made to our overall understanding of the world.

My argument, therefore, that the agapeic pattern of divine love provides us with a coherent, unifying framework of interpretation for all levels of knowledge, is not intended as a reactionary theological take-over bid. I am not wishing to deny the autonomy of these other disciplines. Quite the reverse! Agapeic love respects freedom. To quote John Polkinghorne,

"If it (theology) is to lay claim again to its mediaeval title of the Queen of the Sciences that will not be because it is in a position to prescribe the answers to the questions discussed by other disciplines.... Theology's regal status lies in its commitment to seek the deepest possible level of understanding."[98]

Another scientist, Arthur Peacocke, makes a similar point. Theology, he argues, can serve a fundamental, integrative role. It, "stands at the summit of integrative complexity and wholeness... From this perspective, theology, albeit no longer the mediaeval 'queen of the sciences', might still possibly be accorded the position of a constitutional monarch."[99]

The Bible allows room for different levels of description. It can speak on the one hand of the '*earth*' bringing forth her harvest (eg Mark 4:28, 29), and on the other, of *God* creating certain foods (eg 1 Timothy 4:3). The natural and theological descriptions are set alongside each other as complementary accounts. There is no attempt to reduce the one to the other, but the link between them is important.

---

[98] *John Polkinghorne, 'Science and Creation' (SPCK 1988, Impression 1993) p. 1.*
[99] *Arthur Peacocke, 'Theology for a Scientific Age' (SCM 1990, 2nd edition 1993) p. 23.*

Some distinguished theologians have wrongly sought to keep them separate. Karl Barth (1886–1968) and Emil Brunner (1889–1966), for example, have reckoned that our sinful nature prevents us from recognising the creator within the natural world, and that our best policy is to concentrate solely on his revelation in Christ. Others have declared that theological ideas about creation and scientific ideas about Cosmology have nothing at all in common with each other. It is, "not a scientific description of the beginning of the time series," says J.S. Whale. "Faith in God as creator is not a theory about the origin of the world through a 'first cause,'" writes Gustav Aulen; "The doctrine of creation is not a speculative cosmology," observes Bultmann.[100]

In the opinion of these writers, theological and scientific explanations of the universe have nothing in common, and they are eminent theologians. However, I believe them to be profoundly mistaken. The case for a valid connection between theology and the natural sciences is overwhelming.

There is to begin with the historical link. A.N. Whitehead[101], M.B. Foster and others have argued that science in its modern form could only have arisen within a monotheistic culture. In stark contrast to those ancient Greeks who believed in many gods, pioneers like John Newton were prompted to view the world as an intelligible whole because of their cultural belief in a single, rational, purposive, and faithful God. And in contrast to the ancient Greek tendency to rely on logically determined conclusions drawn from abstract speculation and reasoning, they were led to the conviction that the world's regularities needed to be discerned by concrete observation and experiment. Their belief in a God who freely chose to create ruled out any idea that the universe was rationally pre-determined.

In contrast to those cultures elsewhere in the world where manual labour was regarded by the ruling classes with contempt,

---

[100] *Theologians quoted by Owen R. Jones in 'Philosophical Reflections on Creation', in 'Science and Religion', ed. Ian G. Barbour (SCM 1968) p. 235.*
[101] *A.N. Whitehead, 'Science and the Modern World' (London 1926, Pelican 1938) Chapter 1.*

the western scientists' allegiance to Jesus, the carpenter from Nazareth, meant that they were quite happy to indulge in practical, down-to-earth experiments. They were also inspired by their Lord's teaching to value the individual and to emphasise small details. The undeniable success of modern science is a powerful indication of how helpful to them was their background Christian culture, and how strong the connection that could develop between theology and the natural sciences.

Of course, the old-style natural theology, which sought to 'prove' the existence of God from the way in which the world is ordered, was abandoned some time ago. But if Christians are right in their belief that God made the world, then the way it is constituted must have at least some bearing on God's character and on the way God operates.

> "Natural theology is important," writes Polkinghorne, "because if God is the creator of the world, he has surely not left it wholly without marks of his character, however veiled. There must be a *consonance* between the assertions of science and theology about the world in which we live."[102]

Just how important is our awareness of God's presence and activity within the wider world, becomes most forcibly apparent when Christians engage in mission. It would be difficult, for example, to make sense of Jesus as 'the cosmic Christ' (Colossians1:15–20) and a window onto God our maker, if the universe were fundamentally chaotic and not an ordered cosmos. The gospel offers 'meaning' to our existence, but unless this meaning relates to how we see the world, it remains unintelligible.

It was realising this that made Bishop Hugh Montefiore devote a three-month sabbatical to writing a book[103]. There was no point, he felt, in lecturing on such dogmatic themes as the 'Son of God', unless people believed in a creator.

Archbishop William Temple (1881–1944) once said:

---

[102] *John Polkinghorne, 'One World' (SPCK 1986) p. 78.*
[103] *Hugh Montefiore, 'The Probability of God' (SCM 1985).*

"Only if God is revealed in the rising of the sun in the sky, can he be revealed in the rising of the son of man from the dead."

We saw earlier on how Barth and Brunner objected to natural theology on the grounds that our perception of God in creation has been distorted by sin. Undoubtedly sin has had its effect. But there are two decisive difficulties with their argument. First it may be asked why, if our perception of God in creation is so hopelessly distorted, our perception of God and what he has done for us in Jesus is not similarly obscured? What is the difference? Secondly, if their view was correct, the Church's task of global mission would be impossible. When missionaries go to a place, one of the first things they do is to look for words within the language of that place which correspond to key concepts (such as 'God'), which they will need in order to communicate their message. If the local people's awareness and understanding of God was so hopelessly distorted by sin, they would struggle to find suitable words and be unable to spread the gospel.

Linking theology to science ought to be of mutual benefit. Theology can engage with those ultimate questions which arise from science but which are not themselves scientific in character, whilst science can help theology to root itself more firmly in the way things actually are within nature. The scientific discovery, for example, that the universe has evolved over billions of years will support the notion that God is rather more patient and subtle in the way he operates than Christians sometimes imagine, and is prepared to take much longer than they would wish to achieve his purposes. Fraser Watts appealed in an article in 'The Church Times' for a "substantive and increasingly detailed exchange" between the two disciplines.[104]

A link between science and theology is, in fact, vital because the welfare of society in general and individuals in particular,

---

[104] From 'Two Ways of Making Sense of the World', an article by Fraser Watts in 'The Church Times', 11th November 1994.

benefit so much from it. We live, says Montefiore, in a 'disintegrating society'.

> "If belief in God were no longer marginalised into the private faith of individuals, but if it were the basic presupposition on which the whole fabric of society rests, then there would be a real possibility of society's renewal. As the agnostic Hayek said: 'We have to make him (the individual) admit that the very things of which he had been contemptuous – these beliefs which were preserved by religion and could be preserved only by religious belief – must be recognised, even by a complete agnostic, to have been indispensable conditions of the growth of civilisation'."[105]

'Belief in God' can, of course, mean many different things, and not every belief is either adequate or rationally coherent. When atheists describe to me the God they are unable to believe in, I often find I cannot believe in the God they are describing either. The God to whom I have committed my life is the God revealed in Jesus, the God whose nature and activity is characterised supremely by agapeic love. This love is all around us. It is the love, in fact, in which we live and move and have our being.

---

[105] *Hugh Montefiore, 'The Probability of God' (SCM 1985) p. 176.*

CHAPTER 8

'Agapeic Love and the Cosmos'

We now move on to examine the extent to which the pattern of agapeic love coheres with a modern, scientific understanding of the cosmos. If we are able to show that the universe is a product of divine agapeic love, then I believe we will have a secure framework within which to uphold the dignity and value of humans and all living creatures.

A Dynamic Pattern

Agapeic love is, to begin with, a dynamic pattern of 'being' and 'becoming'. It is not a static 'virtue'. It is rooted in the agency of the Godhead (the eternal *being* of the Trinity), and associated with relationships at every level. It concerns the dynamic promotion of Life in its fullness (the process of *becoming*). I am reminded of the Eastern Orthodox with their distinction between God's 'essence' and his 'energies'; and of St John who combined in his Prologue the Greek and Hebrew understanding of the 'word' as both the 'logos' (rational pattern) and the 'dābār' (dynamic activity) of God (John 1:1).

This dynamic agapeic pattern accords well with the picture of the cosmos painted by scientists. The universe is no longer viewed as a static reality; it is active, open-ended, and full of potential. Particles are not irreducible 'solids' but particles of 'energy'. Heisenberg (best known for his uncertainty principle) once wrote:

"In the experiments about atomic events we have to do with things and facts, with phenomena which are just as real as

121

the phenomena of daily life. But atoms or elementary particles are not as real; they form a world of potentialities or possibilities rather than one of things or facts."[106]

Agapeic love, God's dynamic pattern of activity, entails an historical process of 'becoming' through relationship rather than static, atomistic isolation. This interrelatedness and interconnectedness echoes the description of the world given by scientists. They too speak of interrelatedness and interconnectedness. There is a very real sense, for example, in which we should speak (in the light of Quantum theory) of:

"every fundamental particle, or structure consisted of them (which means everything)... *interacting* to some extent with everything else in the universe."[107]

Springing from a Single Source

The pattern of agapeic love is seen by Christians to spring from a single source, the purposive mind of God.

Not all scientists of course believe in God as this single source, but they do, it would seem, accept the idea of a coherent, unified cosmos which for Christians arises from this belief. And it does explain why scientists can be found so constantly striving to replace either a variety of 'models' with a single 'theory', or else two conflicting theories, with a more complete 'unifying theory'. A dramatic example of this was when the wave-theory of light (developed by Maxwell in the 19th century) and the particle-theory of light (developed in the 20th century) were reconciled without inconsistency in 1927 through Paul Dirac's quantum field theory[108].

---

[106] *Quoted by John Polkinghorne in 'One World' (SPCK 1986) p. 45.*
[107] *Arthur Peacocke, 'Theology for a Scientific Age' (SCM 1990, 2nd edition 1993) p. 42.*
[108] *Paul Dirac (1902–84) was an English theoretical physicist widely regarded as one of the most important physicists of the 20th century.*

Scientists have been amazingly successful in furthering this process of simplification. As Einstein observed,

> "In every important advance the physicist finds that the fundamental laws are simplified more and more as experimental research advances. He is astonished to notice how sublime order emerges from what appeared to be chaos. And this cannot be traced back to the workings of his own mind, but is due to a quality that is inherent in the world of perception."[109]

The diversities and complexities of our world are now seen by scientists to have developed within the limits of just a few basic parameters, such as the speed of light and the mass and charge of an electron, and four 'fundamental forces' – gravity, electromagnetism, and the weak and strong nuclear forces within the atomic nucleus. Physicists have already found a way of uniting electromagnetism and weak nuclear forces within a single mathematical description. Now, as we noted earlier, the search is on for a 'Grand Unified Theory' (GUT), which will be able to incorporate the strong nuclear forces, and finally come to a so-called 'Theory of Everything' (TOE), which will combine the three forces I have just mentioned with gravity, general relativity and particle theory.

In Newtonian physics, the world consisted of 'mass', with 'energy' located in 'time' and 'space'. Each of these four elements of reality could at one time have been considered in isolation, but not anymore. Einstein's Theory of Relativity implies not only that space and time are 'mutually interlocking', but that the common-sense distinction between mass and energy (cf the famous equation $E = mc^2$) has been undermined. As Peacocke rightly asks:

> "... If a 'particle' of matter is but a certain local configuration of space-time, as it is according to the general theory of

---

[109] *Preface by Albert Einstein to Max Planck's 'Where is Science Going?' (Allen & Unwin 1933).*

relativity, how can it be said to 'move in' a 'space' that itself constitutes its own nature?"[110]

Everything in the universe seems to be related in some way to everything else.

"Quantum entities exhibit a counterintuitive *togetherness-in-separation*," writes Polkinghorne, "a power once they have interacted to influence each other however far they subsequently separate. Paradoxically, the atomic world is one that cannot be described atomistically."[111]

We will see in a moment how the growth and development of modern science in western Europe was aided by a belief that we live in a *uni*-verse created by the single agapeic will of God. This belief seems even more plausible today than it did at the time of Newton.

Free and Rational

Agapeic love is a free gift of grace. God is not compelled to love us. God's work of creation (and redemption) is the product of his own free will, not of any logical necessity.

The Greeks had assumed that all essential insights about the world could be acquired by means of philosophical reflection, and that the way the world was constituted was a matter of logical inevitability. As we have already noted, the 17th century pioneers of modern science saw it very differently. They believed that such knowledge could only be acquired through practical observation and experiment. Their methodology coheres well in this respect with the in-built freedom of agapeic love.

It is a rational freedom, not the arbitrary or capricious freedom exhibited by the pagan gods of Rome and ancient Greece. The

---

[110] Arthur Peacocke, *'Theology for a Scientific Age'* (SCM 1990, 2nd edition 1993) p. 33.
[111] John Polkinghorne, *'Reason and Reality'* (SPCK 1991) p. 43.

scientists of the Enlightenment who lived in a culturally Christian Europe, believed in a rationally purposive God, and this gave them both the motivation to look for rational patterns within the natural world and the strength to persevere with their enquiries. Despite the uncovering of the cloudy, fitful world of quantum theory, and more recently the discovery of 'chaos' systems, the openness of the universe to rational enquiry continues to impress scientists, whether or not they have a faith. Einstein famously commented:

"The eternal mystery of the world is its comprehensibility... The fact that it is comprehensible is a miracle."

The astronomer Fred Hoyle observed in like manner:

"When by patient enquiry we learn the answer to any problem, we always find, both as a whole and in detail, that the answer thus revealed is finer in concept and design than anything we could ever have arrived at by a random guess."[112]

The comprehensibility of the universe is based, not on Greek geometry (as the Aristotelians assumed it would be), but on 'the unreasonable effectiveness of mathematics'[113]. Mathematics has proved its ability, not just to reveal the order and structure of our environment sufficiently to enable us to survive, but help us to penetrate to the very depths of physical reality, and to uncover levels of rationality which are both surprising and beautiful in their simplicity. John Polkinghorne explains:

---

[112] *Fred Hoyle (1915–2001) was an eminent English astronomer who formulated the theory of stellar nucleosynthesis, the creation of chemical elements within stars by nuclear fusion. He was also known for his opposition to the 'Big Bang' theory.*
[113] *Eugene Wigner (1902–95) was a Hungarian-American theoretical physicist. In 1963 he was awarded the Nobel Prize in Physics, "for his contributions to the theory of the atomic nucleus and elementary the particles."*

"It is an actual technique in fundamental physics to seek theories which are mathematically elegant and tightly-knit – in a word, which are mathematically beautiful – in the expectation that they will prove the ones to fit the facts. A theoretical physicist on being presented with a theory which is mathematically clumsy and contrived instinctively feels 'That can't be right!' Paul Dirac wrote:

'It is more important to have beauty in one's equations than to have them fit experiment.... because the discrepancy may be due to minor features which are not properly taken into account and which will get cleared up with further developments of the theory'..."[114]

The fact that the human mind has found the universe to be so rational and intelligible, does not 'prove' the existence of a free and rational, agapeic agency behind it all (ie God), but it is consistent with such a belief and a strong pointer towards it.

Purposive

Agapeic love is purposive and hence directional. How is this reflected in the universe in which we find ourselves? The old Newtonian view of the world as consisting of various sized atoms being knocked about like 'billiard balls' and operating solely in accordance with reversible dynamics (like the to-and-fro swing of a pendulum) has long been abandoned. Many events, such as the spread of heat through a metal bar, are now seen to involve non-reversible processes. The direction of time's arrow is generally regarded as a thermodynamic effect and the result of increased entropy (growing disorder). There is in other words an in-built openness to the future.

Nature is all too often viewed by Christians as an inert stage upon which the drama of redemption is enacted. The insights of modern science, viewed within the dynamic framework of agapeic

---

[114] John Polkinghorne, *'One World'* (SPCK 1986) pp. 46.

love, can help us to rediscover the biblical insight that creation is also 'on the move' and part of redemptive history.

Pagans saw history as the manifestation of a directionless, cyclical nature. Israel by contrast worshipped a God of history. She did not see herself as having a direct encounter with God in or through the forces of nature:

> "... where can wisdom be found?... it cannot be found in the land of the living. The deep says, 'It is not in me'; the sea says, 'It is not with me'."
>
> (Job 28:12–14)

And so, writes Berkhof,

> "... the old nature-feasts which Israel inherited from her neighbours, the feast of unleavened bread, the feast of the first fruits and the feast of the booths, were in the course of Israel's history turned into memorial feasts of God's historical deeds (*cf* Exodus 23:14–17 with Deuteronomy 16:1–17). Nature is not so much the realm where God is revealed to man, as the realm in which man, created in God's image, has to realise God's purpose for his creation (Genesis 1:26–30)."[115]

Gradually, nature (and with it a more historical natural theology) is incorporated into this purposive, saving history, either through playing a decisive role in it (eg in the crossing of the Red Sea) or as pre-figuring God's faithfulness to Israel (eg Psalm 104). In Genesis Chapter 1 the priestly writer presents the story of creation as the opening phase in the history of humankind and of God's people. The cosmos is understood within the ongoing pattern of God's purposive agapeic love.

Scientists have quite rightly, from the very beginning, excluded the possibility of a 'purpose' or Aristotelian 'final cause' from their

---

[115] *Hendrikus Berkhof, 'Science and the Biblical World-View' in 'Science and Religion', ed Ian Barbour (SCM 1968) p. 46.*

enquiries. Restricting their field of investigation in this way has been one of the keys to their success, and at times they have understandably reacted quite strongly to any hint of purpose creeping into their discussions. David Attenborough, in his book of the television series, *'Life on Earth'*, makes his position quite clear:

> "In describing the consequences of this process (of the Evolution of Life) it is only too easy to use a form of words that suggests that the animals themselves were striving to bring about change in a purposeful way – that fish *wanted* to climb on to dry land and to modify their fins into legs, that reptiles *wished* to fly, strove to change their scales into feathers and so ultimately become birds. There is no objective evidence of anything of the kind."[116]

Attenborough is undoubtedly right to comment in this way on specific creatures, but when all is said and done, Big Bang cosmology, the evidence for what F.R. Tennant[117] calls 'complexification' – the emergence of more and more complex life-forms, conscious beings in particular, and a growing appreciation of the Anthropic Principle, are all powerful indications of purposiveness in a more general sense. Many have been so impressed by the evolutionary story of life on this planet that for them the probability of there being an overall plan or purpose at work behind it all seems overwhelming. To quote Montefiore:

> "The existence of trends over millions of years as well as repeated occurrence of the same evolutionary process, particular adaptations and changes seem to suggest some kind of overall plan behind evolution."[118]

---

[116] *David Attenborough, 'Life on Earth' (Collins/BBC 1979) p. 8.*
[117] *F.R. Tennant (1866–1957) was a British theologian and philosopher of religion, well known as a proponent of the anthropic and aesthetic principles in debates about the existence of God.*
[118] *Hugh Montefiore, 'The Probability of God' (SCM 1985) p. 96.*

Consistent

The agapeic love of God which Jesus revealed is a consistent, covenant love. It is not here one moment and gone the next. It is constant, unchanging, and unwavering.

It implies an ongoing purposive involvement on the part of God, and excludes therefore any suggestion of an interventionist deity, who only periodically 'comes down' from heaven to redirect the course of history and help or guide us in some way. The God of agapeic love does not 'intervene' from '*outside*' because he is already involved on a continuous basis on the '*inside*'.

If God were seen to be intervening only very occasionally on behalf of particular groups or individuals, we would be tempted to ask why the interventions have not been more frequent and inclusive, to prevent the many terrible tragedies which we read or hear about in the news. The God of agapeic love is not a periodic interventionist God, but a God who cares for the whole cosmos the whole of the time (John 3:16).

Miracles are often defined as the work of an interventionist God who has stepped in to suspend the 'laws of nature', but we need not necessarily view them in this way. We should remember that what we refer to as the 'laws of nature' are simply regular patterns which scientists have observed. They are not written down on unalterable tablets of stone, so breaking one of these patterns is not the same as suspending a 'law'. John in the fourth gospel describes miracles simply as 'signs' (eg John 2:11; John 6:30) and the word literally means 'a wonder'.

The faithful consistency of agapeic love still allows for the possibility of 'miracles'. Polkinghorne suggests that when Jesus performed them, it was not so much a random breaching of God's order as a glimpse into a deeper, higher rationality. He cites the example of how Ohm's law on conduction (in which the voltage has to overcome the resistance and be 'pushed' around the circuit), was found (by Kammerlingh Onnes in 1911) not to apply to certain metals at very low temperatures. Resistance disappeared.

"This discovery of the superconducting state did not mean that physics had suddenly become irrational. It was simply the case that there was a higher rationality than that known in the everyday world of Ohm... The different behaviours correspond to different regimes, characterised by different organisations of the state of motion of the electrons in metal. One regime changes into the other by a phase change (as the physicists call it) at the critical temperature."[119]

Jesus' miracles could be seen as the result of a spiritual 'phase change', when a new level of divine power came into operation. Jesus himself saw no problem in his disciples being able to follow his example and do the things he did (John 14:12). His miracles were not unique to him. Nor ultimately was his resurrection. The latter was at least in part a pointer towards an even more profound (potential) phase change in the history of this planet, the 'first fruits' of a more universal harvest of the dead (1 Corinthians 15:20,23). Oliver O'Donovan sees it as the key to how we should live our lives, the key to Christian ethics:

"We are driven," he says, "to concentrate on the resurrection as our starting point because it tells us of God's vindication of his creation, and so of our created life."[120]

When Christians bring an issue before God in intercessory prayer, it is sometimes thought that they are trying to persuade God to 'intervene' and bring about something which he would not otherwise have done. Intercessory prayer is not like that. When Christians pray *'in Jesus' name'* or make a request *'for the sake of Jesus Christ'*, what they are seeking to do is align themselves with what the Lord would wish to happen, to tune in to the will of God. This indeed is what they mean by 'praying in the Spirit', sensing an alignment with God's will and the direction in which the Holy Spirit is leading them. As Paul puts it:

"We do not know what we ought to pray for, but the Spirit himself intercedes for us with groans that words cannot

---

[119] *John Polkinghorne, 'One World' (SPCK 1986) p. 75.*
[120] *Oliver O'Donovan, 'Resurrection and the Moral Order' (IVP 1986) p. 13.*

express. And he who searches our hearts knows the mind of the Spirit, for the Spirit intercedes for the saints in accordance with God's will." (Romans 8:26b-27)

God's agapeic love brings about a constant and consistent involvement in the world. But this continuous involvement need not exclude the possibility of a response to a specific prayer request. The 'intervention' however is an intervention *by us*. We are opening ourselves to becoming channels of God's grace in ways perhaps which we do not fully understand. And God is responding to our 'intervention' in a consistent, faithful, and loving manner.

A final form of 'intervention', which should be mentioned very briefly if only to reject, is the 'God of the gaps' – the God who is periodically invoked in order to account for currently unexplained phenomena. This 'God' is not only dubious scientifically but theologically unacceptable as well. The God of the Christian is the Ground of *all* existence, not just the ruler of the dark, unexplored corners. As John Baillie says,

"No good will ever come of setting any limit to the advance of scientific knowledge. The relations of science and faith are not such that faith comes in where science stops, or comes in to fill up the gaps and supply the missing links. God is not a stopgap. He is not to be discerned through the cracks of our experience but as giving meaning to the whole. Or, to put it more abstractly, purpose is not to be called in when mechanism fails, or primary cause where no secondary causes can be discovered. Rather is mechanism everywhere, and is everywhere the servant of purpose. The two conceptions are not alternative but complementary."[121]

We have seen how agapeic love implies continuous divine action. Polkinghorne speculates whether the continuous in-built 'gaps' within the physical system (as opposed to the old 'gaps' of

---

[121] *John Baillie and others, 'Science and Faith Today' (Lutterworth 1953) p. 59.*

ignorance) could provide the necessary scope for this providential interaction:

> "... The notion of flexible process helps us to see where there might be room for divine manoeuvre, within the limits of divine faithfulness."[122]

Peacocke dislikes this idea, seeing it as simply a new version of the 'God of the gaps', albeit at a microscopic level. He also objects that 'intervention' implies knowledge of outcome, and to his way of thinking there are too many uncertainties, even at the macroscopic level, for this to be possible.[123] However, what Polkinghorne is proposing, within the openness and flexibility of microscopic systems, is not a 'periodic *intervention*' but a 'continuous *interaction*' which could allow for uncertain outcomes arising from the in-built freedom of response.

Maurice Wiles is so impressed by the continuity and commitment of God's activity that he finds it impossible to say where one 'act' ends and another begins. He prefers to speak of a single creative act. But as Peacocke points out, this fails to do justice to the flexible, personal interaction between God and ourselves such as when we pray. Despite the very real ambiguities highlighted by Wiles, it remains more in line with the pattern of agapeic love to speak of a constant series of divine interactions along the lines suggested by Polkinghorne.

The purposive agapeic will is always consistent and universal in its concern, never random, and this again reflects what we see of God's activity in nature.

A Transcendent Agency

A recognition of the constant, immanent involvement of God in the cosmos should not imply a denial of his transcendence. I noted

---

[122] John Polkinghorne, *'Science and Providence'* (SPCK 1989) p. 31.
[123] Arthur Peacocke, *'Theology for a Scientific Age'* (SCM 1990, 2nd Edition 1993) pp. 154,155. *Arthur Peacocke (1924-2006) was an English Anglican theologian and biochemist.*

earlier how the pattern of agapeic love was rooted in the transcendent agency of God. If this description tallies with the way the physical world actually behaves, we should expect to find indications of it in some form of 'top-down' causality. Peacocke for example suggests that God could perhaps have a general 'top-down' influence

> "... on the world-as-a-whole in a way analogous to that whereby we in our thinking can exert effects on our bodies in a 'top-down' manner."[124]

The input would be akin to 'information' rather than 'energy' and as such, it would be reminiscent of ideas put forward by 20th century process theologians like A.N. Whitehead (1861–1947) and Charles Hartshorne (1897–2000). Process Theology sees God as fully engaged with the evolutionary process, seeking to 'lure' creation with its radical in-built freedom into making choices which will enable it to actualise its potential. Its account of God's interaction with the cosmos fits well with the pattern of agapeic love. It echoes the 'lure' of the moral imperative (for which agapeic love is the summum bonum); it emphasises the freedom of the cosmos (which agapeic love also affirms); and it also coheres with an evolutionary understanding of the universe. To quote Birch:

> "... The modern understanding of the evolutionary process is not at all incompatible with what might be expected to happen if God is a God of persuasion rather than coercion... To be is to act, and an individual creature cannot be constituted by divine action or decisions alone. It must achieve its own creaturely decisions... This may be the reason that nature is not a contrivance, a sheer mechanism."[125]

---

[124] *Arthur Peacocke, 'Theology for a Scientific Age' (SCM 1990, 2nd Edition 1993) p.161*
[125] *L. Charles Birch, 'Creation and the Creator' in 'Science and Religion', ed Ian G. Barbour (SCM 1968) pp. 204, 205.*

Process Theology is far from perfect. Polkinghorne, for example, feels with some justification that it offers too weak a view of providence. Its focus on punctuated 'events' is reminiscent of the 'God of the gaps' and divine, periodic 'interventions'. Even if these 'events' are frequent, the fact that they are not continuous is for Polkinghorne a problem, and the divine 'lure' of process theology seems to him to be insufficient on its own. We ought to be able to say that God can *act* and not just *plead* from the sidelines;[126] and that God, whilst not exercising the rigid control of an autocrat, can still, like the Chess Grandmaster mentioned earlier, guarantee ultimate success.

Why Polkinghorne should also be so critical of Fred Hoyle for siding with Teilhard de Chardin[127], "peering forward to the omega point ..." and speaking of "... a mysterious teleological influence acting from the future to draw the universe towards its eventual fulfilment,"[128] I am not so sure. Whatever the strengths and weaknesses of Teilhard de Chardin's controversial theory, the notion of a 'teleological influence acting from the future' seems to me to be not at all odd or outrageous. Our experience of the moral 'ought' is an obvious everyday example of this future-orientated 'lure' or influence, as are those sudden, 'penny dropping' insights of scientists.[129]

Committed to the 'Real'

Agapeic love relates to people or things *as they are*, not as we would like them to be. It deals with 'the real'; it works with what is actually there. When things go wrong, God's response is not

---

[126] *John Polkinghorne, 'Reason and Reality' (SPCK 1991) p.47*

[127] *Teilhard de Chardin (1881–1955) was a French philosopher, Jesuit priest, paleontologist and geologist, who was involved in the discovery of the Peking Man. He developed the theory of the Omega Point, a maximum level of complexity and consciousness towards which he believed the universe was moving.*

[128] *John Polkinghorne, 'Science and Creation' (SPCK 1988, 5th Impression 1993) p. 56.*

[129] *Charles Coulson refers to such experiences in 'The Similarity of Science and Religion' in 'Science and Religion', ed Ian G. Barbour (SCM 1968) p. 74.*

generally to wipe the slate clean and start again, but to start from where things are, and then heal and mend and build bit by bit on what has gone before. The Bible speaks to us of a long, painful, and frequently frustrating process of growth and development.

The picture it paints is almost evolutionary-like, and it matches surprisingly well our modern understanding of the way in which the cosmos has developed. The natural sciences reveal a world which, as Peacocke says, consists of;

> "a series of levels of organisation of matter, in which each successive member of the series is a 'whole' constituted of 'parts' preceding it in the series, frequently said (as a convention, with no implication of value judgement) to run from 'lower' to 'higher' as the complexity increases."[130]

Agapeic love builds, little by little, upon what is already there. It does not do so in a rigidly uniform manner. As the creatures and cosmos grow and develop, so God encourages development and change in the patterns and dynamics of the various relationships. We could say that God is like the parent of a young child. When children are babies, parents do almost everything for them. Love at this point entails almost absolute control. As children grow older and begin to exercise greater autonomy, however, parents care for them, less by what they do and more by what they say. "Have you cleaned your teeth yet?" "Don't forget your home-work." "Yes, you may have your friend round for tea." The control is still there, but it is looser. When children become adolescents and adolescents young adults, the way in which a parent relates to them changes yet again. The control has effectively gone. Insofar as it is there, it takes the form of gentle persuasion, guidance, support, and encouragement.

Within the cosmos, we observe a similar development in the causal relationships as more and more complex structures emerge. At the 'lower' levels control is more rigidly mechanistic. But

---

[130] Arthur Peacocke, 'Theology for a Scientific Age' (SCM 1990, 2nd Edition 1993) p. 38.

agapeic love fosters freedom, and as freedom emerges, so the relationship of love changes.

With the emergence of mind, explanations at the level of 'mechanistic causality' increasingly give way to explanations on the level of 'meaning'. Let me illustrate what I mean. Imagine for a moment that you are a 'computer'. A piece of paper is fed in to you with squiggles on it, which you do not understand. You find the squiggles on a list and another set of squiggles alongside it. You copy the second set onto a piece of paper, feed it out to the 'computer' operator. You as a machine comprehend neither the information you receive nor the output you produce. Your activity of looking up squiggles on a list and writing down what is alongside them is purely mechanical. It is the human operator outside who understands the squiggles, the information he feeds in and the output he receives, who can perceive the process as meaningful. The first set of squiggles, for example, may be questions in Chinese and the second set of squiggles the answers to those questions (also in Chinese). Human behaviour can be described and 'explained' by scientists, not only on the level of 'mechanistic causality' (ie as akin to that of a computer), but on the level of 'meaning'. The latter is what distinguishes the mind of a human being from the mechanism of a 'clever' computer, and that too is what distinguishes 'lower' structures and organisms from human beings and perhaps one or two non-human species of animals as well.

Eventually a point is reached when these higher levels of organisation become necessary for explaining lower level structures and events, as when for example a boiling kettle has to be explained, at least in part, by the desire of someone to make a cup of tea.

The process of building on what has gone before can lead to genuine novelty. Reductionists argue that the whole can be summed up by a description of the parts, but this is not always true. When particles come together, they can bring into operation relational forces, which were simply not manifest when they were in isolation. The property of 'wetness', for example, created by the coming together of hydrogen and oxygen molecules, cannot be observed when hydrogen or oxygen are looked at in isolation. The sum is greater than the parts.

"The everyday world," explains Polkinghorne, "is constructed out of constituents from the quantum world, but as these entities combine together into systems of greater and greater complexity new possibilities come into being, exhibiting properties (such as life or consciousness) which were unforseeable in terms of the simple constituents out of which they are made, ... Thus growth in organisation produces genuine novelty and each level (biological, human, social) enjoys its own autonomy in terms of concepts which are not simply reducible to those associated with lower levels."[131]

The emergence of genuine novelty enables us to affirm the *uniqueness* of humankind created 'in the image of God'. But it also reminds us of our *solidarity* with the rest of creation. God builds on what has gone before, and it should not surprise us to discover that the basic ingredients of our culture have their roots in the animal kingdom. The ability to learn from experience is thought by some to have begun, for example, in the flatworm. The ability to use elementary tools can be observed amongst chimpanzees. Bees employ a complicated sign language to indicate the direction and distance of a food supply from the hive. Birds express an aesthetic sense of joy and appreciation when they sing (they do not only sing for breeding, survival, or territorial purposes). As Birch has observed:

"Culture, although primarily characteristic of man, does have its rudiments in animals, which learn from their parents part of their way of life."[132]

---

[131] John Polkinghorne, 'Science and Creation' (SPCK 1988, 5th Impression 1993) p. 36.
[132] L. Charles Birch, 'Creation and Creator' in 'Science and Religion', ed Ian G. Barbour (SCM 1968) p. 208.

The issue of causality is highly complex and mysterious, but the emerging lifeforms, cultures, and relationships which we have been describing demonstrate how well a modern understanding of the natural world fits within an agapeic pattern of activity, seeking to promote life in its fullness.

Seeking Life in its Fullness

The dynamic goal or end, towards which God's pattern of agapeic love is directed, is the flourishing of the whole cosmos reconciled to its Maker (Colossians 1:15–20), and, for us as human beings, 'life in all its fullness' (John 10:10).

But how does this relate to our modern understanding of life on earth? One of the great puzzles of the 19th century was the apparent discrepancy between two of that century's most important scientific discoveries, Darwin's Theory of Evolution and the Second Law of Thermodynamics. If the latter was correct in describing an inevitable increase in disorder (entropy) within isolated systems, how was it possible for increasingly complex lifeforms to have evolved so successfully? The answer, it seems, lies in the open-endedness of the systems which the Second Law of Thermodynamics describes.

The amazing 'fruitfulness' of the universe is truly remarkable. Montefiore reflects upon the mysterious way in which living cells began to combine:

> "For billions of years the Earth's oceans had contained various kinds of one-celled living organisms. Now, for reasons entirely unknown, they decided to join forces. We do not even know when this happened, but the fossil record of such multi-celled organisms goes back 870 million years.
>
> Some formed colonies, and these can still be seen today. For example, sponges are aggregates of cells which, even when minced up into individual cells, will join themselves together again. Slime moulds can behave in the most extraordinary ways. Normally this loose association of amoeba feed on bacteria and divide six or seven times a day. But suddenly

some 40,000 of these amoeba come together to form a kind of slow-moving slug. This then lifts itself up vertically and forms a stalk, and a fruiting body develops at the head. When spores are released the whole edifice collapses and the amoeba die. What is the advantage of such behaviour over the more humdrum existence of the amoeba it is hard to see, and why such colonisation developed is unknown."[133]

The fruitfulness of the cosmos is impressive. There is a drive towards life which lies at the heart of its evolutionary ferment we see all around us. One of the most exciting discoveries of modern science has been this unveiling of an in-built openness to development. Deep within its cosmic roots quantum events are interpreted by the majority of experts as 'radically random,' with predictable regularity emerging at higher, macroscopic levels through the statistical law of averages. Some like David Bohm[134] have put forward deterministic explanations, but whilst these accurately describe the phenomena, they suffer from what Polkinghorne calls "an unnatural air of contrivance."[135]

Most scientists accept the existence of random quantum events, but most would also wish to speak about the high level of unpredictability within deterministic systems. The slightest error (and there is always a margin of error) over the angle at which we strike a billiard ball, for example, will rapidly lead to big variations in outcome as one ball strikes another. Even if we assume the (impossible) eradication of the margin of error, we would need to know the gravitational pull upon the balls of every other physical system in the universe, in order to make a totally accurate prediction of the outcome.

It used to be thought that all macro-systems operate in a rigidly deterministic fashion along the lines of Newtonian physics

---

[133] Hugh Montefiore, 'The Probability of God' (SCM 1985) p. 65.

[134] David Bohm (1917–1992) has been described as one of the most significant theoretical physicists of the 20th century. He is best known perhaps for some of his unorthodox ideas relating to quantum theory.

[135] John Polkinghorne, 'Science and Creation' (SPCK 1988, 5th Impression 1993) p. 31.

(eg revolving planets), but scientists know now that this is not the case. There are a large number of dynamic systems ('chaotic systems'), which exhibit a surprising sensitivity to the smallest variations. Polkinghorne has described, for example, how even a simple deterministic equation,

"can produce behaviour which is random to the point of unpredictability."[136]

The slightest variations in one's starting point rapidly leads to widely diverging results and irregular fluctuating sequences, albeit within certain limits.

These open systems create the possibility of new régimes emerging, and indeed, even more than the *'possibility'*. There is within such systems, as we have already noted, an in-built *'propensity'* to produce increasingly complex structures. The dice are loaded, so to speak, in favour of life. And although there are those who, like Jacques Monod in his book, *'Chance and Necessity'*, regard blind chance as the key feature of the universe, I and many others are more impressed by its order and 'fruitfulness'. Structures and organisms seem somehow at every stage of development to be moving towards greater complexities.

People in the 19th century used to speak rather simplistically of evolutionary 'progress' as if it were a single, straight path towards life in its fullness. We now know that there are innumerable paths, random meanderings, cul de sacs and false trails. This of course is not a problem. Freedom, complexity, and rich variety is precisely what we would expect within the divine pattern of agapeic love. Christian love respects and fosters freedom. It allows God's creatures and cosmos room to develop freely. The popular notion, that God exercises a rigid control over everything that happens, does not reflect what we observe in the cosmos, and it is not a particularly Christian view in any case. Agapeic love fosters a balance between order and freedom, stability, and openness to the future.

---

[136] *John Polkinghorne, 'Reason and Reality' (SPCK 1991) p. 36.*

The emergence of homo sapiens is not so readily described these days as 'the crown of creation', but it is impossible to exaggerate the significance of the event. Personhood, Peacocke writes, was a totally unpredictable evolutionary development, "the most intrinsically irreducible of all emerging entities that we know."

> "... we cannot help asking what kind of universe is it, if it can generate such entities as persons?... Does not the very intimacy of our relation to the fundamental features of the physical world, the 'anthropic' features, together with the distinctiveness of personhood, point us in the direction of looking for a 'best explanation' of all-that-is (both non-personal and personal) in terms of some kind of causality that could *include* the personal in its consequences?"[137]

Teilhard de Chardin has been widely criticised for his pantheistic tendencies, his dubious ideas about the 'perfectibility' of this world, his over-simplistic linking of complexity with consciousness, and his assumption that everything was created simply as a means of producing human beings. But leaving all this to one side, his central claim, namely that life is not an 'Epi-phenomenon in the Material Universe' but rather the 'Central Phenomenon of Evolution' still for me rings true.

David Ingram[138] uses an illustration of a Martian who comes to visit our planet. He wishes to know what are the 'important' places for him to see. We fetch a large map and point to a tiny blob indicating London:

> "You see this little dot called London? Now that is really a very important place. Even if you don't go anywhere else, you ought to go there."

---

[137] Arthur Peacocke, 'Theology for a Scientific Age' (SCM 1990, 2nd Edition 1993) p. 111.
[138] David J.E. Ingram, 'Plan and Purpose in The Universe' in 'Christianity in a Mechanistic Universe', ed. D.M. Mackay (IVF 1965) pp. 91, 92.

The Martian laughs and points to the large blue expanse on the map indicating the Pacific Ocean. "Surely that is a more important place to see? It's so much bigger," he says. But the Martian has failed to understand.

> "London is important, not because of its size, but because of what is happening there."

And so it is with human beings. What is happening on Earth with the evolution of life and the emergence of a conscious rational being is of infinite significance. A mind has emerged which seems to detect and to relate to a deeper rationality or mind akin to its own, behind and within the vastness of the cosmos. Life has reached a point where it can begin, however feebly, to understand its own meaning and its true goal.

All-Embracing Goal

Agapeic love is all-embracing. Indeed, when we come to look more closely at the significance of the cross, its supreme symbol, we will see how the life, death and resurrection of Jesus has for Christians truly cosmic significance (Colossians 1:15–20). It is no longer possible to think or speak as if only humans matter, and as if the millions of non-human creatures who have lived on this planet are of no real consequence in the redemptive plans of the creator.

> "We cannot," says Birch, "just look at the crown of creation, man, and ask if the whole process has been worth this. Perhaps no part of the creation is without its value. The whole process should not be conceived as a means to one end, namely man, but as many ends, each with value in itself."[139]

---

[139] *L. Charles Birch, 'Creation and the Creator', in 'Science and Religion', ed. Ian G. Barbour (S.C.M. 1968) p. 214.*

We have noted the slow and costly way in which the pattern of agapeic love must operate, building step by step on what has gone before. Novelist Dorothy Sayers[140] likens the challenges facing the creator to those of an author writing a book. The characters in a book, she explains, take on a life of their own, which limits or constrains the writer in what she can get them to do. These self-imposed limitations lead to 'problems' in the unfolding narrative, which need to be 'resolved' in a process not so dissimilar from God's providential work of redemption.

Arthur Peacocke compares the creator to, "an improviser of unsurpassed ingenuity". He suggests the image of a musical composer who, within certain constraints and structures, introduces a simple initial theme, develops it in a variety of ways, and then draws it all together in a final, full restatement of the original theme.

Self-imposed constraints of a similar kind are faced by the God I have been describing, who creates and upholds the universe, and who strives to promote its fruitfulness and the wellbeing of the creatures who live in it, in accordance with a pattern of agapeic love.

We have seen how effectively agapeic love functions as the 'summum bonum' of the moral dimension, and how comfortably it sits as an interpretative framework for our understanding of the cosmos. The cosmos is a uni-verse; it has shown itself to be remarkably open to rational enquiry; it is a subtle mixture of order and freedom, of cyclical stability and fruitful openness to the emergence of life (the anthropic principle), taking what is there and building step by step on what has gone before. Its characteristics are characteristics shared by the pattern of agapeic love which we were describing earlier; there is to my mind significant coherence between the two. No other theory we have examined, whether scientific, ethical or religious, comes as close to undergirding the two dimensions in such a positive manner. They either

---

[140] *Dorothy Sayers (1893-1957) was an English crime writer and poet. One of her best-known characters was the amateur detective, Lord Peter Wimsey.*

ignore elements within the opposing domain, or else suppress them.

The divine pattern of agapeic love offers a simple, coherent, and unifying framework of interpretation. It lies at the very heart of the universe, at the core of God's being, and at the centre of the truly good life.

CHAPTER 9

'Cruel Cosmos or Caring Creator?'

I have sought to show how our dignity as human beings, the foundation of our moral values, and the fruitfulness of modern scientific enquiry can all be seen to rest upon, or cohere within, a divine pattern of agapeic love.

Highlighting the centrality of agapeic love, however, draws attention to a central paradox of the Christian faith – the paradox of believing in a God of infinite love whilst at the same time recognising the huge amount of evil and suffering clearly present within the world. If God is a God of love, how can so much evil and suffering be allowed to occur? With my recent diagnosis of advanced pancreatic cancer, this question has for me a particularly obvious, pressing, practical, and personal relevance. How can I continue to affirm a belief in God's pattern of agapeic love in the light of what is happening to my body?

Most writers on this subject restrict their discussion of the problem of suffering to human beings. But if the divine agapeic love which I have been describing is all-embracing, the issue of animal suffering and 'nature red in tooth and claw' is no less problematic. In this chapter I will seek to show how God's agapeic love, revealed supremely in Jesus, confronts the problem, embraces all living creatures, and includes the whole cosmos within God's redemptive goal.

Christian Concern for God's Creatures

"If a robin redbreast in a cage
Puts all heaven in a rage,

145

How feels heaven when
Dies the billionth battery hen?"
                    Spike Milligan

In January 2008 the celebrity chef, Jamie Oliver, launched a campaign to persuade the general public to refrain from eating battery-reared chickens. A series of television programmes were broadcast, highlighting the cramped and sordid conditions in which the birds are kept and the stress from which they suffer.

Jamie Oliver's campaign helped to raise awareness of the issue amongst the general public, but it also predictably aroused antagonism. On 9th January 2008, Allison Pearson wrote sarcastically about the chef's latest venture in the *Daily Mail*:

> "Forget malnourished old people in lack-of-care homes. Forget teenagers on remand held in conditions so bleak they hang themselves. Forget the two new mums who died within hours of giving birth with hospital hygiene the likely culprit. Today, ladies and gentlemen, we are going to be concentrating on the health and welfare of something really important. I refer, of course, to the chicken..."

She, like many others, was unwilling to consider the plight of the battery hen to be a significant matter of concern and accused campaigners of being unrealistic, sentimental, and out of touch with the real issues of the day.

When asked what might be the cause of such hostility and indifference, animal welfare activists often blame the Church. Western culture, they say, is rooted in Christian beliefs and values, and people routinely justify their exploitation of animals on theological grounds. Thomas Aquinas, the great medieval theologian, believed for example that there was a hierarchical order within creation, that the lower orders existed for the sake of the higher orders, and that animals existed for the sake of human beings. The 'dominion' given to Adam in the Garden of Eden (Genesis 1.28) bestowed on him a God-given right to use them in whatever way he chose.

Until relatively recently Aquinas' view was accepted by Christians almost unquestioningly, but with the growth of the animal welfare movement and an increasing concern about environmental issues, attitudes within the Church have begun to change. A growing number of Christians are questioning this inherited outlook.

It has been noted that Aquinas' teaching about animals owes more to hierarchical ideas of certain Greek philosophers like Aristotle than to the Bible. His interpretation of the Hebrew word translated in English as 'dominion' has been seriously questioned. Since humanity is 'made in the image of God' (Genesis 1:26, 27), God's gracious character is to be reflected in the actions of the people to whom he has entrusted his creation. The biblical notion of 'dominion' does not imply a self-centred tyrannical rule, but the reign of a good and gracious God whose care for his 'subjects' is supremely revealed in Jesus, the servant-King.

> "Your attitude," wrote St Paul, "should be the same as that of Christ Jesus: Who, being in very nature God, did not consider equality with God something to be grasped, but made himself nothing, taking the very nature of a servant..." (Philippians 2:5–8)

> "... whoever wants to become great among you must be your servant..."
> (Mark 10:43)

Christian lordship and dominion entail responsible service:

> "The Lord God took the man and put him in the Garden of Eden to work it *and take care of it.*" (Genesis 2:15)

The notion that every living creature was created for human use is absurd. Dinosaurs lived and died long before we arrived on the scene, and there are creatures in the depths of the oceans and jungles of whose existence we are barely aware.

> "The Animals, you say, were 'sent'
> For man's free use and nutriment.

Pray, then, inform me, and be candid,
Why came they aeons before Man did?"[141]

Some passages in scripture, such as the one in which God gives Noah permission to kill animals for food (Genesis 9), appear to encourage a more exploitative attitude. But these should be seen in the context of the Bible's primeval vision of peace (Genesis 1:29, 30) and its ultimate goal depicted in Isaiah's famous prophecy:

"The wolf will live with the lamb... They will neither harm nor destroy on all my holy mountain..." (Isaiah11:6–9. See also Isaiah 65:25)

The covenant with Noah is an expression of God's temporary, *permissive* will rather than God's *ultimate* purpose. And whilst we may not interpret Isaiah's prophecy literally, it does indicate the direction in which Christians are called to be moving as they look to God's eventual creation of a 'new heaven and new earth' (Revelation 21:1). Paul the apostle embraces a vision which goes far beyond the mere salvation of human souls or the renewing of society. Jesus as the 'Second Adam' inaugurates a new humanity, and God calls all who are in Christ to move towards this final vision of cosmic peace and redemption:

"...*the creation itself* will be liberated from its bondage to decay and brought into the glorious freedom of the children of God." (Romans 8:21)

Christ's redemption is all-embracing:

"...[God] made known to us the mystery of his will... which he purposed in Christ,... to bring *all things* in heaven and on earth together under one head, even Christ." (Ephesians1:9, 10; see also Colossians1:19, 20)

---

[141] *Henry S. Salt (1851–1939), 'The Sending of the Animals'.*

The speed at which this vision can be realised is, of course, a matter of judgement. Jesus held a dynamic view of when developments should occur. He spoke of a 'right time' ('kairos') for certain things to happen (e.g. Mark1:15). During his ministry, for example, he felt the time had come to re-evaluate the application of the traditional Levitical laws concerning clean and unclean foods, and following his resurrection his followers effectively abandoned them. Over the years other issues such as slavery, racism, child labour and misogyny have arisen and Christians have felt the time has been right to address them too. Today, many would say the time has come to embrace the biblical vision of cosmic redemption, to take far more seriously than before our responsibility to care for the environment, and to challenge and actively oppose the widespread abuse and exploitation of animals.

Sentimental Idealists?

In James Vance Marshall's novel, *'Walkabout'*, first published in 1959, two children, Mary and Peter, find themselves alone in the Australian desert. They are the sole survivors of a plane crash. Their chances of staying alive seem remote until, quite unexpectedly, they encounter an Aboriginal boy on 'walkabout'. The latter's skill and experience in finding food and water is remarkable, but this fact is completely lost on the 13-year-old Mary. Despite her obvious inability to cope with the hostile desert environment and her total dependence upon the Aboriginal, she is blinded by her prejudice and utterly convinced of the superiority of her own culture.

> "Brother and sister were products of the highest strata of human evolution... Coddled in babyhood, psycho-analysed in childhood, nourished on predigested patent foods, provided with continuous push-button entertainment, the basic realities of life were something they'd never had to face. It was different with the Aboriginal. He knew what reality was..."[142]

---

[142] *James Vance Marshal, 'Walkabout' (Heinemann New Windmills 1977) Ch. 5, pp. 20, 21.*

'*Walkabout*' highlights the extent to which our modern society has become enmeshed in its comfortable, concrete, urban existence, and lost touch with the natural world.

We who live within a highly developed culture can be almost oblivious to the harsher side of life, to the way, for example, in which creatures prey upon each other for food. Animal lovers from the western world seem particularly prone to adopt a sentimental, rose-tinted view of the world which is totally at odds with reality.

If however the pattern of agapeic love reflects the core purpose and nature of God revealed in Jesus, if it is as all-embracing as I have been suggesting it is, and if it includes caring for both our fellow human beings and all living creatures, then it must be seen to cohere with what we find in the natural world. It would be odd to maintain that caring for our fellow human beings and for domestic and farm animals is the will of God, whilst at the same time believing that God is happy for creatures in the wild to suffer disproportionately and unnecessarily as victims of 'nature red in tooth and claw'. It would look as if Christians were trying to superimpose purposeful moral values on a meaningless mayhem, like a child who is trying to spot meaningful shapes and patterns amongst the random formations of clouds passing overhead.

Richard Dawkins, a well-known professor of zoology and biology and a militant atheist, regards the immense suffering of animals in the natural world as 'proof' that God cannot exist:

> "In a universe of blind physical forces and genetic replication, some people are going to get hurt, other people are going to get lucky, and you won't find any rhyme or reason in it, nor any justice. The universe we observe has precisely the properties we would expect if there is, at bottom, no design, no purpose, no evil and no good, nothing but blind pitiless indifference."[143]

---

[143] *Richard Dawkins, 'River out of Eden: A Darwinian View of Life' (London: Phoenix 1995) p. 133.*

I believe such scepticism to be unwarranted. To my mind, belief in a loving creator motivated by agapeic love is consistent, not only with the existence of cruelty wrought by humans, but also with the seemingly endemic suffering within the natural order.

God and Moral Goodness

Evil is quite rightly a problem for people who believe in a God of love. But as we have seen from the outset, those who abandon belief in such a God in favour of a purely secular morality also face significant difficulties. Values cannot ultimately be derived from 'brute facts'. It may be a 'fact', for example, that you *feel* revolted by behaviour X (emotivist theory), but this does not prove that you *ought* to be revolted by it. It may be a fact that you wish to 'prescribe' to others a particular moral principle Y (prescriptivist theory), but this does not mean that you *ought* to prescribe it. 'Facts' concern the way things *are*, but as we noted in our discussion of the naturalistic fallacy in Chapter 4, the way things are can never logically entail how they *ought* to be. Purposive goals and values originate from purposive minds, not from brute facts. That is why atheists, who deny the existence of God, tend so often to locate the source of our moral and spiritual values within the conscience of an individual or the culture of a society. The only purposive mind or minds of which they are aware are human.

But interpreting moral experience as a purely human phenomenon fails, as we also saw earlier on, to reflect the way in which we actually encounter it. All of us, I suspect, can recall moments when we have been challenged, deep down, to oppose some needless cruelty or injustice inflicted upon an animal or human being and to recognise in such situations what Kant describes as a 'moral imperative', a universally, morally binding call to do something about it.

However, we have also seen that, although the source of this imperative may be mediated *through* our conscience or *through* the communities to which we belong, it never appears entirely to originate *from* them. Rather, it manifests itself, more often than not, either as a challenge *to* the individual or as a judgement *upon* the community. To share one small example, when I began in the late 1970's to learn about the exploitative practices of intensive farming, and to move, by way of a personal response, towards a more vegetarian diet, the moral challenge was not something which I had anticipated, willed or welcomed. It came, so to speak, from completely 'out of the blue'. Prior to that moment, I had been an enthusiastic carnivore, living in a society in which intensive farming was accepted almost unquestioningly, and in which vegetarians were dismissed as cranks. The challenge could not have been a product of my own wishful thinking; nor could it have originated from the flesh-eating society in which I lived. Its moral authority and power had to be derived from elsewhere, from a moral dimension 'beyond' and 'above' both me as an individual and society. Now for Christians (and other theists too), transcendent moral values are suggestive of a transcendent moral valuer, or in other words, God.

There is no obvious alternative. We have noted previously how some philosophers like W.D. Ross[144], impressed by the transcendent character of our moral experience, have argued for the existence of objective *prima facie* obligations or values without reference to God. But the idea of values floating around in a meaningless universe independent of a 'valuer', or of a purposive set of morals outside of a mind, seems to me to be intuitively implausible. The broadly theistic alternative, that the moral dimension is rooted in the mind of God, offers a far more intellectually satisfying explanation, and a far more promising basis upon which to found a philosophical ethic.

Our perception of the moral dimension can, of course, be coloured and distorted by personal circumstances, interests, feelings, and cultural background. It is far from perfect:

"Now we see," says Paul, "but a poor reflection as in a mirror…"

(1 Corinthians13:12)

---

[144] *William David Ross (1877–1971), 'The Right and The Good' (OUP 1930).*

However, the inadequacy of our moral awareness need not necessitate total skepticism any more than the fallibility of our ordinary senses. What is required is a degree of humility, and a recognition that some perceptions may be less complete or adequate than others. The Christian understanding of divine revelation should lead us to expect a degree of moral development and spiritual progress:

> "You have heard that it was said to the people long ago, 'Do not murder, and anyone who murders will be subject to judgement.' *But I tell you* that anyone who is angry with his brother will be subject to judgement..."
>
> (Matthew 5:21, 22)

Jesus repeatedly challenges us to move on to a new level of understanding.

Non-theistic thinkers often assume that Christians can leave this transcendent experience of revelation to one side when addressing moral issues, and operate within a purely secular framework. But an encounter with God in Jesus shapes a Christian's entire outlook. Revelation provides them with the all-important framework within which to interpret the moral dimension, gauge the relative importance of different imperatives, and see how it all fits together. As C.S. Lewis once wrote:

> "I believe in Christianity as I believe that the Sun has risen – not only because I see it, but because by it, I see everything else." [145]

God and the Problem of Evil

Plato's 'God'

We have seen how a moral concern for humans and animals, grounded in a purposive God of love, may be more coherent and

---

145 *Quoted by Alistair McGrath in, 'Creation' (SPCK 2004) p. 2.*

philosophically attractive than the non-theistic alternatives. But we still face the problem of how belief in a God of love, working out his purposes through a pattern of agapeic love, can be reconciled with the presence of evil and suffering in the world.

The problem is avoided, of course, by those who divorce their encounter with God from what they see round about them, by declaring the material world to be either eternally existent or else created by another lesser god (we shall examine this dualistic belief shortly). Such people argue that God in his holiness and perfection is totally 'above' and 'beyond' the imperfect material world and has only limited involvement with it.

Plato in his dialogue, 'The Republic', described an eternal world of forms *above and beyond* the world in which we live. In his famous allegory of the cave, he compared the plight of human beings to prisoners held in a cave. They could only see, by the light of a fire, shadows of shapes and figures cast upon the wall in front of them. To glimpse the reality which lay beyond them, they needed to be set free, and allowed to turn around and journey to the entrance of the cave:

> "The prison dwelling corresponds to the region revealed to us through the sense of sight... The ascent to see the things in the upper world you may take as standing for the upward journey of the soul into the region of the intelligible;... the last thing to be perceived and only with great difficulty is the essential form of goodness. Once it is perceived, the conclusion must follow that, for all things, this is the cause of whatever is right and good...'[146]

Plato drew the distinction between the material world experienced through our senses and the spiritual world grasped by the intellect. There were similarities between the two because material objects reflected the eternal forms, but Plato was always keen to emphasise the difference between them. Matter, he observed, was subject to

---

[146] Plato, 'The Republic', translated by F. MacDonald Cornford (OUP 1941) Part 3, Ch. 25.

change and decay and inherently imperfect. The creator (or 'Demiurge' as he was generally known in Plato's *'Timaeus'* dialogue) was not responsible for bringing it into being; he merely shaped and moulded what was already there, like a potter working with poor quality clay.

In relieving God of responsibility for what he saw as the imperfections of the natural world, Plato fostered a potentially negative attitude towards it and indeed towards our whole physical existence. This negative outlook influenced the so-called Gnostic sects, which flourished at the time of the early Church. These taught that our souls are 'sparks' of the divine trapped in a corrupt and evil world of change and decay. Jesus, they said, had been sent by a transcendent God of perfect goodness (who had nothing to do with creating this material world), to set us free and enable us by means of secret 'knowledge' ('gnosis') to be reunited with him. Salvation for gnostics was not about *redeeming* the world but rather *escaping* it.

Such a rejection and abandonment of the natural order was, of course, unacceptable to mainstream Christians. The opening story of creation in Genesis Chapter 1 declares that *everything*, at every stage and at every level, has been created by God and has an intrinsic value in his eyes. The whole cosmos is caught up within the creative pattern of agapeic love:

"God saw *all* that he had made, and it was very good..." (Genesis 1:31)

I am reminded of the time when, as a Curate in Chatham, a group of children came to my door with something to show me. "It's in here," they said, holding out a basket.

I peered inside to see, to my horror, a grass snake. Ever since I had been confronted as a young boy by a bamboo snake outside our home in Hong Kong, I had had a fear of snakes. I imagined them to be slimy, horrible creatures. But of course I did not want to disclose such thoughts or feelings to these young children. I had spoken to them quite recently in a school assembly about the importance of appreciating and caring for God's creatures. Here was a clear challenge to 'practice what I preached'. So when the inevitable invitation came to hold the snake, I picked it up, held it in my arms, and talked to them about how they should perhaps best care for it by returning it to where it came from. It was one of the most difficult things I have ever had to do. But as I did so, a curious change came over me. It was like a conversion experience. My fear evaporated and my appreciation of the grass snake, which of course was not at all 'slimy' but really quite beautiful, grew. I knew, from that moment on, that it too, like every other creature, was loved and cherished – a precious part of God's creation.

The beauty, order, intelligibility, and fruitfulness observed in the cosmos are positive signs both of the creator's intimate involvement and of his authorship. As Gerard Manley Hopkins notes in the opening lines of his poem, *God's Grandeur*,

"The world is charged with the grandeur of God..."

God is involved with his world from start to finish. The eternal 'Word' *(logos)*, God's rational, creative principle, is present and active in both creation (John1:3) and redemption (John 1:14). We cannot simply speak of God as *beyond* and above us, however helpful that might be in distancing him from the evil and suffering within nature. We must recognise that God is also present and active *among* us.

Dualism

Christians wish both to affirm God's presence (Matthew 1:23) and involvement in the world, and also at the same time to deny God's responsibility for evil. Dualists resolve the tension by invoking the idea of two equal and opposite spiritual powers. Evil, they argue, is attributed, not just to the imperfections of matter as Plato maintained, but to the work of an eternal and intrinsically evil deity. Before his conversion to Christianity St Augustine (354– 430) belonged to a dualistic sect known as the Manicheans, named after their founder, Mani (215–276). The Manicheans believed that good things were attributable to a good god and bad things to a bad god.

It was a simple and seemingly straightforward theory, but to the newly converted Augustine it had serious flaws. In his book, 'City of God', he rejected dualism and sought to show how *everything* that exists is the work of a single, good, all-powerful creator.

Evil, he argued, cannot exist in and of itself. Consider a diseased or injured animal, for example. Why do we regard the disease or injury as bad? It is because we recognize the creature which has been hurt to be 'good' and of intrinsic value. If it were seen as 'bad', we would presumably rejoice at its destruction, and if it were of no value, any damage or destruction would be a matter of indifference. Evil can only ever exist as a corrupting parasite, spoiling something which is good; it can only ever be, as St Augustine would put it, a 'privation of the good', because it always presupposes the existence of something of value which it is harming.

The dualist assumption that evil *'things'* and good 'things' can exist in two distinct and separate groups is therefore false. Good and evil are, in reality, bound up in *relationships* and subjective *attitudes*. As Augustine observed, thorns may be regarded as 'bad' when they prick people, but for the bush on which they grow, they are simply a means of protection. The thorns are bad relative to the people they prick but good relative to the bush they protect. Don Marquis' book, 'Archy and Mehitabel', records the cynical observations of a free-verse poet who has been reborn as a cockroach called Archy. Archy notes how people's notions of good and evil are often relative to their own interests and wellbeing:

> "... I have heard people
> say how wicked it was
> to kill our feathered
> friends
> in order to get
> their plumage and pinions
> for the hats of women

and all the while
these same people
might be eating duck
as they talked
the chances are
that it is just as discouraging
to a duck to have
her head amputated
in order to become
a stuffed roast fowl
and decorate a dining table
as it is for a bird
of gayer plumage
to be bumped
off the running board of existence
to furnish plumage
for a lady's hat
but the duck
does not get the sympathy
because the duck
is not beautiful ..."[147]

Dualists see things in black and white. They assume that humans are born either good or bad, and that angels are either angels of light or angels of darkness. Augustine, however, knew from his own experience of God's saving grace the reality of conversion. Change is possible. The division between those who are good and those who are bad is not fixed.

God wants to create the possibility of genuine goodness and love, and so bestows upon us the gift of free will. Genuine goodness and love require that we are free and responsible. God could not simply program us to be good. If that were so, we would be little more than robots. However, the granting of freedom requires that God relinquishes a degree of control. If creatures are to be

---

[147] *Don Marquis, 'Archy and Mehitabel' (Faber & Faber 1958) Poem No.38: 'Unjust'.*

genuinely free, it must be possible for them to make a morally wrong choice. Moral evil presupposes wrong choices, and wrong choices are the product of what Augustine calls a 'bad will'. When we come across moral evil in the world – when animals, for example, are tortured or abused – Augustine believes that we should blame those who are inflicting the cruelty and misusing their freedom, rather than God who gave them the gift of freedom for the purpose of doing good.

Angels and Humans

As an explanation of *moral* evil, Augustine's appeal to the so-called 'Free Will Defence' has much to commend it. His attempt to use it however to explain *natural* evil as well as moral evil – in order to account for nature 'red in tooth and claw' – is rather more problematic. He maintains that this world was originally a paradise, perfect and complete, and that it was only spoilt when Satan with a group of angels rebelled against God and tempted Adam and Eve to do the same. Their rejection of their God-given goodness caused not only a distortion of their own natures but a corruption of the wider environment as well. From this primaeval 'Fall', Augustine argues, came earthquakes, tsunamis, famines, and plagues. Evil is not God's fault; it is the result of angelic and human rebellion.

Christians who view the first three chapters of Genesis as a literal account of creation, find in Augustine's theodicy a broadly satisfying explanation of evil. To their way of thinking it constitutes *the* biblical account. When Adam and Eve ate from the 'tree of knowledge of good and evil' (it was not an apple tree), death entered the world (Genesis 2:17; 1 Corinthians15:21), human relationships were distorted (Genesis 3:16), relationships with the animal kingdom represented by the serpent were spoilt (Gen.3:15), work on the land degenerated into toil (Genesis 3:17–19), and the close fellowship with God enjoyed by the two archetypal humans in the garden was broken (Genesis 3:23). The Bible tells the story of how the problem began, and how God redeemed the situation through Jesus, dealt with the consequences of the fall and paved the way for a restoration of paradise.

Variations on this Augustinian idea of a 'fall' from perfection are widespread, especially among those from a more conservative evangelical background. However, there are many Christians, arguably the majority, who take a rather different view. The Augustinian explanation conflicts with the mainstream findings of modern science. Anyone who accepts the astronomical, geological and fossil evidence for a slow, evolutionary development of the universe, from the formation of stars to the comparatively recent emergence of the first human beings, must also accept that earthquakes, volcanoes and other such phenomena have been an intrinsic part of the process by which seas, rivers, mountains, and valleys have been formed. The continents and oceans did not appear 'just like that'; creatures were living and dying long before the arrival of homo sapiens; and death could not have entered the world in a literal way through the sin of Adam and Eve.

Augustine sees redemption as a return to the original perfection enjoyed by Adam and Eve in the Garden of Eden. But this raises serious questions about the Christian hope of salvation. If it was possible for the original paradise to be corrupted, how sure can we be that, when God's redemptive work is complete, things will not go wrong again? It would seem on this basis that we are condemned to a perpetual cycle of fall and redemption.

Creative Environment

The idea of an historical 'fall' from perfection is often defended on the grounds that it is 'biblical'. But there have been many scholars who from quite early times have interpreted the opening chapters of Genesis in a very different way. Prior to their act of disobedience, they argue, Adam and Eve were in a state of moral *innocence* rather than moral perfection; they had not tasted the 'tree of knowledge of good and evil' (Genesis 2.9). When Jesus came as the second Adam, he took us *beyond* the first Adam and raised humanity to a new level of existence. There was no return, in other words, to how we were at the beginning:

"...The first man Adam became a living being; the last Adam, a life-giving spirit... The first man was of the dust of the earth, the second man from heaven... And just as we have borne the likeness of the earthly man, so shall we bear the likeness of the man from heaven." (1 Corinthians15:45–49)

The biblical story of salvation is a slow and painful development, akin, some might say, to an evolutionary process – the story of a people gradually being drawn into a deeper relationship with God and a fuller understanding of God's will.

Before the time of Augustine, there was a leading Christian thinker called Irenaeus (c. 130–202) who thought along these lines and argued in terms of a development, a 'rise' from innocence rather than a 'fall' from perfection. Irenaeus shared Augustine's belief in the goodness of creation. A good God, he said, would not have brought into being inherently evil creatures. That would have been contrary to God's nature. But God could not have created them morally perfect either. If they had been perfect, they would not have succumbed to sin. They must have begun in a state of innocence, neither good nor bad. When the writer of the first Genesis creation story described men and women as made in the 'image' *and* 'likeness' of God (Genesis 1. 26), Irenaeus interpreted this as referring to two stages of development: humans began in the 'image' of God, with the potential for rational thought and moral reflection, but grew into his 'likeness', to become God's children and attain eternal life.

Irenaeus believed in the supreme values of love and moral virtue, but recognized, as Augustine would do later on, that God could not have created these things instantaneously. Moral goodness presupposed responsibility, responsibility demanded freedom, and genuine freedom meant that wrong choices (together with their consequences) were almost inevitable.

The natural world was for Irenaeus a soul-making environment, in which creatures could potentially become morally good. Natural evils were a necessary part of this environment. A hedonistic paradise devoid of natural evil would never enable the desired spiritual development to occur. God did not actively want humans to make wrong choices or creatures to suffer pain on account of natural evil, but this was the price which would inevitably have to be paid, if beings capable of genuine moral goodness and love were to be created. Evil was the result therefore of God's *permissive will*, not God's *active will*.

Irenaeus' broad notion of a development from innocence accords well with modern scientific theories of evolution, and it is perhaps not surprising that so many modern philosophers and theologians have employed similar lines of reasoning. Brian Hebblethwaite, for example, has argued for the inevitability of natural evil within the creative process:

> "there may well be logically necessary conditions which make it impossible to create an ordered physical universe containing organic creatures without the possibility of accident and pain... [modern science has shown us more clearly than ever] that it is the operation of the same general laws that both has led to the evolution of sentient and conscious life, with all its possibilities for good and creativity, and also makes inevitable the kind of accident and damage and pain which constitute the problem of physical evil. To wish away the evils is to wish away the conditions of all life and growth as well.'[148]

Austin Farrer makes the point even more forcefully. To the skeptic who wants to know why God, "rooted the higher forms of existence in lower forms, with all the inevitable stupidity and mutual disregard; or why God gave these lower forms freedom to run themselves, instead of moving like pawns on a chess board," he simply retorts:

> "If you raise such questions, I shall be driven to the rudeness of telling you that you do not know what you are talking about. You suggest that God might have made some such

---

[148] Brian Hebblethwaite, *'Evil, Suffering and Religion' (SPCK 2000) p. 77.*

higher forms as he has made, without rooting them in the action and being of lower forms. I reply, that we have no power to conceive anything of the kind. And as to your suggestion that natural forces might have been kept on divine leading strings, I can only say that, so far as I know, running oneself one's own way is the same thing as existing. If God had made things to exist, but not to run their own way, he would have made them to exist, and not to exist.'[149]

The philosopher John Hick[150] has noted that, for creatures to enjoy an authentic existence, and not simply to function as an extension of God's being (like an arm or a leg), they must be allowed to develop at an 'epistemic distance' from their maker.

> "The personal being of creatures... necessarily requires some such kind of context as is provided by a material evolving universe... Personal beings so constructed, have the chance in such an environment, to be themselves before being wooed or called into relation with their maker..."[151]

Conceding that a universe with a degree of in-built freedom might need to exist, critics like David Hume have objected that the amount of pain and evil in the universe is still excessive. But suggestions as to how God might reduce the amount of pain and evil have never to my mind been very clear or convincing. Hume for example suggested that pain as a defence mechanism, to alert creatures to infections or other dangers to their bodies, was unnecessary, and that the experience of a mere 'diminution of pleasure' would have sufficed. But as a matter of empirical fact, we know that creatures which lack the ability to feel pain tend to injure themselves more easily and find it harder to survive. A mere diminution of pain does not prompt a sufficiently rapid response. Indeed, if it did, it is hard to understand why pain as a defence

---

[149] *Austin Farrer, 'Saving Belief' (Hodder and Stoughton 1967) p. 52.*
[150] *John Hick (1922–2012), theologian and philosopher of religion.*
[151] *Brian Hebblethwaite, 'Evil, Suffering and Religion' (SPCK 2000) p. 77.*

mechanism should have become so universal in the evolutionary development of species.

There have been attempts to play down or even deny the problem of animal pain. The French philosopher Descartes (1596–1650) argued that animals are driven by mechanical impulses. They have no centre of consciousness and are incapable of experiencing pain. Twentieth century behaviourists claimed that the animals observed in their experiments simply 'reacted' to 'stimuli' in a quasi-mechanistic fashion. Their ideas have had a profound influence upon our understanding of other creatures. Many fishermen for example still assume that their quarry is incapable of experiencing pain, and huntsmen continue to claim that the deer and fox they pursue suffer only minimal distress during the chase and kill. But whilst the experience of pain can vary enormously from person to person and from animal to animal, this effective denial of animal pain and suffering is becoming increasingly untenable. The dualist division between soul and body, which Descartes proposed, is widely rejected both on philosophical and biblical grounds. The similarity between human and animal nervous systems is very significant, and the capacity for self-awareness and speech in a number of 'higher' animals has further undermined the neat division that is frequently drawn. Few today would support Descartes' implicit denial of animal suffering. Animal suffering is real and cannot lightly be dismissed or ignored.

Critics impressed by the amount of suffering in the world often make great play of the popular image of nature 'red in tooth and claw'. But whilst the amount of in-built suffering is significant, its quantity and intensity has at times been greatly exaggerated. Popular television documentaries about animals in the wild are frequently dominated by violence, because it is more interesting for the viewer to watch a lion catching an antelope, for example, than to see him enjoying a siesta! It is important we recognize that this emphasis on hunting and killing is motivated by the need to 'entertain' more than by a desire to communicate the way things actually are. It is like the media reporting only bad news. David Quammen, a two-time winner of the National Magazine Award for his science essays and other work in *Outside* magazine comments on the way in which nature programmes on the television exaggerate the violence within the natural world and distort our view of reality.

> "Time is always compressed, context is often concealed or altered or flouted, in a filmic composition. Nature in reality is more diffuse, more tedious, less satisfactorily dramatic... The drab truth is that you could stand under the Amazon canopy for a month, with a good set of binoculars, while the microbes ate your feet, and never catch a single glimpse of copulating monkeys or a snake in the act of swallowing a bird."[152]

When we take into account the whole process of creation from beginning to end, including its future goal, there seems quite clearly to be a far greater preponderance of good over evil, Life over death. The charge that this world is not worth having, says Austin Farrer, and that life is not worth living is absurd:

> "... Who can take such a charge seriously? The suicide, in a moment of black despair, desires to be relieved of his existence. And why? Because he is deprived – deprived of the health, or the companionship, or the scope of action which belong to human life in this world. His complaint, whatever he may say, is not that existence is a curse, but that he is cut off from its blessings. The very intensity of the indignation or the grief we feel over the affliction or destruction of God's creatures is a testimony to the esteem in which we hold happiness and the mere life of the creatures affected."[153]

Assessing the amount of suffering in the world is difficult at the best of times. People are so different. An American entertainer, Tim Cridland, for example, known as 'The Torture King', was

---

[152] David Quammen, 'The Boilerplate Rhino' (Touchstone 2000) p. 202.
[153] Austin Farrer, 'Saving Belief' (Hodder and Stoughton 1967) p. 48–49.

interviewed on Radio 4 on 5th November 2007. He was found in tests to be able to withstand 40% higher levels of pain than the average man-in-the-street simply by training his mind in a certain way.

Life, *taken as a whole,* is good. Hebblethwaite notes how responsible, loving parents intuitively sense the basic goodness of life when, despite all the dangers in the world, they decide to have a child. Bad things can happen, but even the poet Tennyson, grieving over the untimely death of a friend, is able to affirm his belief that the good outweighs the bad:

> "I hold it true, whate'er befall;
> I feel it when I sorrow most;
> 'Tis better to have loved and lost
> Than never to have loved at all."[154]

Irenaeus' idea of a soul-making environment has much to commend it. However, it has its problems. It assumes to begin with an extremely narrow purpose. Everything is subordinated to the salvation of human beings. And granted the reality of free will, we cannot assume that everyone will choose the path to life. If only a limited number attain salvation, might we not wonder whether the price is too high – whether the pain and suffering endured by countless humans and animals who fail, for whatever reason, to 'make the grade', renders the final triumph a hollow one. The suffering of animals in particular is dismissed in Irenaeas' theodicy as simply an unfortunate but necessary means to achieve human redemption. Is this acceptable?

Irenaeus saw God's purpose as the creation of beings capable of moral goodness and love. But whilst this may well be an important goal, it is not necessarily the only one. According to Genesis (Genesis 1:10, 12, 18, 21, 25, 31), *everything* created by God is 'good' in God's eyes, even the rocks, rivers and lifeless planets. He values them as an artist values a painting. It is not

---

[154] *Alfred Tennyson, 'In Memoriam', XXVII.*

essential for such things to possess 'eternal life' in order for them to be important, and the same is true of 'lower' life forms.

Quentin Smith, an atheist philosopher, maintains that it is 'essential to the idea of God in the Judaeo-Christian-Islamic traditions that if he creates a universe he creates an animate universe' [a universe which contains living organisms or creatures]. William Lane Craig however begs to disagree. He points out that,

> "if we take Aquinas as our guide, that does not seem to be the case. On his view, rational creatures enhance the goodness of the universe, but there is no necessity that God creates them."[155]

God could quite easily have chosen to create a universe without either a single creature living in it or a single soul being 'saved', and in weighing up the relative amounts of good and evil in the cosmos, all sentient creatures could still have a significant value, even if they do not live for ever.

The Pattern of Divine Love

Irenaeus' assumption that the world is purely a soul-making environment for human beings seems in its classic form to be far too anthropocentric[156].

Anthropocentric ways of thinking tend to encourage anthropomorphic ideas about God, creating God in our own image and picturing him as a human being writ large. Peter Geach reckons that, if we truly appreciated the harsh brutality of the natural world, we would realise how hopelessly anthropomorphic are many of the attributes we ascribe to God. We would not even speak of divine 'goodness' and 'love'. The evolutionary process, he argues, is more suggestive of a creator who is indifferent to animal pain and suffering:

---

[155] *William Lane Craig and Quentin Smith, 'Theism, Atheism and the Big Bang', (Clarendon 1995) p.261, 262.*
[156] *'Anthropocentric' means putting human beings at the centre of your world view and seeing everything as revolving around their interests.*

"The spectacle of the living world... is a manifestation of great power and of great wisdom, for which no detail is too small; but there is no evidence or hint that the whole show is organized to minimize pain; nor, for that matter, is there any evidence that pain as such is elaborately contrived, as by Lewis's Devil. The creator's mind, as manifested in the living world, seems to be characterized by mere indifference to the pain that the elaborate interlocking teleologies of life evolve. How can we then avoid picturing God in the likeness of the unfeeling vivisector in H.G. Wells *The Island of Dr Moreau*?"[157]

God and human beings are clearly very different. The infinite creator is not a frail, finite creature (Isaiah 40:18). Certain virtues such as courage and chastity, which we quite rightly attribute to people, could not possibly be ascribed in the same way to the infinite, eternal source of life. God, it could be argued, need never show courage in the face of death, because God is immortal; and chastity is irrelevant, because God does not engage in sexual intercourse. Crude, anthropomorphic descriptions of God are clearly inappropriate.

But are Christians wrong to speak of divine love? Love, at its most basic level, is closely associated with creaturely experiences and emotions. But the divinely revealed pattern of agapeic love which I outlined earlier possesses characteristics which underlie not only important aspects of human relationships, but features which undergird the non-human, natural world as well. It is consistent, universal, life promoting, and respectful of in-built freedom.

Participation in Suffering

The balance we observe within the cosmos between consistent order and freedom, the necessity for this balance in nurturing creatures capable of genuine goodness, and the unavoidable

---

[157] Peter Geach, *'Providence and Evil'* (CUP 1977) p. 77.

possibility of sin and evil within such an environment, go some way to explaining the presence of evil and suffering at an intellectual level. But pain can be felt at a very personal level, and philosophical explanations often sound cold and detached.

However powerful the rationale, can it ever be enough to justify the cruel and pointless suffering of the innocent? In Dostoevsky's classic novel, 'The Brothers Karamazov',[158] Ivan declares that the suffering of even a single innocent child is too high a price to pay. He relates the incident of a young boy who hits one of his master's dogs with a stone whilst playing. The master has him stripped, chased, and torn to pieces by his hounds in the presence of his mother. To Ivan's way of thinking, a God who allows such things to happen cannot be worthy of worship. Ivan sees God as behaving like some kind of cosmic sadist.

> "If the sufferings of children go to make up the sum of sufferings which is necessary for the purchase of truth, then I say beforehand that the entire truth is not worth such a price... We cannot afford to pay so much for admission. And therefore I hasten to return my ticket of admission... *I accept God, understand that, but I cannot accept the world that he has made.*"

Ivan's protest cuts to the core, but this is the moment when we must turn to the mystery of the cross and the crucified God. As the philosopher and theologian, Jürgen Moltmann, has pointed out, the problem here lies with the traditional notion of God as an eternal, immutable, and omnipotent being who can neither suffer nor die:

> "A God who is incapable of suffering is a being who cannot be involved. Suffering and injustice do not affect him. And because he is so completely insensitive, he cannot be shaken

---

[158] 'The Brothers Karamazov' was Fyodor Dostoevsky's final novel. It was originally published as a serial in 'The Russian Messenger' from Jan. 1879 to Nov. 1880.

or affected by anything. He cannot weep, for he has no tears. But the one who cannot suffer cannot love either. So, he is also a loveless being. Aristotle's God cannot love; he can only be loved by all non-divine beings by virtue of his perfection and beauty..."[159]

Moltmann sees the answer as lying, not in the traditional notion of a transcendent God (who is above and beyond our human joys and sufferings), nor in protest atheism (which assumes there is someone or something to protest against), but in the immanent God of Golgotha, the God who was fully present on the cross:

> "The mainstream church maintained against the Syrian monophysites that it was impossible for God to suffer. God cannot suffer like creatures who are exposed to illness, pain, and death. But must God therefore be thought of as incapable of suffering in any respect? This conclusion is not convincing either. Granted, the theology of the early church knew of only one alternative to suffering and that was being incapable of suffering *(apatheia)*, not-suffering. But there are other forms of suffering between unwilling suffering as a result of an alien cause and being essentially unable to suffer, namely active suffering, the suffering of love, in which one voluntarily opens oneself to the possibility of being affected by another. There is unwilling suffering, there is accepted suffering, and there is the suffering of love."[160]

The God revealed in Jesus is a crucified God, who takes responsibility for evil in the world by embracing it himself and sharing in the suffering of his creatures. God's Spirit who was in Christ, is present in his followers and indeed the whole of creation, 'groaning' amongst them and within them (Romans 8. 22–26).

The cross here is absolutely central to our coming to terms with the 'problem' of suffering. The God of agapeic love does not

---

[159] *Jürgen Moltmann, 'The Crucified God' (SCM 1974) p. 222.*
[160] *Jürgen Moltmann, 'The Crucified God', (SCM 1974) p. 229, 230.*

remain aloof. For agapeic love is involved; agapeic love is vulnerable. The God we know in Jesus shares our pain. He is the 'Crucified God', striving (within the limitations of the pattern of agapeic love) to bring us through to the fuller life of his Kingdom. Donald Evans writes:

> "Belief in a God of indignant compassion involves a belief in a God who suffers, God as depicted by Bonhoeffer when he wrote 'Christians stand by God in his hour of grieving.' Bonhoeffer's image is valid and daring. In a Nazi prison, he interprets his own grieving for humanity as a participation in God's grieving. It is as if he were standing by a friend who grieves over the sufferings of a friend's child. His own grieving is as nothing compared to his friend's. His own compassion for the child is a sharing in his friend's compassion. Similarly a man's finite concern for others is a way of sharing in the infinite divine concern."[161]

Such sentiments are what give substance and depth to those well-known biblical passages which speak of the Christian's crucified life in Christ:

> "... If anyone would come after me, he must deny himself and take up his cross and follow me." (Mark 8:34)

> "Jews demand miraculous signs and Greeks look for wisdom, but we preach Christ crucified... For the foolishness of God is wiser than man's wisdom, and the weakness of God is stronger than man's strength."
>
> (1 Corinthians 1:22-25)

As William Blake wrote, there is a continual sharing of God in the suffering of every single animal and human being. Parents cannot stand idly by when they know that their child is suffering, and nor can God:

---

[161] Donald D. Evans, 'Differences Between Scientific and Religious Assertions' in 'Science and Religion', ed. Ian G. Barbour (SCM 1968) p. 107.

"... And can he who smiles on all
Hear the wren with sorrows small,
Hear the small bird's grief and care,
Hear the woes that infants bear,

And not sit beside the nest,
Pouring pity in their breast;
And not sit the cradle near,
Weeping tear on infant's tear...

... He doth give his joy to all;
He becomes an infant small;
He becomes a man of woe;
He doth feel the sorrow too."[162]

If God's crucified presence is to be found wherever a creature suffers, then God's own suffering must be infinitely greater than anything we could possibly know or imagine. Yet like a parent who has decided to bring a child into the world, he has chosen to create us, to risk the consequences, and to embrace the cost. God has acted through his infinite wisdom and goodness. The issue for us, with our limited knowledge and understanding, is whether or not we dare to trust him.

Conclusion

The problem of evil and suffering is *emotionally* difficult, and at a pastoral level there are rarely any easy, pain-free answers. But I have tried to show, at a philosophical level at any rate, how the 'problem of evil' might begin to be addressed.

Faith in the Christian God of love is both plausible and coherent. Atheists struggle to create their own meaning. But whether they favour Nietzsche's amoral assertion of the human 'will to power' ('might is right') or a more humanist construction of supposedly 'rational' values, the basis of their ethic always

---

[162] *William Blake, 'On Another's Sorrow' (1789).*

seems to me to be somewhat fragile. An inevitable tension exists between the personal meanings and purposes they construct and what they regard as the ultimate meaninglessness of the cosmos. Richard Dawkins professes a belief in the possibility of moral goodness. And this is a welcome, heartwarming declaration, especially when we remember the scorn he so often heaps upon empirically unproveable 'beliefs'. But the tension between his moral ideals on the one hand and what he regards as the meaningless forces of nature on the other, remains. It is almost palpable:

> "At the same time as I support Darwinism as a scientist," he writes, "I am a passionate *anti-Darwinian* when it comes to politics and how we should conduct our human affairs."[163]

Christians who serve the crucified God of love, share to my mind a far more coherent outlook. They see both the natural world and the moral world as the work of a single creator, reflecting the same pattern of divine love, and fostering a concern for peace, justice, and compassion in their dealings with fellow human beings and non-human creatures. This pattern of divine love is rooted, not simply in human dreams and wishes, but in a divine reality. In the words of Timothy Rees' great hymn:

> "... Sin and death and hell shall never
> o'er us final triumph gain;
> God is love, so love for ever
> o'er the universe must reign."[164]

---

[163] *Richard Dawkins, 'A Devil's Chaplain: Reflections on Hope, Lies, Science, and Love', (Boston: Houghton Mifflin 2003) p. 10, 11.*
[164] *Timothy Rees (1874–1939), from the hymn, 'God is Love: let heaven adore him' (A.R. Mowbray & Co. Ltd.).*

CHAPTER 10

'The Creator's Cross'

The cross is the key. We have seen in the previous chapter how crucial a part it can play in coming to terms with the problem of evil. This of course is because it is central to a Christian understanding of God's agapeic love, the creator's amazingly inclusive care for human beings and non-human creatures in all their diversity.

The cross is the main symbol of the Christian faith and of the agapeic love which we proclaim. Go into a church or place of worship and you will almost invariably find it prominently displayed on an altar, on a wall or in a window, as a focus for prayer, worship, and meditation.

The cross and events surrounding it occupy a significant proportion of the New Testament gospels. It was an integral part of Jesus' mission; he was 'a king born to die'. His crucifixion came about, not as a sudden, unfortunate, premature end to what might otherwise have been a promising teaching and healing career, but as the fully expected climax to his ministry and something towards which everything else pointed. It was for him a necessary and unavoidable part of the divine plan:

> "...the Son of Man *must* suffer..." (Mark 8:31 *cf* Mark 9:31; 10:33)

Paul the apostle insisted on the centrality of the cross.

> "...we preach Christ crucified..." (1 Corinthians 1:23)

> "May I never boast except in the cross of our Lord Jesus Christ ..." (Galatians 6:14)

He told readers in Corinth that he would resolve to know nothing while he was still with them "... except Jesus Christ and him crucified." (1 Corinthians 2:2)

Key rituals within the Church all relate to the cross in one way or another. When Christians are baptised, the water which is either poured over them or in which they are immersed, symbolises a mystical union with Jesus in his death and resurrection, a sharing in his crucified and risen life:

> "... don't you know," wrote Paul, "that all of us who were baptised into Christ Jesus were baptised into his death? We were therefore buried with him through baptism into death in order that... we too may live a new life."
>
> (Romans 6:3, 4)

Holy Communion is closely linked in the gospels to the Last Supper eaten by Jesus and his disciples before his arrest and execution. The bread and wine received by worshipers during the service 'in remembrance' of his sacrifice signify their participation in the blessings derived from his death.

> "For I received from the Lord," said Paul, "what I also passed on to you: The Lord Jesus, on the night he was betrayed, took bread, and when he had given thanks, he broke it and said, 'This is my body, which is for you; do this in remembrance of me.' In the same way, after supper he took the cup, saying, 'This cup is the new covenant in my blood; do this, whenever you drink it, in remembrance of me.' For whenever you eat this bread and drink this cup, *you proclaim the Lord's death* until he comes." (1 Corinthians 11:23–26)

Mainstream Thinking about the Cross

Given the importance of the cross, one might have expected it to be central to any Christian proclamation of God's love for the *'world'* (John 3:16). Yet surprisingly, whenever the cross' significance is discussed or expounded, this divine love for the cosmos is almost invariably reduced to a love for *human beings*! Consider for example the introductory words to the Church of England's *'Times and Seasons'* liturgy for Good Friday:

> "God sent his Son into the *world*,
> not to condemn the *world*,
> but that the *world* might be saved through him.
> Therefore we pray to our heavenly Father
> for *people* everywhere according to their needs."[165]

The intercessions which accompany these opening words cover an impressively wide range of topics: the Church, the nations of the world and their leaders, God's ancient people the Jews, those who do not believe, the suffering and the oppressed, ourselves and all God's children, yet noticeable by their absence is any reference to the animal kingdom or the wider environment. It seems that when many Christians read the word 'world' in the Bible, they automatically take it to mean humanity-apart-from-God. This means that there is a hidden exclusiveness built into the expression, as if humanity was the only part of creation that matters; that humanity alone is beloved of God and everything else either doesn't matter or only matters insofar as it can be used or exploited to serve the desires, needs and wants of humanity.

A popular book written for confirmation candidates by Peter Jackson and Chris Wright, *'Faith Confirmed'*, shows how widespread and deeply entrenched this narrowly anthropocentric way of thinking has become:

> "Christians," they write, "believe that through his death Jesus mended the broken relationship *between God and humanity* which had been caused by sin."[166]

---

[165] *'Times and Seasons' (Church House Publishing* © The Archbishops' Council 2006) *p. 316.*
[166] *P. Jackson & C. Wright, 'Faith Confirmed' (SPCK 2013 reprint), p. 27.*

No explicit mention is made of the role which the cross plays in healing non-human 'relationships' with animals or in caring for an environment corrupted by the sinful structures of fallen humanity.

All the mainstream theories of atonement taught to students at theological college rest upon the assumption that God's problem is *human sin* and that saving *humanity* is his primary concern. Thinkers like Peter Abelard (1079–1142) and Hastings Rashdall (1858–1924), for example, representatives of the so-called 'exemplarist' theory, look upon the cross as a supreme expression of God's love aimed at stirring *human* hearts into some kind of positive response. Isaac Watts' great hymn, '*When I survey the wondrous cross*', is a good example of this approach:

> "...Were the whole realm of nature mine,
> That were an offering far too small.
> Love so amazing, so divine,
> Demands my soul, my life, my all!"[167]

The 'classic' or 'dramatic' theory expounded by the likes of the reformation pioneer, Martin Luther (1483–1546), pictures Christ as engaged in a spiritual war against the devil and the forces of evil:

> "...With force of arms we nothing can,
> Full soon were we down-ridden;
> But for us fights the proper Man,
> Whom God himself hath bidden.
> Ask ye, Who is this same?
> The Lord Sabaoth's Son;
> He, and no other one,
> Shall conquer in the battle..."[168]

---

[167] *Isaac Watts (1674–1748), from the hymn: 'When I survey the wondrous cross'.*

[168] *Martin Luther (1483–1546), from the hymn: 'A safe stronghold' ('Ein' feste Burg'), tr. Thomas Carlyle (1795–1881).*

Note again, however, how the decisive victory won by Jesus on the cross is for Luther a victory won on behalf of humanity rather than the wider creation.

The 'judicial' approach favoured by writers such as Anselm (1033–1109) and John Calvin (1509–64) emphasises the costliness of forgiveness through the analogy of a debt for *human* sin being paid to God as the righteous judge:

> "...There was no other good enough to pay the price of sin;
>
> He only could unlock the gate of heaven, and let *us* [not animals] in."[169]

Each of these major 'theories of atonement' has its own strengths and weaknesses, but what they all have in common is a preoccupation with *human* sin and mortality. Indeed, they can all fairly easily be mapped onto the dominant social and political structures of the times in which they were developed. For example, Anselm's judicial and satisfaction theory reflected the feudal society in which he lived where the dignity of the serf's lord was offended (and therefore 'satisfaction' and not just repayment of lost income, was required). Calvin's primary concern was with establishing justice and social order in the mercantile setting of the growing city of Geneva and thus the development there of a living example of what Augustine of Hippo called 'the city of God.' What all this means is that each historical theory of the atonement is at least partially an example of the cross of Jesus being related to people's concerns at a particular time. Humanity's needs for certain kinds of 'justification' are read back into the cross.

Of course we need to be aware of the way emerging theories of atonement in our own time are open to the same criticism of cultural relativity: the cross as an exemplar of supreme love, for example; the suffering of Christ as a sign of his being in solidarity with the poor; or even the cross as God's act of solidarity with all creation.

---

[169] *Cecil Frances Alexander (1818–95), from the hymn: 'There is a green hill far away'.*

A deeper reading should *start* from the cross, working out the implications of John's expression that 'God so loved the world that he gave...' and reflecting as critically as possible on our cultural preoccupations to see whether or not they are valid, sound, and proportionate.

It could be said for example that non-human animals are innocent creatures incapable of sin and that they have no need to be 'saved'. Anselm[170] argued along these lines in his famous work *'Cur Deus Homo?'* (Why did God become Man?). But there are at least two problems with this proposition. First, it assumes that atonement is only concerned with forgiveness; atonement involves, as we shall see, much more than that. Secondly, it relegates non-human animals and the environment to the sidelines, viewing them as little more than irrelevant bystanders in relation to events surrounding the passion of Christ.

The Need for a More Inclusive Understanding

Viewing non-human animals as irrelevant bystanders has serious implications. When a central aspect of the Christian gospel like the cross is understood in a narrowly anthropocentric way (as being there solely for the benefit of human beings), wider creation is not only sidelined but positively devalued. It becomes a mere stage upon which God's great drama of human salvation is enacted, and this in turn gives the unfortunate if unintended impression that God has only a limited interest in non-human creatures; that issues relating to animal welfare and the environment are of only secondary importance. It loses contact with the great insight of the psalmist who, while giving voice to the praise of God and the call to holiness, cries out, 'The earth is the Lord's, and everything in it...' (Psalm 24:1)

At a period in our history when public concern about animal welfare is on the rise and there is a growing global awareness of environmental issues, the Church's failure to emphasise the wider

---

[170] *Anselm (1033–1109) was a leading theologian and philosopher of his time, and a Benedictine monk at Bec who later became Archbishop of Canterbury.*

cosmic relevance of the gospel is short-sighted, even tragic. Jesus was always acutely sensitive to God's timing. When he began his public ministry, for example, he did so because he knew 'the time' had come' – his *kairos*, the appropriate moment. This particular period of heightened concern for environmental and animal welfare issues is our *kairos,* our God-given moment, our opportunity to proclaim God's love for the whole of creation. Our failure to seize this moment will be a stumbling block for many potential enquirers, who will sadly dismiss the gospel as irrelevant to their concerns. There is an issue here which the Church urgently needs to address.

I write now out of a conviction that the cross serves a much wider purpose than is commonly supposed: that Jesus died for 'the world' in its totality, humans and non-humans alike; that our Saviour's redeeming love is truly inclusive; and that the time has come to challenge narrowly anthropocentric assumptions about the cross which have dominated Christian thinking for so long.

The Cosmic Dimension of the Cross

It is strange how the wider cosmic significance of the cross has been so comprehensively ignored or forgotten, especially when one considers the frequency with which the Bible explicitly alludes to it. The book of Revelation describes four living creatures, representatives of the whole created order – humans, birds, and beast – surrounding God's throne:

> "The first living creature," we are told, "was like a lion, the second was like an ox, the third had a face like a man, the fourth was like a flying eagle." (Revelation 4:7)

They share not only in the great song of *creation* (Revelation 4:6b–11) but also more importantly in the song of *redemption.* They are active witnesses and participants in the final completion of God's purposes:

"To him who sits on the throne and to the Lamb," they cry, "be praise and honour and glory and power, for ever and ever!" (Revelation 5:13b)

The letter to the Colossians declares Christ Jesus to be "the firstborn over all creation" by whom "all things were created: all things in heaven and on earth" (Colossians 1:15, 16), and the entire cosmos to be the object of God's redeeming work.

God is "... pleased... through [Christ Jesus] to reconcile to himself *all things*, whether things on earth or things in heaven, by making peace through his blood, shed on the cross." (Colossians 1:19)

The letter to the Ephesians reinforces this all-inclusive message:

"[God] made known to us the mystery of his will according to his good pleasure, which he purposed in Christ... to bring *all things in heaven and on earth* together under one head, even Christ." (Ephesians 1:9, 10)

It is often said that the Old Testament tells the story of God's Chosen People and their developing relationship with him. This is true as far as it goes, but as the Book of Deuteronomy constantly reminds us, the wellbeing of the people is inseparable from the wellbeing of the land which God gives them and the creatures who inhabit that land (eg Deuteronomy 11:8–17).

The cosmic scope of God's redemption is paralleled by the cosmic implications of sin. In the story of 'the Fall' (Genesis 3) problems of division and conflict exist at every level. The two archetypal human beings, Adam and Eve, find themselves alienated not only from God (v. 23) but also from each other (v.12,15), the animal kingdom (v.15) and the environment (v.17–19), and cast out of the 'garden'.

In the narrative we see that at the heart of this tragedy lies the arrogance of Adam. In stark contrast to Jesus the Servant-King (Philippians 2:5–11) he seeks equality with God (Genesis 3:5) and tries to abuse the 'dominion' which he has been given. Human 'dominion' as described in Genesis (Genesis 1:26) was never intended to be a license to exploit animals for selfish purposes. It was, as we have already seen, a call to share in God's royal rule and to reflect his image.

> "Rulers in the ancient world set up images in regions under their control. The images were there to represent their rule. You and I are like those 'images' in our relationship with God. We have been given the ability to represent his rule – to act as his vice-regents. We have been tasked with caring for creation. In the primeval world described by the writer [of the Genesis creation narratives], humans are initially vegetarians (Genesis 1:29; 2:15–20) and although this state of affairs does not last (Genesis 4:4; 9:3), there is a feeling within the Bible that this is how it ought to be – that God's ultimate purposes will somehow entail peaceful relationships devoid of suffering."[171]

God is concerned for the whole cosmos. When we turn to the prophecies of redemption, descriptions of a liberated people are accompanied by visions of a renewed environment – streams flowing through the desert and fields bursting with produce. The prophecy in Isaiah Chapter 11 envisions universal peace and harmony:

> "A shoot will come up from the stump of Jesse;
>   from his roots a branch will bear fruit.
> The Spirit of the Lord will rest on him -
>   the Spirit of wisdom and of understanding,
>   the Spirit of counsel and of power,
>   the Spirit of knowledge and of the fear of the Lord -
> and he will delight in the fear of the Lord

---

[171] *Hugh Broadbent, 'Thinking about Animal Testing' (Anglican Society for the Welfare of Animals).*

The wolf will live with the lamb,
  the leopard will lie down with the goat,
the calf and the lion and the yearling together;
  and a little child will lead them.
The cow will feed with the bear,
  their young will lie down together,
  and the lion will eat straw like the ox.
The infant will play near the hole of the cobra,
  and the young child will put his hand into the viper's nest.
They will neither harm nor destroy
  on all my holy mountain,
for the earth will be full of the knowledge of the Lord
  as the waters cover the sea." (Isaiah 11:1–3, 6–9)

From the very beginning God purposed to redeem and reconcile, not just the human race, but the whole created order.

Atonement as a Process

A technical term which is commonly used in relation to the redemptive work of Christ is 'atonement'. The word literally means 'a bringing together', an 'at-one-ment', whereby God draws all creatures into deep, harmonious communion with himself and with each other.

Atonement is not the result of a single event like the crucifixion, but of a much longer process which is still on-going – a barrier-breaking process in which we are constantly being called to participate. When the shepherds were invited to become the first witnesses to the birth of Jesus, for example, an important social barrier was overcome (Luke 2:8–20). Shepherds were looked down upon by some of the orthodox because the work they did made it harder for them to attend services and festivals and could make them neglectful of their religious duties[172]. Throughout Jesus' earthly ministry, the all-embracing and radically inclusive

---

[172] G.B. Caird 'The Gospel of St. Luke' (Penguin Books Ltd 1963, this edition 1968 A.& C. Black Ltd), p. 61.

nature of the gospel led to cultural, moral, and spiritual barriers, which separated people and animals from God and from each other, being challenged or removed.

Jesus sought at every level to spread God's gracious rule, bringing them together in his love and furthering the work of at-one-ment. Many of us will be familiar with the ways in which this happened, with the Lord reaching out to the poor, the sick, the marginalised and the rejected. Numerous examples could be cited from the gospels: befriending the despised tax collectors (Mark 2:13–17), allowing a sex worker to wash his feet (Luke 7:36–50), touching ritually unclean lepers in order to heal them (Mark 1:40, 41), taking time out to bless young children who in those days were regarded as being of little importance (Mark 10:13–16), or commending a Roman soldier, one of the hated alien invaders, for his faith (Luke 7:1–10). Even plants and non-human creatures came within the scope of God's providential care. Echoing Psalm 104, for example, Jesus spoke of God clothing the lilies of the field (Matthew 6:28, 29) and knowing about even the tiniest sparrow sold for a penny in the market place (Matthew 10:29).

The Word made Flesh

We have spoken of a process of atonement and of bringing the whole created order together in God, but there is of course a sense in which everything has already been united in the person of Jesus through the 'incarnation'. John's prologue connects Jesus as the incarnate Word (John 1:14) with all that has been brought into being through the Word (John 1:3), and with the Word that enlightens every human being (John 1:5).

> "In the beginning was the Word... Through him all things were made... In him was life, and that life was the light of men." (John 1:1–4)

There is a distinction which we should note between the 'light' brought to humanity and the 'life' given to the wider natural world. But the Word made flesh in Jesus is responsible for both of them, and this reinforces the idea we find in the letter to the Colossians that "all things were created" by Christ (Colossians 1:16); that God is already here with us in the world as the one in whom we live and move and have our being. (Acts 17:28)

The implications of this are profound. The practical theologian John B. Cobb Jr. puts it in stark terms:

> "To think of all living things as embodying Christ must give us pause. A creature in whom we see Christ cannot be *only* a commodity to be treated for our gain or casual pleasure."[173]

Athanasius (c. 296–373), the great bishop of Alexandria, understood the inextricable link between God as creator and God as redeemer. He saw how the same divine Word or Wisdom who brought the world into being and continuously sustains it, also became flesh in Jesus in order to renew humanity's broken image and make a reality the fullness of life which he promised. He saw too how the same Spirit, who in the beginning moved over the primeval waters of chaos, is today at work not only in drawing men, women and children ever more deeply into the love of God, but also in bringing non-human creatures to share in that divine fellowship. In his first letter to Serapion[174] he wrote:

> "The Spirit does not belong to the created order, but is proper to the Godhead of the Father, in whom the Logos also deifies[175] created things."[176]

---

[173] John B. Cobb Jr, 'All Things in Christ?' from 'Animals on the Agenda' ed. Andrew Linzey and Dorothy Yamamoto (SCM 1998) p. 177.

[174] Serapion was an Egyptian monk and theologian, Bishop of Thmuis, and leading supporter of Athanasius in his fight against the Arian heresy.

[175] 'Deification' was an understanding which was developed by Athanasius and some other early Church fathers, who saw that all living beings would finally be taken up into Christ and fully become participants in the divine nature. During the subsequent history of the Church 'deification' has proved to be both a profoundly important and controversial insight. For a biblical reference to sharing in the divine nature see 2 Peter 1:4.

[176] Quoted by Denis Edwards in 'Creaturely Theology', ed. Celia Deane-Drummond & David Clough (SCM 2009) p. 90.

It was love for the world, not just the human race, that prompted God to come amongst us in the 'flesh'.

> "In the beginning was the Word," writes St. John in his Prologue, "and the Word was with God, and the Word was God. ... The Word became *flesh* and made his dwelling among us..." (John 1:1,14)

Some will suggest that, because it was human 'flesh' that God assumed and not the form of a non-human animal, God could not have had any interest in saving non-human animals. If this line of argument were to be pursued to its logical conclusion, however, we could equally well say that because Jesus was born a Jewish boy in first century Palestine, God was only interested in saving male Jews living in that particular Roman province at that particular time! This is clearly nonsense. The moral and spiritual significance of Jesus extends far beyond his own particular cultural or biological circumstances.[177]

The gospel is inclusive. When followers of Jesus within the early Church known as 'Judaisers' suggested that Jesus' Jewish ethnicity meant he had only come for the Jews and that Gentiles should therefore be excluded from becoming his disciples, their error was quickly exposed (Acts 10:44–47; 11:18). God's coming in Jesus inevitably entails the divine Presence being restricted to a particular, finite creature. But this does not render it irrational or unworthy of a perfect, infinitely wise mind. If God's love had only ever been revealed as a love for 'everyone in general but no-one in particular', it would have been incredibly weak and far too dilute

---

[177] *It is perhaps worth noting here that the Catholic/Anglo-Catholic argument against admission of women to the priesthood is, in part, linked to the fact that Christ assumed male flesh – only men, on the basis of this argument, can act in persona Christi at the altar. As S. Gregory of Nazianzus points out in his letter to Cledonius, however: "That which he [God] has not assumed he has not healed; but that which is united to his Godhead is also saved. If only half Adam fell, then that which Christ assumes and saves may be half also; but if the whole of his nature fell, it must be united to the whole nature of Him that was begotten, and so be saved as a whole."*

to have had any significant, transformative effect. God needed to embrace the 'scandal of particularity' if the depth of the divine love was truly to be conveyed. We must simply recognise that the particularity of the revelation should never be seen as a denial of God's wider inclusive intent.

When in the Prologue to his gospel John talks of the Word made 'flesh', he intended the word 'flesh' to be understood as,

> "... an inclusive term for all living things, with roots in the Hebrew *basar*, used frequently in the Old Testament to refer to all living creatures".[178]

God's warning to Noah about the flood uses the phrase 'all flesh' in this inclusive sense, to indicate nature's solidarity with humankind:

> "God saw how corrupt the earth had become, for all the people ['flesh'] on earth had corrupted their ways." (Genesis 6:12)

Elihu reminds poor suffering Job that, if God gathered to himself the breath of life he had given to his world, 'all flesh' would die (Job 34:14, 15). There are occasions, such as in some of Paul's letters, when 'flesh' is used to describe sinful human nature, but generally speaking the word has a much broader and more positive meaning when referring to God coming 'in the flesh' (*cf* Ephesians 2:14; 1 John 4:2).

The expression 'made flesh' is intended to show that Jesus is in solidarity with all living things, both fully divine and fully *in the flesh*, and that this solidarity is in both life and death. David Clough makes the point in a somewhat startling and controversial fashion:

---

[178] *David Clough, 'On Animals Volume 1' (Bloomsbury T&T Clark 2013 pb) p. 85.*

"If we are right to understand that God took on creatureliness and animality in the incarnation, then it is *as a creature* and an animal that Jesus Christ is put to death on the cross."[179]

I am not sure that I would wish to make the point in quite such a stark fashion. But if Jesus died as a human being, he certainly did so as a human being in solidarity with 'all flesh', as the cosmic Christ.

The Bible frequently compares Jesus on the cross with a pure and innocent lamb led to the slaughter (Isaiah 53:7 *cf* 1 Peter 1:19; Revelation 5:6). Scripture speaks of Jesus as 'the Word made flesh' giving himself to death on the cross in solidarity with all created beings, human and animal, and in this moment the first Christians were quick to understand that the need for any further animal sacrifice had been brought to an end. This in fact is one of the main reflections in the New Testament letter to the Hebrews. Jesus was bearing the cost of salvation for the whole of creation, not just the human race.

When Jesus once famously referred to himself as the Temple which would be destroyed and raised again in three days (John 2:19 *cf* Mark 14:58), he was in the first instance referring very simply to his own crucified and resurrected body. The apostle Paul described our bodies in a similar vein as temples of the Holy Spirit (1 Corinthians 6:19). But the Temple also has a much wider, cosmic significance. Tom Wright[180] in his book '*Virtue Reborn*' reminds us how it was designed, not as a refuge from the world but as a representation of it, a 'creation-in-miniature'.

"Its dimensions, its furnishings, its ornaments, its priestly robes and activities – all were supposed to reflect and sum up the great cosmos itself... It was an advance sign of what

---

[179] *David Clough, 'On Animals Volume 1' (Bloomsbury T&T Clark 2013 pb) p. 128.*
[180] *N.T. Wright is a New Testament scholar and was Bishop of Durham from 2003 to 2010.*

God intended to do with and for the whole creation. When God filled the house with his presence, that was a sign and foretaste of his ultimate intention, which was to flood the whole world with his glory, presence, and love."[181]

By describing himself as the embodiment of the Temple Jesus was emphasising the *cosmic* significance of his passion. It was not just him as an individual who was being killed and raised to new life. He, as the 'Temple', the cosmos-in-miniature, was anticipating God's ultimate goal – the birth of a whole new creation (Revelation 21:1). In the visionary language of St John, God and the Lamb replace the Temple:

> "I did not see a temple in the city, because the Lord God Almighty and the Lamb [the crucified Christ] are its temple... [with] the river of the water of life... flowing from the throne of God and of the Lamb." (Revelation 21:22, 22:1)

They become the source of life for the whole redeemed cosmos.

Atonement Completed on the Cross

No creature is omitted from God's work of at-one-ment in Christ. All things are reconciled through the blood of the cross (Colossians 1:19). Jesus found the heavy handed and wooden application of the Levitical and Deuteronomic laws of purity a major barrier in reaching people and creatures on the margins. The lepers Jesus touched (Luke 5:12, 13), for example, the woman with the flow of blood (Luke 8:43–48) and the tax collectors with whom he shared a meal (Luke 5:29–32) were all strictly speaking ritually unclean. Engaging with them in the way he did involved breaking the purity laws, which understandably incurred the wrath of the religious leaders who could not understand why God's Messiah should wish to flout instructions laid down in the law of Moses. It

---

[181] N.T. Wright, 'Virtue Reborn' (SPCK 2010 pb) p. 73.

was one of the main reasons for Jesus' eventual arrest, trial and execution.

Jesus' death was not only a *result* of his earthly ministry of reconciliation contravening these purity laws; more than that, it was its final consummation. Nailed to the cross Jesus himself was rendered ritually unclean. According to the law of Moses (Deuteronomy 21:22, 23), the body of an executed criminal hung or impaled on a tree or stake was deemed to be accursed. It 'polluted' the land and had to be disposed of – utterly rejected.

Jesus on the cross was, according to the law of Moses, accursed, unclean, and rejected by God. Yet in the wake of his resurrection, his followers became convinced that God had vindicated him as his Messiah. How could this be? I am reminded of the words spoken to Peter during his vision of the sailcloth:

"… Do not call anything impure that God has made clean."
(Acts 10:15)

Jesus on the cross had come alongside the supposedly unclean; he had reached out to the estranged and the alienated in a supreme act of solidarity. Rowan Williams writes:

"[He] included everyone and everything and overcame enmity. Something of the same argument is behind the strange statement in 2 Corinthians 5:21 that God has 'made him [Jesus] to be sin for us'." [182]

This extraordinary expression of solidarity has profound implications, not only for our relationship with fellow human beings who have been rejected and are feeling alienated from the Church and perhaps society[183], but for our dealings with non-human animals

---

[182] *Rowan Williams, 'Meeting God in Paul' (SPCK 2015) p. 62. Rowan Williams is a theologian and was Archbishop of Canterbury from 2002 to 2012.*
[183] *This has significant implications, I believe, for Christian thinking about such issues as gay relationships and gay marriage, which are often opposed on the basis of the purity laws in the Book of Leviticus. It paves the way for Christians to affirm all committed and caring relationships which promote human*

too. It is significant to note, for example, that not long after Jesus' death and resurrection the Church abandoned the old distinction between clean and unclean animals laid down in the Torah. All were to be regarded as equally precious. If Jesus on the cross was deemed by God to be pure and holy, a focus of God's presence, even after he had supposedly been rendered ritually unclean, then as far as Jesus' first followers were concerned, the old division between clean and unclean could no longer apply.

Atonement and Forgiveness

Jesus' death is perhaps most frequently associated in the minds of Christians with God's covenant of forgiveness. The cross represented in itself the greatest act of sinful rebellion that one could imagine – the killing of God's one and only Son. Yet Jesus at the Last Supper transformed this heinous act into God's supreme offer of mercy and forgiveness:

> "... Jesus took bread, gave thanks and broke it, and gave it to his disciples, saying, 'Take and eat; this is my body.' Then he took the cup, gave thanks and offered it to them, saying, 'Drink from it, all of you. This is my blood of the covenant, which is poured out for many for the forgiveness of sins'."
>
> (Matthew 26:26–28)

---

flourishing in line with patterns of agapeic love. As in the case of slavery, we must avoid 'proof texts' and seek rather to discern the overall direction in which Jesus' atoning, agapeic love (together with any new scientific findings) is taking us. Great care needs to be taken in handling scriptural passages relating to gay relationships. Romans 1:26, 27, for example, is not in my view the direct condemnation of faithful, committed homosexual relationships as many assume. It is part of an argument designed to show how Gentiles and Jews alike are guilty of idolatry (Romans 2:1), and refers to sexual activity relating to the worship of false gods. Note how the apostle Paul uses 'akatharsian' in Romans 1:24, the same Greek word as is found in the Septuagint to describe cultic prostitution. Jewish idolatry also sometimes involved sexual rituals (Leviticus 17:7; 18:3,21, 22; 20:2–5,13; Deuteronomy 23:17–18).

The resultant reconciliation through Christ's atoning death was in this respect undoubtedly intended primarily for humans. Some recent thinkers have suggested biblical, historical and zoological grounds for supposing that some non-human animals may be capable of sinful behaviour and in need of God's forgiveness [184]. Clough, for example, cites interesting studies of an ape punished by others for infanticide and of certain medieval trials of animals. But most, I suspect, would not wish to go this far.

Andrew Linzey and others (including myself) prefer to emphasise the innocence of animals.

> "According to Christian theology," writes Linzey, "humans alone are morally responsible because they have free will whereas animals have no such freedom. But the logical conclusion of this train of thought is that since animals cannot sin, they must be closer to the state of natural blessedness that God intended. Since their lives have not been disfigured by sin, they still possess an original innocence in a way that humans do not." [185]

The matter is clearly open to debate. But be that as it may, those of us who are drawn more and more deeply into the pattern of divine, all-embracing agapeic love will all find ourselves needing God's forgiveness, not only for sins against our fellow human beings but for the terrible abuse and exploitation of animals and the environment.

Solidarity in Creaturely Suffering

We saw in the previous chapter how God's fullness was in Christ, reconciling all things to himself, "through the blood of the cross" (Colossians 1:19) and sharing in our trials and sufferings as well as in our joys. (Hebrews 4:15-end)

---

[184] D. Clough, 'On Animals Volume 1' (Bloomsbury T&T Clark) Ch. 5.
[185] Andrew Linzey, 'Creatures of the Same God' (Winchester University Press 2007) p. 109.

This distinctively Christian picture of the creator as the incarnate, 'crucified God' casts the problem of evil in a totally new light. It shows God accepting responsibility for the universe and the creatures he has brought into being and sharing in the consequences of the in-built freedom he has bestowed upon them. The sustaining and renewing power of God can be seen to be present, not only in the anguish of Jesus hanging on the cross, but in the suffering of every single creature that exists or has ever existed.

All categories of suffering, even those which we feel are of such a different order as to require separate treatment, are embraced by the all-inclusive God of the cross: the courageous protester, for example, who is tortured in prison because of the peaceful stand which he or she is making against some blatant abuse or injustice, or a loved one who is dying from a terminal illness. The eye of faith and heart of compassion also recognises that he is there with the broiler chicken hanging on the conveyor belt when its throat is cut, with the exhausted fox when it is caught and torn apart by the hounds, or with the mouse toyed with by the cat.

Atonement and the Second Adam

The work of at-one-ment, revealed supremely through the cross, shows how God from a divine perspective comes alongside the suffering and rejected. From our own more human perspective, we experience God reaching out to us through the cross, drawing us into at-one-ment with his all-embracing love. Our love for God is ignited in response:

"We love because he first loved us." (1 John 4:19)

Spearheaded by Jesus' humble obedience even unto death (Philippians 2:5–11), we are drawn into the birth of a new humanity, a radical development in our evolutionary history. The first Adam, the original archetypal human being in the Genesis creation narratives, represented our *old fallen humanity*; Jesus represents and embodies our *new humanity*. He is our second Adam. In the words of J.H. Newman:

> "O loving wisdom of our God!
> When all was sin and shame,
> A second Adam to the fight
> And to the rescue came."[186]

By the grace of God and the paradoxical power of the cross we find ourselves being led into closer and closer conformity with the pattern of our risen Lord Jesus, the Second Adam, held ever more deeply in the infinite love of God and the ongoing life of the Holy Spirit.

The first Adam is associated with the original creation stories in Genesis 1 and 2; the second Adam is linked in a similar manner to the new creation which God is bringing about (2 Corinthians 5:17). Michael Gilmour[187] notes how the writer of the Fourth Gospel organises his material around various 'signs', the first of course being the miracle at the wedding in Cana where he turns water into wine (John 2:1–11). There are seven signs in total performed during the course of Jesus' earthly ministry, and these according to N.T. Wright follow the sevenfold sequence of the old creation. The eighth is the resurrection. This occurs, as John emphasises by mentioning it twice, "on the first day of the week" (John 20:1,19) – a new day, a new week. It marks the start of a new creation. The good news of Easter is not simply about the resurrection of human beings, but about the birth of a whole new heaven and earth. (Revelation 21:1)

At the heart of God's new creation is Jesus, the second Adam. Paul has the penetrating insight that:

> "... The first man Adam became a living being; the last Adam, a life-giving spirit. The spiritual did not come first, but the natural, and after that the spiritual. The first man was of the dust of the earth, the second man from heaven. As was the earthly man, so are those who are of the earth;

---

[186] *John Henry Newman (1801–90) 'Praise to the holiest'.*

[187] *Michael J. Gilmour, 'Eden's Other Residents' (Cascade Books 2014) p. 68.*

and as is the man from heaven, so also are those who are of heaven. And just as we have borne the likeness of the earthly man, so shall we bear the likeness of the man from heaven." (1 Corinthians 15:45–49)

Gilmour interestingly observes how on the first Easter morning, at the dawn of this 'new creation', while it is 'still dark', our risen Lord is mistaken by Mary Magdalene for being 'the gardener' (John 20:15). This is perhaps a deliberately ironic detail as there is a sense in which Jesus as the second Adam *is* indeed the new gardener. The first Adam had failed in his God-given task of tilling and caring for the garden of God's world (Genesis 2:15). Jesus and those who share his risen life will not fail. The key to godly dominion over creation is humble conformity to God's purposes:

"Your attitude should be the same as that of Christ Jesus: Who, being in very nature God, did not consider equality with God something to be grasped [as Adam did], but made himself nothing, taking the very nature of a servant, being made in human likeness. And being found in appearance as a man, he humbled himself and became obedient to death – even death on a cross! Therefore God exalted him to the highest place and gave him the name that is above every name, that at the name of Jesus every knee should bow, in heaven and on earth and under the earth, and every tongue confess that Jesus Christ is Lord, to the glory of God the Father." (Philippians 2:5–11).

The New Testament scholar Richard Bauckham notes how during Jesus' temptations in the wilderness the wild beasts were 'with' Jesus, the second Adam, in a positive way as his companions (Mark 1:13)[188], just as in the Genesis narratives they were with the first Adam before his 'Fall'. Those of us who seek to follow

---

[188] Richard Bauckham, 'Jesus and the Wild Animals (Mark 1:13): A Christological Image for an Ecological Age' in 'Jesus of Nazareth Lord and

Jesus are called to exercise our God-given dominion in a right
way, to share in his victory over the forces of sin and death, to
walk as he did the path of humble obedience, and to live at peace
as far as we can, not only with our fellow human beings but with
all God's creatures. We must stop discussing animals and the environment as if their wellbeing were simply a matter of enlightened
self-interest, something about which we must concern ourselves if
the human race is to survive, and start to cherish them as God
does – for their own sakes, as being of intrinsic value. In 2006 I
was moved to write the following hymn on this theme:

> Across a sea of chaos, dark and brooding,
> The Spirit stirs; our Maker brings to birth
> His plan for life ablaze with love and beauty,
> And countless creatures on a fruitful earth.
> Our fath'ring God within his heart rejoices
> As he beholds their wonder and their worth.
>
> Beneath a sea of violence and injustice
> This precious life is drowning day by day.
> Creation smeared by cruel exploitation;
> The selfish path we tread with feet of clay,
> We reach the end, our dignity distorted,
> And see the Maker's image fade away.
>
> Upon the sea a fragile ark is drifting,
> A sign of hope that rises with the flood.
> For Man becomes a servant of redemption
> To bird and beast, as now he seeks their good.
> The rainbow-God shows in a dove his mercy –
> His love for all more clearly understood.
>
> The chaos gone! Our God one day will conquer.
> His love will bring a harmony complete,

Christ. Essays on the historical Jesus and New Testament Christology'. Ed. Joel
B. Green & Max Turner. Grand Rapids, MI: Eerdmans 1994.

As grief and pain, the sorrow all around us,
Are swallowed up in victory so sweet.
The Lamb of God will reign on high for ever,
As living creatures worship at his feet![189]

Atonement and Sacrificial Love

The cross is linked to discipleship. Christians are called, after the pattern of Jesus the Servant King, to deny themselves, take up their cross and follow him. (Mark 8:34)

> "My command is this," said Jesus: "Love each other *as I have loved you*. [Jesus of course loved us even unto death]. Greater love has no-one than this, that he lay down his life for his friends." (John 15:12–13)

The cross symbolises the life of self-giving love, caring for everyone and everything: fellow human beings, non-human creatures, and the whole environment. Jesus famously described himself as the good shepherd who, in stark contrast to the false shepherds or religious leaders condemned by Ezekiel for their abuse of power (Ezekiel 34:11ff), was ready to lay down his life for his sheep. (John 10:14, 15)

Bearing in mind the wider, inclusive, cosmic significance of the word made 'flesh' which we discussed earlier, we should now of course appreciate the fact that the sheep here do not simply represent human beings. They are quite literally sheep and indeed any non-human animal in need of our help. The way in which we behave towards our fellow creatures is of real importance. Paul in his letter to the Romans hints at a causal connection between the redemption of non-human animals on the one

---

[189] My hymn, 'Across a sea of chaos dark and brooding', can be sung to the tune of 'Finlandia'. It was first used at an Animal Welfare Sunday service at St Bartholomew's church, Brighton in 2006, a service organised in conjunction with the Anglican Society for the Welfare of Animals (ASWA).

hand and our newly redeemed nature as children of God on the other. He notes how:

> "... we ourselves, who have the first fruits of the Spirit, groan inwardly as we wait eagerly for our adoption [as God's children]" (Romans 8:23),

prefacing it with the hope that;

> "... creation itself will be liberated from its bondage to decay and brought into the glorious freedom of the children of God." (Romans 8:21, 22)

Conclusion

The Christian life is a response to God's pattern of agapeic love revealed supremely in Jesus – his life, death, and resurrection. I have sought in this book to show how it is foundational to an understanding of how and why the universe exists; how it undergirds the value and the dignity of every human being and living creature; and how, supremely in the mystery of the cross and the transforming, renewing power of the resurrection, it confronts and triumphs over a suffering world 'red in tooth and claw'.

Ever since I became a Christian it has been my overriding desire to be drawn into ever closer conformity with God's pattern of agapeic love revealed in Jesus, to embrace its unwavering, inclusive, life-enhancing nature, and to live in harmony with it. A chorus to one of the songs I wrote for a musical, *'The Clown'*, based on the life of St. Francis, provides perhaps a fitting summary:

> "When the love of him who made us
> Begins to fill your heart,
> You will start to love as he does
> The world in every part.

You will care for one another,
See creatures as your sister and brother,
Share in the love of the greatest of lovers,
Share in the love of God."[190]

---

[190] 'The Clown' is a musical that I wrote based on the life of St Francis of Assisi.
It was performed at Holy Trinity, Bromley Common in May 1994.

Chapter 11

'My Journey into Agapeic Love'

For me, believing in the God of agapeic love has had profound practical implications. It has shaped everything I am, everything I stand for, and everything I do. Living in the embrace of God's agapeic love is living with reality. God calls me to join in the action, not just appreciate it from a distance like a mildly interested spectator.

The Christian writer, John Ortberg, suggests that joining in the action with God is like walking through an open door of boundless opportunities.

> "Of unlimited chances to do something worthwhile; of grand openings into new and unknown adventures of significant living; of heretofore unimagined chances to do good, to make our lives count for eternity."[191]

For me there are five 'key components' which have opened the door to my walk with God.

Quiet Times

One of greatest privileges and joys of following Jesus is being able to come into the presence of God in prayer. Love lies at the core of God's being, and it is my fervent desire as a Christian to make his

---

[191] *Gerald Hawthorne, 'Colossians', self-published commentary 2010, quoted by John Ortberg in 'All the Places to Go' (Tyndale 2015) p .5.*

agapeic love central to my life also. Spending quality time with him every day helps me to achieve this. It keeps me grounded in who I am (his child) and what I am seeking to do (his will).

Each day I tend to read a portion of the Bible, the importance of which I explained earlier on in Chapter 3, to spend some time in quiet reflection, and then to pray. I refer to this as my 'Quiet Time' but the name is not important. What matters is the outcome – whether my relationship with God is deepened and strengthened.

Many people struggle with prayer. They 'meditate', perhaps, pray for help when faced with a crisis, or recite set prayers when attending a church service. But doing more than that – cultivating a personal prayer life – seems somehow beyond them. Whilst they might admire Jesus' ethical teaching, they are tempted to regard prayer and worship as at best an optional extra, and at worst a time-consuming distraction from the down-to-earth business of caring for others and 'loving their neighbour.'

Prayer for me is a joy, not a burden. It opens the door to my inner relationship with the God I love and the God who loves me, an inner relationship from which my devotion and practical service all ultimately spring. Jesus treasured the times he spent in prayer alone with God. We know that he regularly took himself up into the mountains (Mark 6:46) or to a solitary place of quiet, early in the morning in order to pray (Mark 1:35). Before he chose his twelve disciples he spent a whole night on a mountain praying about who he needed to have with him (Luke 6:12). Shortly before his arrest, Jesus went with his friends to a garden, the Garden of Gethsemane, to pour out his heart before his heavenly Father in prayer (Luke 22:39–46).

Jesus was perfectly at one with God (e.g. John 17:21). There was a mystical union between them. He spoke of God as his heavenly 'Father' (e.g. Mark 14:36) and encouraged his followers to do the same (Matthew 6:9 *cf* Romans 8:14–16). The reason why we feel able as Christians to approach God and relate to him in the way we do – expectantly (Matthew 7:7–12), persistently (Luke18:1–8), and boldly (Hebrews 4:14–end) – is because of Jesus and what he has shown and taught us. God is our heavenly

Father, a God of infinite love, totally committed to our wellbeing. No wonder that when his disciples saw him praying, as they often did (eg Luke 9:18), they saw something very special and wanted to learn from him and imitate him (Luke 11:1).

Prayer for me is two-way, a dynamic response to the living God as I encounter him in the world, and it takes many forms. The beauty of creation for example will often evoke in me a sense of awe and wonder and celebratory praise. The example set by 'big name' Christians like St Francis of Assisi and Janani Luwum[192], or unnamed Christians, can prompt me to praise God, to give thanks for them, and pray that I may live like them too. Things I have said or done which I should not have done, or things which I have failed to do, will make me want to repent and pray for forgiveness and inner renewal. If I meet with cruelty or injustice I will feel challenged to pray for both the victims in their suffering and the perpetrators too, that God will turn their hearts; to give thanks for those who are seeking to bring relief; and to dedicate myself to combating all that is wrong and working for a better world.

I try to 'listen' and respond to what God is 'saying' to me. It is not always easy; sometimes it is even quite uncomfortable. But it is why humility, honesty and openness to the truth are such important virtues to cultivate. Jesus tells a story about a publican and Pharisee who go to the Temple to pray. The publican returned home 'justified' (in a right relationship with God), because he listened to what God was saying to him and repented; the Pharisee could not be 'justified', because he listened only to himself (Luke 18:9–14).

Jesus warned against people whose lives are all show and no substance. In his culture this even applied to the way people prayed. (Matthew 6:1–8). The real purpose of prayer is to be with God, to be close to him, to 'listen' to him, and to discern his will. The first word which Jesus taught his disciples was 'Father', and

---

[192] *Janani Luwum was the archbishop of the Church of Uganda from 1974 to 1977. He was arrested in February 1977 after protesting to the President, Idi Amin, about human rights abuses. Shortly afterwards he was murdered on the orders of Amin.*

the very next was '*your* will be done' (Matthew 6:10). What Jesus wants is for his disciples to tune in to God's pattern of agapeic love and to discover what he is calling us to be and to do. There are many things which I may desire and be tempted to pray for which are selfish or ill-considered and ought to be left to one side. When I conclude a prayer, I often use a phrase like 'in Jesus' name' or 'for the sake of Jesus Christ our Lord', to remind me to check and make sure that what I am praying for is likely to be in accordance with God's pattern of agapeic love, and is a prayer which Jesus would have been happy to pray himself.

God, who was fully present in Jesus, is here amongst us even today through his Holy Spirit. The God of agapeic love is never far away. God is Immanuel, 'God with us', present and active always and everywhere. When I pray, I can sense him not only 'speaking' *to* me but speaking *with* me as my 'Advocate' or 'Counsellor' (John 15:26; 16:7–15), guiding me as to how I should pray. When I pray, it is as if God is 'at both ends of the telephone'. Some Christians call it 'praying in the Spirit'. God prays through us, and we in the process become channels of his grace.

> "In the same way, the Spirit helps us in our weakness. We do not know what we ought to pray for, but the Spirit himself intercedes for us with groans that words cannot express. And he who searches our hearts knows the mind of the Spirit, because the Spirit intercedes for the saints in accordance with God's will." (Romans 8:26, 27).

Some people try to manipulate God when they pray. They look upon him as some kind of cosmic genie, there simply to grant them their wishes. Simon the sorcerer in Acts (Acts 8:9–25) seems to have thought of prayer along these lines. For Christians however it can never be like this. For them it is always the other way round. We do not pray for God to help us with *our* agenda; we seek through prayer to discern and cooperate with *his* agenda: 'Your kingdom come; *your* will be done'. He is the God of agapeic love. We love God and everything he stands for.

Church

Jesus was the supreme agent of agapeic love. He loved to be with people and to call people together. Although he frequently prayed and ministered on his own, he also chose twelve (far from perfect) disciples to accompany him on his travels, and sent them out in pairs, not singly. He attended local synagogues regularly on the Sabbath to worship with his fellow Jews (Mark 1:21, 3:1; Luke 4:15, 13:10) and his disciples did the same. When Paul went on his missionary journeys to different cities around the Mediterranean, he usually had someone like Barnabas, Timothy, or Silas with him as a companion. And his first port of call was invariably the synagogue, the Jewish equivalent of a church. As the Christian community grew in different places, they made regular meeting together their priority. There were no church buildings then, so they met wherever they could – in people's homes, by the river bank, in the market place.

No church is perfect, but then none of us are perfect either. If I ever found a church that was completely as it ought to be, I should probably hesitate to become a member for fear of spoiling it! We are all sinners. But God loves us and, despite our many weaknesses and failings, can still do amazing things through us. We have our strengths. I have been blessed in countless ways from being part of a fellowship. I have learnt so much. And when all is said and done, the Church is the only organisation on this planet dedicated to the task of living and proclaiming the agapeic love of God revealed in Jesus. Without the gentle support and encouragement of the Christian community at various critical moments in my life, I might well have drifted off and lost my way. My spiritual life would certainly have been weaker and poorer if I had tried to 'go it alone'.

Jesus recognised our need for one another. That is why he chose his twelve disciples to accompany him, and that is why the Church exists. Many of us think of the church as a building where we go to worship. More fundamentally however it is a community of faith to which we belong. The Greek word for 'church' (ekklesia) means 'a gathering' or 'assembly'. The first followers of Jesus realised the importance of fellowship and community (Acts 2:42). They used to meet regularly in each other's houses. New Christians were baptised and welcomed into the community of faith, the 'body of Christ' (1 Corinthians 12:13), and as members they became like limbs and organs of the body (Romans 12:4–8; 1 Corinthians 12:12–end) each with their own distinctive contribution to make.

Jesus clearly enjoyed being with others for prayer, worship, teaching, encouragement, and support; so did his first followers; and so do I. I want to celebrate agapeic love and I want to celebrate my relationship with fellow Christians. I love being part of the church:

- I go to worship – The English word comes from the Anglo-Saxon, 'weorthscipe'. The word literally means 'worth-ship', 'attributing to someone or something its true worth'. I look at the amazing world we live in and find myself moved to thank and praise the amazing God who brought us all to life. I also want to do this with other Christians who feel as I do, who have also experienced God's love in Jesus as I have, and who want to express their love for him (Philippians 4:4–7).[193]

- I go to pray with my brothers and sisters – Jesus taught his followers that there was a particular value in praying together. "For where two or three come together in my name", he said, "there am I with them" (Matthew 18:20). In the 'Prayers of Intercession' we bring before God the needs of his world as well as our thankfulness for all that is good.

- I go for teaching – The word 'disciple' means a 'learner', and although I have been an ordained minister in the Church of England for many years, I am still a learner. I still wear my

---

[193] *I have written a small booklet for the Anglican Society for the Welfare of Animals (ASWA) on the subject of worship entitled 'Worshipping with the Whole Creation'. It explores the Greek and Russian Orthodox belief that worship is not something which begins and ends at a certain time in church, but is rather an endless activity which we all too briefly enter into with the whole of Creation.*

'L' plates. I meet with other Christians at church because I want to learn from them. During a normal act of Christian worship the Bible is read, opened up and applied to practical Christian living through the sermon (eg Colossians 1:28, 3:16). The quality of preaching can vary! But it is always possible to find something to take home from what has been said, to reflect upon and to pray about. I also find the words of the hymns and the prayers used in the service a rich source of spiritual nourishment[194].

- I go for fellowship – The New Testament Greek word for fellowship, 'koinonia', literally means 'sharing in common'. I look upon my fellow Christians as 'brothers and sisters in Christ'. We are all part of God's family. It is wonderful when we can help and encourage one another, share each other's joys and sorrows, and be held together in God's agapeic love.

- I go for Holy Communion – Ever since Jesus ate his final meal with his friends, the main act of Christian worship has centred around a service with bread and wine. The first Christians regularly 'broke bread' whenever they met. Receiving communion could never be for me an optional extra. 'Do this in remembrance of me', is a command from the Lord, not a request. But it is also a joy and a great blessing. What we *do* in remembrance can be so much more powerful than what we merely *say* or *hear*.

When I receive the bread and wine, I look *back* at what Jesus did for me, dying on the cross ("This cup is the new covenant in my blood; do this, whenever you drink it, in remembrance of me." 1 Corinthians 11:25b); I look *around* at my brothers and sisters in Christ with whom I am sharing the one bread and one cup and pray for them; I look *forward* to the 'messianic banquet', the ultimate victory of God's Love, symbolised by the bread and wine, and renew my

---

[194] *This is one of the advantages I find of being given a hymn book and prayer book or service sheet, which I can use to reflect upon before, during or after the service.*

hope in Christ; and as I consume the elements, I always look *inward* at the inner transformation that God is seeking to bring about in my life through his Holy Spirit.

- I go to share the good news – When we are together, we can work as a team. There are things we can do as a Christian fellowship which we could never do on our own – or at least, never as effectively. We are called and commissioned to share the good news of God's agapeic love in Jesus, to make disciples, and work together to promote his kingdom (Matthew 28:18ff) "on earth as it is in heaven" (Matthew 6:10). At the end of every communion service we commit ourselves to this practical task in a concluding prayer: "... We offer you our souls and bodies to be a living sacrifice. Send us out in the power of your Spirit to live and work to your praise and glory"[195]. The last words in our communion service are amongst the most important of all. "Go in peace, to love and serve the Lord." They bring the focus of our faith to where it really belongs and where it can make a real difference – to God's agapeic love for *the world* and to all that share the gift of life in it.

It has been truly amazing to see over the years how people, within very different church fellowships with widely differing resources, have selflessly sought to serve their communities and put this prayer into practice through an amazing kaleidoscope of initiatives.

Daily Life

God's agapeic love is all-embracing. He loves the whole world, not just 'the nice bits'. God's commitment to the wellbeing of his creation is constant and unwavering.

The ancient Greeks held work in contempt. The good life was for them a life free from toil, and the gods they worshipped indulged in carefree leisure. The God of the Bible is, in stark

---

[195] *Common Worship: Services and Prayers for the Church of England (Church House Publishing ©The Archbishops' Council 2000).*

contrast, a worker from the very beginning, creating the universe and providing a 'garden' for the animals and the first primeval man and woman. God is a craftsman:

> "The heavens declare the glory of God; the skies proclaim the work of his hands." (Psalm 19:1)

The work is ongoing. God as Creator labours continuously to sustain the natural world (Psalm 104:10–22) and protect the people (Psalm 121). Jesus in the New Testament holds work in high regard:

> "As long as it is day," he says, "we must do the work of him who sent me."
>
> (John 9:4a)

Human beings are made in the image of God and called as such to be fellow workers. The link between God as a worker and you and me as workers is made clear in the fourth of the Ten Commandments:

> "Six days you shall labour and do all your work... For in six days the Lord made the heavens and the earth..." (Exodus 20:9,11)

Work of course can degenerate into toil as the story of 'the Fall' makes clear (Genesis 3:17–19), and rest and recreation are also important. But as we are drawn deeper and deeper into God's agapeic love, our love and concern for the world will become more and more constant and unwavering. Every single moment will be an opportunity to express our devotion, to show that we care for this world which God has made, and for which his Son came to die, and that we are prepared to do everything we can to enable it to flourish. Whether we have somehow found ourselves involved in a major media headline event, or are simply engaged in the task of helping a neighbour in need, or rescuing an ant or snail from a public footpath where it is in imminent danger of being crushed under foot, it matters not. Every encounter will bring with it the chance to be a channel of grace: to rescue, reassure, affirm, help or encourage. Through these moments of meeting we will show and share the love of the One who created us:

"... whatever you did for one of the least of these brothers of mine," said Jesus, "you did for me." (Matthew 25:40)

Even activities which seem irredeemably dull can offer unexpected opportunities to do this. A crucial lesson I learnt when I was a curate, for example, was the importance of administration – filling in forms, drawing up rotas, and writing letters. I always tended to dismiss such tasks as mundane and unspiritual, and of little importance when set alongside tasks like writing a sermon or leading an act of worship. Gradually however I came to realise that efficient administration helped the wheels of the organisation to turn more smoothly and make the work of the Church as an agent of agapeic love more effective.

The 17th century Carmelite friar, Brother Lawrence (born *Nicholas Herman*) was for many years a kitchen hand in a busy, hot, noisy monastery kitchen. His collected teachings and letters were put together by Father Joseph de Beaufort in a spiritual classic, *'The Practice of the Presence of God'*. For Brother Lawrence there was no distinction between work and worship, prayer, and play. He was aware of God's presence with him whether he was busy in the kitchen or praying in church. He found

"That it was a great delusion to think that the times of prayer ought to differ from other times...

That we ought not to be weary of doing little things for the love of God, who regards not the greatness of the work, but the love with which it is performed...

That the whole substance of religion was faith, hope and charity, by the practice of which we become united to the will of God; that all besides is indifferent, and to be used as a means that we may arrive at our end, and be swallowed up therein, by faith and charity."[196]

Justice

We have seen how God's agapeic love can give shape to our life at a very personal level. But the personal cannot ever be separated completely from the public environment and the wider world in which we live. God loves not just the whole of my life but the life of every single person and every living creature. God's agapeic love embraces whole communities, countries and entire wildlife habitats. By the power of love, God is ushering in his 'kingdom' "... on earth as it is in heaven,"[197] so living in harmony with this love has enormous political and social implications.

When I vote in a General Election, I do not simply look to my own interests. I try to consider prayerfully which of the various parties or candidates standing for election will best promote a fairer, happier society in which everyone can flourish. Policies affecting animals, the environment and the most vulnerable members of our society can be particularly revealing when trying to discern which party is most in tune with what God's all-embracing agapeic love is seeking to bring about.

Employment should never be sought simply on the basis of the salary it offers or the social kudos it may carry. We should, as far as possible, seek work which will contribute to the enrichment of the community, and help the world become more as God would wish it to be. I know people can sometimes be forced to take on morally dubious jobs, simply to survive or put food on the table for their families. It is scandalous that they should ever be put in such a position. But most of us, I suspect, are not like them. We do have a choice. Work occupies a considerable proportion of our time, and discerning and choosing a job which is pleasing to God

---

[196] Brother Lawrence, 'The Practice of the Presence of God', 4th Conversation, (Spire Books, 16th Printing, May 1980) p. 24, 25.
[197] The Lord's Prayer, Matthew 6:10.

and in tune with his pattern of agapeic love ought to be possible in a genuinely just society.

'Live more simply that others may simply live', said Gandhi. Love demands it. As we become increasingly aware of the impact that our relatively comfortable lifestyle can have upon the poor of the world, the environment, the wildlife threatened by loss of habitat, and the non-human victims of our intensive farm systems, we have seen the need to adjust the way we live.

The 'LOAF' principles offer a helpful checklist for reflecting upon how we might do this. I was first introduced to them by 'Christian Ecology Link', an organisation committed to promoting and encouraging, "the propagation, among Churches and the public, of a better understanding of the integrity of creation and of the human role as steward of creation." The letters stand for:

Locally sourced,
Organically grown,
Animal friendly, and
Fairly traded.

If we buy '*locally sourced*' items, apples which have been grown in the United Kingdom for example rather than in New Zealand, we will lessen the environmental impact of transportation and fuel costs.

Purchasing '*organically grown*' produce whenever possible can help reduce the damage to the environment and wildlife which we might otherwise inflict by the over-use of chemical fertilisers and pesticides.

Being '*animal friendly*', in whatever way we understand that phrase, seems to me to be an intrinsic part of living in harmony with God's all-embracing agapeic love for the world[198]. It was

---

[198] *There are numerous animal welfare organisations such as Compassion in World Farming (CIWF). The Anglican Society for the Welfare of Animals (ASWA) (https://www.aswa.org.uk) and SARX (https://sarx.org.uk) are two Christian ones.*

shortly after I was ordained[199], for example, that I was made aware of the horrifically cruel treatment of chickens on our factory farms, and decided to become a vegetarian.

'*Fairly traded*' is the fourth and final principle. People matter to the God of love. A practical agapeic commitment to their wellbeing, especially the poor and vulnerable, entails to my mind a practical commitment to the 'fairly traded' principle. I remember when concern about 'fairly traded' goods was first voiced in churches around the late 1970s and early 1980s. The Christian charity Traidcraft was, I believe, the first to pioneer fair trade in the United Kingdom. It advocated (and still does)

> "the importance of organic farming, sustainability and transparency to the lives of growers and artisans around the world."

It was founded back in 1979, published its first catalogue in the same year, and not long afterwards introduced the first fairtrade tea, coffee, and sugar to the United Kingdom. In 1992 it co-founded the Fairtrade Foundation, and has been going strong ever since.

Many of us are aware these days of the scandal of cheap clothes made in 'sweat shops' in India and elsewhere. But these are not the only products of which we should be wary. Whenever something is sold at a significantly lower price than elsewhere, it is worth asking ourselves 'Why?' 'What are the pay and conditions of the workers like who are producing it?'

The LOAF principles are to my mind a useful checklist. But we must be aware, when important principles are stated as simply as this, that putting them into practice may not be as simple as at first it may appear. We are called to live in the real world where everything we eat, wear and use comes out of a complex matrix of agriculture, industry and trade which is worldwide.

---

[199] *This was at a time when vegetarians were regarded as cranks and vegans as totally beyond the pale. If you wanted to buy beans and pulses you often had to go to a specialist food shop. Very little was available in the supermarkets.*

It is encouraging to see how far society has come. Supermarkets stock many more products suitable for vegetarians and vegans than they did thirty or forty years ago. Products these days are also much better labelled than they used to be, which helps if you are looking for food that is fairly traded and organically grown, or for cosmetics that have not been tested on animals.

I cannot in all honesty say that I have been as successful in putting the LOAF principles into practice as I might wish. It is definitely for me a 'work in progress'. Applying the principles is not always straightforward. If one tries to be more 'animal friendly', for example, by eating less meat or becoming vegetarian or vegan, it can be harder to stick with 'locally sourced' products, as many beans and pulses are imported. Organic food can be significantly more expensive, which can create budgetary problems for any of us on tight incomes. And on the health front, I am painfully aware that the medicines I am currently being given to treat my pancreatic cancer and help ease the symptoms have either been tested on animals or actually contain animal products. My own personal rule of thumb has always been that taking a life requires serious justification. If it is necessary for health[200] or survival[201], that for me could provide potential justification, though it still makes me feel uncomfortable.

Vocation

The basic life of agapeic love is a calling common to us all. The fruit of the Spirit listed by Paul, for example, is a blessing which we pray will grow in every one of us.

But we are individuals, and the God of love values us as individuals. We have different skills, hobbies, and interests, and we can all be called to use what God has given us in different ways. I am very grateful for the opportunity I was given to learn

---

[200] Hugh Broadbent, 'Thinking About Animal Testing' (Anglican Society for the Welfare of Animals).
[201] Hugh Broadbent, 'Thinking About Vegetarianism' (Anglican Society for the Welfare of Animals) p. 5.

the piano and guitar, and during the course of my ministry I have been able to play these instruments in playgroups, holiday clubs, assemblies, and acts of worship. Others I know, with a keen interest in football, have channelled their love of 'the beautiful game' into organising football matches for church youth groups; and still others have used their love of cooking to prepare special meals for the church or wider community.

A vocation or calling comes from God. It is never of our own making. Often we may find ourselves resisting it, so a sign of its authenticity can lie in the fact that it refuses to go away even when we wish it to do so. I am reminded for example of the excuses which Moses made when he was called to go back to Egypt to rescue the Israelites from slavery (Exodus 3:1; 4:17), or Jeremiah complaining that he was too young to do what God was asking him to do (Jeremiah 1:6). Their calling was not the product of wishful thinking but quite the opposite.

A vocation or calling should always be tested. If it is simply the product of selfish ambitions or desires rather than a wish to serve in line with God's pattern of agapeic love, then that would suggest it is not a genuine calling, and that it comes from us rather than from God.

The opinion, advice and encouragement of other people can be helpful. When they give us positive encouragement to take on a particular task or project, that can often help provide the assurance we need. And in the same way, when we recognise gifts or callings in others we need to be ready to nurture them and offer the encouragement they need.

Callings often come to us through other people. My decision to go to Kenya between school and university to teach in a small, rural harambee school came about as a vocational response to a suggestion by my grandmother; my decision to join the Anglican Society for the Welfare of Animals and serve on its central committee was also a response to an invitation from an existing committee member.

The vocations I have mentioned have mainly concerned the gifts, hobbies, and talents that people have. But the most important callings in my life have been to do with relationships: when

God called me to follow Jesus; when I was ordained as a deacon and a priest in the Church of England; when I married Jane, the love of my life; when we decided to start a family and were blessed with our two beloved children. My calling to all of the parishes in which I have ministered has come through the diocesan bishop of the time or through the Bishop's Council. These vocations have all called for a commitment either to God or to certain people, and they have all entailed specific responsibilities which have been unique to me.

Conclusion

The agapeic love I have been describing may seem to some people overly demanding – clothed, so to speak, with too much 'duty' and 'discipline' and not enough 'joy'. If that is the case, I am sorry. I do not mean it to come across like that. Knowing God's agapeic love in my life has been for me an unreservedly liberating, life-enriching blessing.

But deep joy, it seems to me, often requires duty and discipline. The thrill of athletic success, for example, only comes to those who are willing to commit themselves to the discipline of training; and the joy of deep relationships only comes to those who are willing to give to them and stay committed to them when the going gets tough. I am reminded of Ignatius Loyola's famous prayer:

> "Teach me, dear Lord,
> to give and not to count the cost,
> to fight and not to heed the wounds,
> to toil and not to seek for rest,
> to labour and not to ask for any reward,
> save the JOY of knowing that we do thy will."

Sharing in God's work of agapeic love involves discipline and duty, but it is nevertheless a huge privilege and joy, and it has been for me quite literally life-changing.

> "We... are being transformed into his likeness with ever-increasing glory, which comes from the Lord, who is the Spirit." (2 Corinthians 3:18)

> "... if anyone is in Christ, he is a new creation; the old has gone, the new has come!" (2 Corinthians 5:17 *cf* Galatians 6:15)

God's Spirit, I believe, has been at work in me, and over the years has transformed me in all kinds of ways. My hope and prayer is that he may touch your life also, and that what I have written will encourage you as readers to know this love which surpasses understanding (Ephesians 3:17b–19); which is above all, through all, and in all. Love is an overworked word, and talking about it can sometimes feel rather simplistic and superficial. But to my mind, 'agapeic love' is the phrase which most truly encapsulates my experience of God and my journey with him (1 John 4:7–12). It undergirds everything that for me is of ultimate importance, everything that I hold dear, and everything that is rooted in the eternal, gracious God I know in Jesus.

Deo Gratias

APPENDIX

'Collection of Hymns and Poems'

Over the years I have written various hymns and poems on the themes of creation and cosmic redemption, for use in worship:[202]

1. Across a sea of chaos, dark and brooding,
    The Spirit stirs; our Maker brings to birth
    His plan for life ablaze with love and beauty,
    And countless creatures on a fruitful earth.
    Our fath'ring God within his heart rejoices
    As he beholds their wonder and their worth.

    Beneath a sea of violence and injustice
    This precious life is drowning day by day.
    Creation smeared by cruel exploitation;
    The selfish path we tread with feet of clay,
    We reach the end, our dignity distorted,
    And see the Maker's image fade away.

    Upon the sea a fragile ark is drifting,
    A sign of hope that rises with the flood.
    For man becomes a servant of redemption
    To bird and beast, as now he seeks their good.
    The rainbow-God shows in a dove his mercy –
    His love for all more clearly understood.

---

[202] *Prayers and liturgical resources which I have written or compiled can also be found in 'Animal Welfare Patterns of Worship' published by the Anglican Society for the Welfare of Animals (ASWA).*

The chaos gone! Our God one day will conquer.
His love will bring a harmony complete,
As grief and pain, the sorrow all around us,
Are swallowed up in victory so sweet.
The Lamb of God will reign on high for ever,
As living creatures worship at his feet!

Words: Hugh P.C. Broadbent;
Tune: 'Finlandia'.

2.   Behold our God rejoicing
In all that He has made:
His order and His beauty
In wondrous power displayed;
A mystery unfolding –
His vision near to birth
Of peace and love embracing
All things in heaven and earth.

Behold our Maker grieving
As Man usurps His throne,
Abusing fellow creatures
He thinks that he can own.
God sees the callous tyrant,
The needless blood he's spilt.
He hears the cry for mercy
– Our judgement and our guilt.

But now the Man for Others,
A Second Adam, reigns!
In love He comes amongst us
To share Creation's pains.
He rides a lowly donkey
The humble path to peace.
Old Adam will be vanquished
And all oppression cease!

We praise the faithful Shepherd,
His changeless love proclaim,
Who nurtures us and guides us
And calls us each by name.
He risks His life to save us;
For love He lays it down ~
Each child a priceless treasure,
His joy, His pride, His crown.

In Christ, the faithful Shepherd,
May we be faithful too.
In Christ, the Second Adam,
May God our minds renew:
Remoulded in the pattern ~
Of Christ, the Servant-King
To care for all His creatures,
Our lives our offering.

Words: Hugh P.C. Broadbent;
Tune: 'Cruger' or 'Thornbury'.

3. *Come, shout for joy!*
Let earth resound with praise
To God revealed as Love
In all his ways.

Brought into being by his mighty Word,
Nature proclaims the glory of the Lord.
Come, shout for joy ...

Even the swallows in his Temple nest,
Knowing how all in him can find their rest.
Come, shout for joy ...

Noah received an olive branch of peace
Brought by a dove – God's sign the Flood would cease.
Come, shout for joy ...

When to the desert poor Elijah fled,
God through the ravens brought him daily bread.
Come, shout for joy ...

When Balaam's donkey saw where danger lay,
He saved the prophet – stopped and turned away.
Come, shout for joy ...

Gently the donkey bore his precious load,
As to his Passion Jesus humbly rode.
Come, shout for joy ...

God, give us grace your goodness to perceive.
Open our hearts your blessings to receive.
Come, shout for joy ...

> *Words: Hugh P.C. Broadbent;*
> *Tune: 'Crucifer'.*

4.   How can it be
      That children of a Father-God
      Can be so blind
      To suffering so plain,
      That we should make
      Compassion seem a dirty word
      And stop our ears
      To cries of fear and pain?
      O God of love,
      In You Creation's hope revives.
      In You each creature's worth is understood.
      O God of love,
      Have mercy on their broken lives.
      For as our Father-God you purpose only good.

      How can it be
      That bird and beast should languish so
      On fact'ry farms,

From birth to death confined.
They never feel the sun above or earth below,
But simply serve
The greed of humankind.
A price too high!
Abused, exploited, cheaply sold –
The hidden cost
To fill our groaning shelves!
A price too high
When we become so callous-cold
And bring such shame and deep dishonour on ourselves.

When will it be
That we embrace our Christian call
To bring the peace of God upon the earth,
So Man and beast,
In slavish toil through Adam's Fall,
Are freed to share
His new Creation's birth?
O God of love,
Like fire, consume our selfish pride.
O God of love
Come warm our hearts of stone.
O God of love
Come light the Way. Our footsteps guide
Towards the dawn of grace Your risen Son has shown.

Words: Hugh P.C. Broadbent;
Tune: 'Londonderry Air'.

5. Image of gold,
   Erected once in Babylon,
   Sign of a ruler's lust to domineer –
   Bullied and beaten,
   Brazenly downtrodden,
   All in its shadow
   Lived as slaves to fear.

Idols of gold
Can still corrupt our lives today,
Driven by profit, greed will take its toll:
Conscience sedated,
Nature decimated,
Gaining the world
Whilst forfeiting the soul!

Image divine!
In Adam God desired to see
Mirrored in us His care for all He's made:
Tilling and tending,
Man and Nature blending,
Living in peace,
His glory thus displayed.

Image renewed!
In Christ we can be born again,
Mirror the Lord, th'eternal God of grace.
May we be worthy,
Worthy of our calling.
May bird and beast behold in us His face.

Words: Hugh P.C. Broadbent;
Tune: 'Finlandia' or 'Lord of the Years'

6.   Lord of life and love unbounded,
Blessèd Holy Trinity,
From the dark primeval chaos
You have brought Your world to be.
May we glimpse in all Your creatures
That same goodness which You see.

Called to share in Your dominion;
Exercising royal rule,
We must follow You in Jesus,
Servant-king, not tyrant cruel.

Help us tend the world, Your Garden,
Groaning, waiting for renew'l.

May our minds embrace Your vision
Of the prophet's holy hill:
Wolf and lamb at peace together,
Love's shalom, Your perfect Will.
Like an ocean, come salvation!
All Creation flood and fill!

Words: Hugh P.C. Broadbent;
Tune: 'Regent Square' or 'Rhuddlan'.

7.　　O Lord, across the centuries
Down labyrinthine ways,
Your love pursues us with a zeal
Which nothing can erase.
And though we plumb the darkest depths
And soar to heights unknown,
We cannot flee the Hound of Heav'n,
For all is but Your own.

In forest, field, with bird or beast
No refuge can we find.
The chase begun – the Hound of Heav'n
Is always close behind.
And still Your voice we hear above
His slow, unhurried tread:
'The earth is mine and all therein,
And by my hand you're fed.'

No place to go, we stand at bay,
The Hound of Heaven's eyes
Now penetrate our deepest thoughts
Which we cannot disguise.
He bears the marks of grief and pain;
His message blazoned red:

'With ev'ry creature you have harmed,
I've suffered too, and bled.'

Our fear and guilt all melting in ~
The warmth of Love's embrace.
Redeemed, renewed, we gladly join
The Hound in heav'nly chase.
For through His eyes the wonder of ~
Each creature now we see,
And heed His call to make the world
As it is meant to be.

> *Words: Hugh P.C. Broadbent;*
> *Tunes: 'Vox Dilecti' or 'Kingsfold'*
> *(inspired by Francis Thompson's poem,*
> *'The Hound of Heaven').*

8. Our Father in heaven, by His mercy and grace,
    Has called us and led us to serve Him in this place.
    The seed of His Word of Life in us He sows.
    Let us pray that the fruit of His Spirit grows.

    Praise Him, you people ev'rywhere!
    Praise the Creator who holds us in His care!
    As freely He gives to us, so freely we share
    For the sake of the Gospel we're called to bear.

    The Lord is our Maker and his Purpose is good,
    Yet we have rebelled, disobeyed, misunderstood.
    We have nailed our rejection to a cross of wood
    And have failed to obey as we know we should.
    Praise Him, you people ev'rywhere...

    The Lord of the Harvest knows our ev'ry need.
    So let go of your cravings, your selfishness and greed,
    Pollution – the spoiling of this earth – must cease
    So all Nature may enter His Reign of Peace.
    Praise Him, you people ev'rywhere...

The birds and the animals on farm and in field
Are more than the products of economic yield.
They're loved by their Maker; they deserve to be
Treated well with compassion and dignity
Praise Him, you people ev'rywhere...

He's God of the wealthy and He's God of the poor,
And the plight of the needy He never will ignore.
Let's trade so they benefit; let's share and let's give,
That we all of his bounty may taste and live.
Praise Him, you people ev'rywhere...

Words: Hugh P.C. Broadbent;
Tune: 'Lord of the Dance' (Shaker Tune).

9. Praise the Father of Creation;
    Its wonders behold,
    See the order with its purposive ~
    Patterns unfold.
    See the joyful, wild profusion
    Of the creatures brought to be.
    No machine-like fatalism –
    They're born to be free!

    Born free! Born free!
    In the wisdom of their Maker
    They're born to be free!

    Where no cows graze in the meadows
    And birds never fly,
    Where the basic nat'ral instincts
    We humans deny,
    God is grieving o'er our sinning
    O'er the world he wills to be.
    And the whole of his Creation
    Cries out to be free.

Be free! Be free!
And the whole of his Creation
Cries out to be free!

Gracious Father, you're renewing
The face of the earth,
And the children of your kingdom
You're bringing to birth.
With the harvest of redemption
Comes the fruit of harmony ~
'Twixt the Maker and his creatures.
We all shall be free!

Be free! Be free!
In the love of the Redeemer
We all shall be free!

> *Words: Hugh P. C. Broadbent;*
> *Tune: 'The Sans Day Carol'.*

10. Today as we remember
the tragedy of war,
the countless men and women
whom loved ones see no more,
we glimpse the Maker's vision
in Christ our Lord revealed:
a world where all can flourish
and ev'ry hurt be healed.

Through war God's fruitful Eden
becomes a barren hell,
as forest, field and mountain
are blitzed by bomb and shell,
and Nature's blameless creatures
are forced to pay the price
for human violence trampling
its way through paradise.

Enrolled within the armies
on each and ev'ry side,
embroiled within this nightmare,
too many beasts have died.
Yet humble, ever faithful
to humans in their plight,
they witness in our darkness
to God's redeeming light.

So now at this Remembrance,
we look towards the day
when swords are turned to ploughshares
and war is done away;
and we by grace are agents
of harmony and joy
to all of God's Creation
which nothing can destroy.

> *Words: Hugh P C Broadbent;*
> *Tune: 'Aurelia'.*

11. God of Time
    And Master of Eternity,
    Down through the ages
    Your love has shaped our history.
    Alpha, Omega,
    The Source of Life,
    The Final Goal,
    Grant that Your Vision
    Inspire each living soul.

    God of Truth,
    Whose light so clear in Jesus shone,
    You can illumine
    The hearts and minds of everyone.
    Knowledge is soaring
    With Babel-pride to dizzy height.

Grant us the wisdom
To use our pow'r aright.

God of Love,
In Jesus you were one with us –
Boundless compassion,
Self-giving, dying on a cross.
Crucified Saviour,
Our hurts, confusions you still share.
Faithful, unfailing,
We know you're always there.

God of Hope,
The centuries have passed us by;
Two thousand years
Since you first unveiled the reason why.
Now to your future
With thankfulness and joy we turn,
Ready to further
Your Rule for which we yearn.

'Millennium Hymn'
Words and Tune ('New Start'): Hugh P.C. Broadbent.